CREATIVE HOMEOWNER PRESS®

PLANNING YOUR ADDITION

CREATIVE HOMEOWNER PRESS®, Upper Saddle River, New Jersey

Editorial Director: Timothy O. Bakke
Art Director: Annie Jeon

Editor: David Schiff
Associate Editor: Lynn Elliott
Copy Editor: Candace B. Levy, Ph.D.

Graphic Designers: Heidi Garner
John Larimer
Illustrators: Jerry Germer
Insight Design Group

Cover Design: Annie Jeon
Cover Photo: Susan Gilmore
Photo Researcher: Georgette Blau

Manufactured in the United States of America
Electronic Prepress: TBC Color Imaging, Inc.
Printed at: Webcrafters, Inc.

Current Printing (last digit)
10 9 8 7 6 5 4 3 2 1

Planning Your Addition
Library of Congress Catalog Card Number: 97-075262
ISBN: 1-880029-99-5

CREATIVE HOMEOWNER PRESS®
A Division of Federal Marketing Corp.
24 Park Way, Upper Saddle River, NJ 07458

Photo Credits

CONTENTS

Introduction 5

Chapter 1   ASSESSING YOUR NEEDS 6
Assessing Your Space Needs ♦ Six Additions that Work

Chapter 2   FORMING A PLAN OF ATTACK....................21
Move or Improve ♦ How Much Will It Cost? ♦ Finding Financing
What to Do Yourself–What to Hire Out ♦ Using Outside Design Help

Chapter 3   DEFINING THE PROJECT 35
Legal Limitations ♦ Planning the Site ♦ The House

Chapter 4   FROM DREAM TO DESIGN 55
Designing on Your Own ♦ Planning the Layout ♦ Shaping the Exterior

Chapter 5   DEFINING THE SUPERSTRUCTURE 75
Foundations and Footings ♦ Floor Structures
Structural Walls ♦ Framing the Roof

Chapter 6   ENVELOPE DECISIONS 98
The Skin ♦ Insulation ♦ Doors ♦ Windows and Skylights ♦ Roofing

Chapter 7   FINISHING THE INTERIOR 129
Walls and Ceilings ♦ Floor Finishes ♦ Trimming the Interior ♦ Cabinetry

Chapter 8   CREATING COMFORT IN YOUR ADDITION 154
Conservation First ♦ Mechanical Heating Equipment ♦ Ventilation
Plumbing Rough-In ♦ The Electrical Systems ♦ Planning the Lighting

Chapter 9   BUILDING THE ADDITION 175
Contract Documents ♦ The Construction Phase ♦ You as General Contractor
Entrusting Construction to a General Contractor ♦ Some Final Words

Glossary 187
Index 188

INTRODUCTION

Chances are that your home was designed to meet the needs of another owner in another time. If the house is part of a subdivision, it was designed and built for an unknown buyer whose needs were assumed by the developer. In either case, the home was not designed for you or your household, so you've thought about building an addition.

Or perhaps your house once was fine for your needs, but those needs have changed, and you think adding more space might be the solution. You may be, for example, one of the millions of professionals who have brought their workplace home over the past few years and noticed that setting up your computer in a spare bedroom didn't create a space in which you can work. You found that the space itself isn't sufficient or family dynamics make working there difficult.

Like many people these days, you may be spending more leisure time at home. Does your house have the kind of spaces that are conducive to home-based recreation? Is there sufficient space for each person to pursue his or her leisure activity without conflicting with others? If you have taken up a regular exercise routine, do you have a workout area large enough to accommodate the equipment? Maybe you face lodging an elderly parent in your home, but the current layout can't accommodate the space needed, guarantee privacy, or provide handicap access.

It could be that you are looking forward to a healthy, active retirement. You may want to open up your floor plan and convert the unused kids' bedrooms into spaces for pursuing interests and hobbies.

But wait. Before you get to work planning your addition, you have a crucial decision to make. That decision is, of course, whether you should undertake this project in the first place. Perhaps you simply should move to a house that better suits your needs. The first two chapters of this book will help you make that decision. Chapter 1 will show you how to set your priorities, then take you on a tour of six actual home additions. The owners of these homes were selected because they are happy with their additions. These homeowners will share with you how they worked with architects, builders, and tradesmen to realize their dreams. They'll tell you what, if anything, they would do differently. You'll get some important insights from the architects who designed these additions, as well. An architect may be able to tell you, for example, that there's a good chance you don't need as much new space as you think. What you may really need is a small addition that ties together a new floor plan.

In Chapter 2 you'll learn about options for paying for your addition and what types of additions will return your investment at resale time. You'll learn the roles of the professionals and tradesmen you'll work with along the way, and you'll find help in deciding what work, if any, you should take on yourself.

Still want to build that addition? Read on. The rest of this book is designed to help you make the myriad decisions—from foundation to roof shingles—that will transform your home into a place that fits your present and future needs and your budget. You'll learn enough about your house's structure and mechanical systems to talk intelligently to the architect, designers, contractors, and tradesmen you may hire.

Rarely is building an addition an easy experience. After all, you are about to hand a big pile of money to a bunch of strangers. You owe it to yourself to make sure those people give you exactly what you want. There is, however, no reason why the experience can't be a fun, exciting adventure. You simply need the confidence that comes with being a well-informed consumer. Giving you that confidence is what *Planning Your Addition* is all about.

Decide what kind of space suits your needs. Here, a sun-filled living room (left) takes advantage of a garden view (above).

Chapter 1

ASSESSING YOUR NEEDS

Any family is a collection of diverse personalities, needs, and desires. And every member of the family likes certain things about their home and dislikes other things. Everybody probably could mention a feature or two they'd like to include if they were designing their home from scratch.

The first step in planning your addition is a family conference to catalog everybody's thoughts about your home. In this chapter, you'll find some suggestions for issues to discuss at the family meeting. To help you get the ideas flowing, we'll take a tour of six successful additions. The homeowners were nice enough to invite us in to share why their additions work for them.

The famous architect Frank Lloyd Wright reportedly spent his first meeting with new clients by asking them about their political views, hobbies, food preferences, and other personal questions. When Wright got up to don his well-known hat and cloak, the clients would protest, "But you haven't asked us about our new home yet." Wright would answer that he had all he needed to begin the design, then he would depart.

Whether or not the story is true, the point is that Wright believed he could better understand his clients' space needs by understanding their personalities, rather than by querying for those needs directly. In the same way, you can get your planning off to a sound start by taking an inventory of your lifestyle and that of your household. Then move onto how your home meets the needs of each person's lifestyle. Besides being fun, this tactic can reveal needs of which you might not have been aware. It might even eliminate a problem you thought needed addressing.

You might begin the inventory with everyone sitting around the table, stating general areas where the house works for them and where it doesn't. Once you get the ball rolling, you won't come up short of opinions.

Your adolescent son complains about the lack of privacy in the downstairs bathroom he shares with his two younger brothers. Also, now that he is a teenager, he doesn't want to share his bedroom with his 8-year-old brother. Your husband points out that his new work schedule requires him to leave home at 6:30 a.m., and it would make his life easier if he didn't have to dig his car out from snow and ice on winter mornings. You point out how you would really like a quiet place to read the paper when you come home in the evening. With the kids monopolizing the living room for TV or music, there is no place for more-peaceful leisure. Talking about leisure, it occurs to you and your spouse that you have both gotten into regular exercise programs in the past few years, and you can't always get to the local gym. Maybe an exercise space at home ought to be part of the plan. How about including a spa? While we're at it, why couldn't this room be a place to grow plants in? And so on.

ASSESSING YOUR SPACE NEEDS

Now comes the task of bringing everyone back to reality. Some items that come out of the meeting are critically needed; others are more in the category of "wouldn't it be nice to have. . . ." You can begin sorting out your household's space and functional needs with a four-step process that starts with listing each member's issues and concerns in the order in which they come up. Then you prioritize the issues and concerns, matching them with possible solutions. The result will be a design program—the basis of a design concept, whether you do your own design or hire a specialist. Here's how the concerns expressed above could be turned into a program for design.

1. List the current problems and desires of each member of the household.

▲ Find a solution for the rush-hour traffic jam in downstairs bathroom.

▲ Solve the conflict between TV/audio use and quiet uses or conversation in the living room.

▲ Add more bedrooms.

▲ Need a garage.

▲ Want an exercise room for exercise equipment and spa.

▲ Want a sun room for solar heat and growing plants out of season.

2. Prioritize the list. Write down the problems in order of importance.

1. Cramped bathrooms.
2. Insufficient bedrooms.
3. Lack of area for quiet leisure.
4. Garage.
5. Sun room.
6. Lack of area for exercise, spa.

3. List possible solutions to the right of each problem, as shown in Table 1-1 on page 8.

4. Refine the list of possible solutions into a design program, as shown in Table 1-2 on page 8.

Before etching this last list in stone, one more thing to consider is how the situation will change over the foreseeable future. Will your household grow or shrink? Will any facilities added now improve the value of the home? Can those facilities be converted to other uses? Thorny questions, all. Maybe it's not feasible to improve your home to satisfy the design program you have formulated. We'll look at some of the costs and alternatives in the next chapter. Meanwhile, seeing how other homeowners have met their space needs might spark your thinking.

One way to begin thinking about planning your addition is to look at other additions that have been built. If you know friends who have built an addition, ask them about it. What did they want the addition to accomplish? Is it working the way they hoped? What would they do differently?

TABLE 1-1

Problem/Need	Possible Solutions
1. Cramped bathrooms	Schedule usage of facilities Add another basin Add a shower above existing bathtub Add a separate shower Add new bathroom(s)
2. Insufficient bedrooms	Add new bedroom
3. Lack of area for quiet leisure	Schedule usage of facilities Add new entertainment room Add new quiet/space room
4. Garage	Add new garage
5. Sun room	Add new sun room
6. Lack of area for exercise, spa	Add space for exercise and spa

TABLE 1-2

Problem/Need	Solution To Explore
1. Cramped bathrooms	See if facilities can be subdivided, add space if not
2. Insufficient bedrooms	Add new bedroom
3. Lack of area for quiet leisure	Add rec room for noisy entertainment, keep living room primarily for sitting, reading
4. Garage	Add new garage
5. Sun room	Add sun room to accom- modate exercise equipment and spa
6. Lack of area for exercise, spa	

SIX ADDITIONS THAT WORK

The homeowners in the examples that follow are diverse in many ways: location, lifestyle, family size, and the type of home with which they started. The household all shared one thing in common, however: the need for additional space. Each of the families met this need in a different way by adding outward or upward and sometimes by combining an addition with a major rehabilitation of the existing house. After comparing the before and after floor plans of each project, you can see how dramatically an addition can change a house. The examples should inspire you to think through your own situation, and you may even walk away with an idea or two.

Rotating Rooms in Rockville

More space wasn't the issue in Steve and Janice Brose's decision to add on to their house in Rockville, Maryland. The issue was more a matter of how the space was used. The house was built around 1960, and the floor plan just didn't work for the family.

"It was a very dark, closed-up house with a beautiful golf course in the back," Janice said. "The view of the golf course wasn't being taken advantage of."

The only previous space additions to the house were a small breakfast room with lots of windows overlooking the golf course and a slight bump-out added to an existing back porch. A large deck was added at the back to create an inviting outdoor space that takes further advantage of the view. Although the additions were small, most of the house was virtually gutted to rearrange many of the rooms. In fact, the first step was to finish off the basement with a kitchenette so that the Broses could live down there during the six months of house renovation. The two sons, who are away at college, now use the basement when they are home as a recreation room to entertain friends.

The Broses never considered moving. They had lived in the house for 10 years before the renovation and knew from the start that the house itself was not really what they wanted. Steve is an attorney, and Janice is a nurse. The house is near both their jobs, in a beautiful neighborhood and in close proximity to Washington, D.C., with all the cultural advantages and events the national capital has to offer.

"We bought the house for the location," Steve said, adding that the couple waited a decade to remodel their house because "We wanted to do it all at once, do everything that needed to be done, and we wanted to use the best materials."

When they were finally ready, the Broses invited several architects and builders to their home to discuss

The Broses' addition consists of two semi-octagonal bump-outs: the breakfast nook (left) and the three-season porch (right). Although small, the additions make a big difference in the use of downstairs space, and they integrate the house with the deck and yard.

the project. One of the builders was Alex Dean, president of The Alexander Group, a design and renovation firm in nearby Kensington, Maryland. Alex had been recommended by one of Steve's colleagues who had used Alex's services.

Alex is not an architect, although he designs some additions himself. His approach is to meet prospective clients to see whether he is interested in the job and whether the clients are interested in working with him. If that relationship clicks, Alex selects an architect he thinks is right for the job and introduces the clients to the architect. If a deal is struck, Alex signs a contract with the clients and subcontracts the design work to the architect.

This approach is different from the traditional relationship between client and architect, and not all architects like to work this way. Traditionally, the architect is hired and paid directly by the client. With no financial ties to the builder, the architect acts as the client's agent, overseeing the work and making sure the client gets what he paid for.

Alex believes the traditional architect-client relationship has drawbacks that outweigh concerns of financial ties.

"Let's say, for example, that the architect accidentally draws the foundation 2 feet too short and the contractor pours it that way," Alex said. "Who is responsible? If I'm the builder, there's no question. I'm responsible."

More importantly, Alex believes that mistakes and misunderstandings are less likely to happen under his kind of arrangement. He has an established working relationship with the architects on his jobs. Because he and the architects are on the same team, he can work closely with them to realize his clients' visions.

Terry Cook, of T. Michael Cook in Gaithersburg, Maryland, is the architect who designed the Broses' remodel. Terry also works directly for clients in the traditional way. He said he enjoys working with Alex because, "If Alex gets the job, I know I will see it built, and I know it will be built right."

In addition, Terry said, Alex does the cost analysis for projects and provides Terry with feedback during the design process. This communication avoids wasting time designing something that is outside the client's budget.

"We had other people come over," Steve said. "We found that Alex and Terry were the people who knew what we wanted and had good ideas."

"That house had a lot of square footage, but it was built like a rabbit warren," Terry said. "There were lots of turns and walls."

Over the course of several meetings, Terry saw that the downstairs rooms were in the wrong places. The guest room in the back of the house, for example, received a lot of natural light and had a great view, but it was only occasionally used. Meanwhile, the family room was a cramped space tucked in the front corner of the house. The Broses, however, liked having each of the rooms that existed downstairs, so Terry rearranged the floor plan.

"Terry made that mental leap to move all the rooms around," Alex said.

The Broses' breakfast nook takes full advantage of the view and opens the home to natural light.

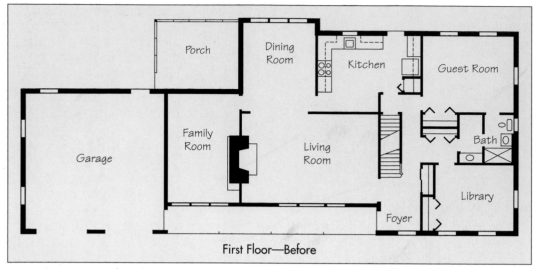

Drawing 1-1 *Before the remodeling, the guest room, which was the least-used room in the Broses' house, enjoyed the best view.*

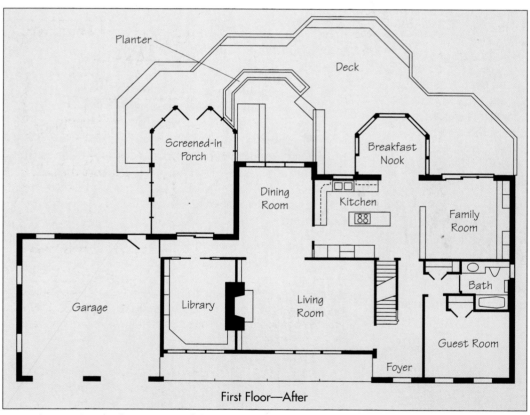

Drawing 1-2 *The largest part of the Broses' remodeling involved rearranging the existing floor plan. In the end, the remodeling required only two bump-outs to add space—a breakfast room and a screened-in porch.*

"We had three or four meetings, and we began by talking in the most vague terms," Janice said. "Then Terry came back with rough drawings that showed exactly what we wanted."

Terry came up with a design that called for moving the family room to the old guest room location at the back of the house. The wall that divided the old guest room from the kitchen was replaced with a waist-high, built-in bookcase that's topped with the same elegant black granite as the new kitchen countertops. The bookcase separates the family room from the kitchen without blocking light. Glass patio doors from the new family room to the new deck replaced the old guest room windows. The breakfast nook added another bank of windows. Now the house is flooded with light, air, and view.

The next problem was, where to put the new guest room and bath? The first thought might be to simply swap places with the old family room. It would be costly to install plumbing in that remote part of the house, though, so Terry moved the guest room to the old library location. Making that switch allowed Terry to keep the plumbing right were it was while redesigning the bathroom and making it accessible to the new guest bedroom. The quiet, remote location of the old family room was perfect for a library.

The old porch had jalousie windows, which obscured the view. With their new family room, the Broses didn't anticipate using the porch except in the nicest weather, so a screened-in porch was the best answer. Bumping the porch out a bit mirrors the breakfast nook and gives the back of the house a balanced look.

With their sons no longer in full-time residence, the Broses felt it was time to stretch out upstairs. The couple still wanted three bedrooms, however, because there are still times when both boys are at home. Besides, eliminating bedrooms would slash the resale value of their home. The first move was obvious: Get rid of that virtually useless sitting room that was robbing the master bedroom of one-third of its space and much of its light and view. Grab some room from one of the bedrooms to make

The wall that had once closed off a bedroom is now a low book-case that divides the family room from the kitchen. Black uba tuba granite tops the kitchen island and the bookcase, elegantly tying the scheme together.

space for a walk-in closet in the master bedroom and a spacious master bath to replace the old, cramped master bath. Lastly, the old upstairs hall bathroom and closets were reconfigured to make space for a comfortable modern bathroom.

Looking back at the process of planning their addition, Steve and Janice remember feeling a bit overwhelmed at first by the number of decisions they had to make.

"I went into this saying there are certain things I must have," Steve said. He originally was adamant that a fireplace be worked into the scheme, for example, but it turned out that there was no practical place to put one. Even if there was space, the fireplace would have drained a great deal of money out of the budget. "I learned there were a lot of things I thought I wanted that I didn't really need. I think the most important decision we made was that whatever we did, we wanted it to be top quality. That limited our choices right there."

A Kit House Grows Up

In the years between 1908 and 1940, you could sit down with a catalog from Sears Roebuck Honor-Bilt Modern Homes and order a kit house by mail. The Sears houses were modest homes; most cost under $2,000. For your money, you got the entire house with numbered parts, instruction booklets, paint, and nails.

One of these homes was built in 1920 at the end of a quiet, tree-lined, dead-end street in Chevy Chase, Maryland. Because this pleasant suburb borders Washington, D.C., property values are quite high. Still, when the realtor first showed Joe and Elonide Semmes the little beige two-bedroom bungalow, they were not impressed.

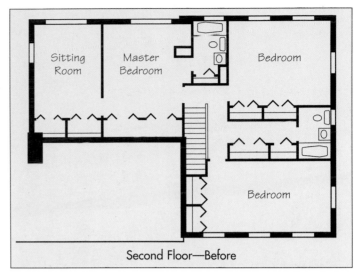

Drawing 1-3 *Originally, the second floor of the Broses' home was laid out so that the sitting room took a considerable amount of space from the master bedroom.*

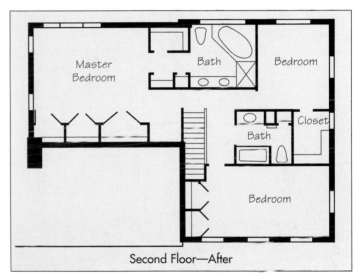

Drawing 1-4 *The Broses' redesigned master bedroom now bousts a walk-in closet and a luxuriously sized bathroom. Note that the bathroom and closets between the boys' rooms were reconfigured, too.*

"When I first saw the house, I had no interest in it," Joe said. "It looked like a shack. We came through the house, through a small kitchen to a porch at the back. Then I saw this big lot with an explosion of trees in the back. The room I really liked was the outdoors."

The location of the little house was appealing, too. It's a quick drive to the hospital where Joe is an emergency-room doctor. Elonide, a marketing consultant, works out of a home office. The house is conveniently located for receiving clients.

The house was a bargain considering the size of the lot, so the Semmeses bought it with the intention of adding on. With their four children, the couple endured the cramped conditions for a year before work began on the addition.

When the Semmeses bought their home, it was a two-bedroom Sears kit house in a great neighborhood.

With additions at the front and the back, the Semmeses' house now has room for a family of four.

For the amount of money the Semmeses invested in the house and addition, they knew they could have bought one of the nice new houses on the big lots that are popping up a little farther from the city.

"We thought about moving out of the city," Joe said. "But we belong to a country club about two blocks away. If we moved out, we'd have to get into traffic. And we thought that if we stayed in this neighborhood long enough, the house would hold its value. The plantings are mature. Schools and markets are nearby. If you want to live in a nonamazing place you can live anywhere. We wanted a sense of community, that we were around people who read and streets that work."

Joe had been through two other home renovations before buying the bungalow, so he had a pretty good idea of what he was looking for in a builder and architect. Joe and Elonide talked to a number of professionals about their addition. They hit it off with Alex Dean and Terry Cook, the same team who did the Broses' addition.

With his two earlier renovations, Joe said, the architects didn't really design within a budget. Because Alex was involved in meetings during the design phase, Terry was kept aware of budget concerns, while Alex was intimately aware of what the Semmeses wanted. As a result, Joe said, the job went smoother than it would have if Alex was just working from plans.

As design discussions began, it was immediately clear that most of the new space would be added at the top and rear of the house. The lot was simply too narrow to add sideways. There was room for expansion above the front porch, but if the house was too tall, it would look awkward among its low-slung neighbors. The

challenge was to make the house bigger without sacrificing its cozy cottage character.

As experienced remodelers, Joe and Elonide came to their first meeting with a list of what they wanted:

▲ Add two additional bedrooms upstairs.

▲ Build an office with a separate entrance for Elonide in the basement.

▲ Improve traffic flow in the front entry area.

▲ Add a family room, breakfast area, and new deck.

▲ Expand the dining room.

▲ Build a kitchen to accommodate an industrial cook top and oven.

▲ Provide special lighting and spaces for their art collection.

▲ Retain the first-floor bedroom and bathroom in case, in retirement, Joe or Elonide became unable to use the stairs.

▲ Soundproof the master bedroom to enable Joe to sleep during the day when he works the emergency-room night shift.

▲ Select low-maintenance building materials.

▲ Maintain a rear yard suitable for badminton, croquet, and other family sports.

Achieving all these goals in a narrow footprint was going to require some compromises. In the new plan, for example, you have to walk through the kitchen work area to get to the family room and breakfast area at the back of the house. This traffic pattern would drive many cooks up the wall. But Elonide didn't much mind. As long as she got her efficient, airy, well-equipped kitchen, Elonide figured she could live with a little traffic.

This compromise allowed Terry to improve the traffic pattern in the rest of the downstairs. In the old plan, the front door was at the middle of the house. To get to the kitchen you had to walk through the middle of the living room and the middle of the dining room, which made furniture placement awkward. In the new plan, the door was moved to one side, almost directly across from the main staircase so that a small part of the living room instantly became a foyer. A new door was added next to the staircase so that you can get to the first-floor bedroom without going through the living room or dining room.

The Semmeses also had to give up a beautiful old stone retaining wall and patio at the back of the house to make room for the breakfast area, family room, the new deck off the family room, and the home office below. The office doesn't feel like it is in a basement because the lot slopes down and away from the front of the house, and the door and windows at the back of the home office are not below ground.

The upstairs of the house had undergone a previous remodel to create one large master bedroom, a master bath, a home office, and some storage areas. As part of the new project, a small dormer at the front was replaced by a much larger one to create a large bedroom. The dormer steps back just a bit before becoming full width. The extra corners make the facade a little more interesting and make the new dormer less imposing and more proportional to the rest of the house. A third bedroom was created using most of the space that had been occupied by the old master bedroom. The new master bedroom occupies most of the rear addition. The old master bath was reconfigured to make room for a new master bath and a hall bath.

A last-minute inspiration was a little bay at the back of the master bedroom that Terry said reminds him of

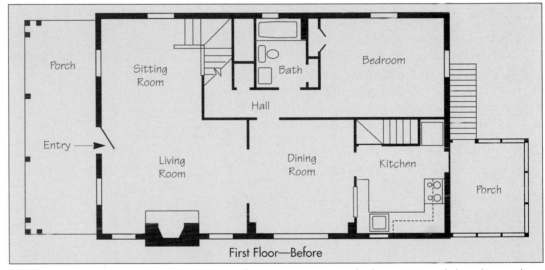

First Floor—Before

Drawing 1-5 *The awkward entrance in the Semmeses' Sears kit house opened directly into the living room. The small kitchen also needed to be redesigned.*

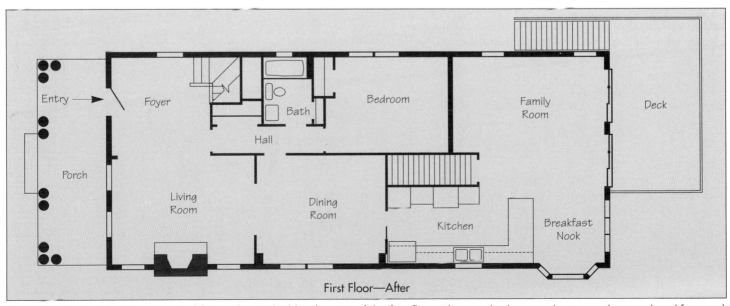

First Floor—After

Drawing 1-6 *The Semmeses' addition almost doubles the size of the first floor. The new kitchen is adjacent to the new breakfast nook and leads into the family room.*

a tree house. The original plan called for the second-floor roof to extend all the way over the back of the house. While framing the addition, the head carpenter, Mike Watson, remarked to Elonide that it was a shame to block the view with the roof. Together they developed the idea for stepping the main roof back to create a bay with windows on three sides, including an arch-top window in the gable end.

Now the Semmeses have a family house, Joe said. When friends and family come to town, Joe and Elonide can put them up.

"Having enough room for family and friends makes an enormous difference in your connectedness to people," Joe said.

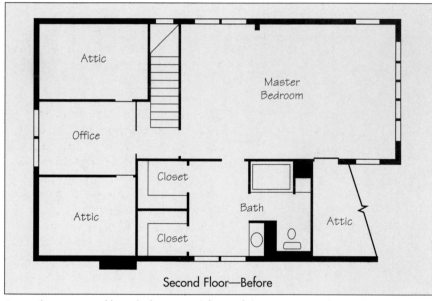

Drawing 1-7   *Although the second floor of the Semmeses' house had been remodeled before, much of the space could only be used for attic storage.*

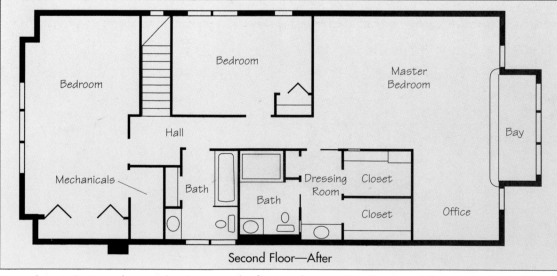

Drawing 1-8   *By enlarging the dormer in the front and expanding the second floor in the back, the Semmeses comfortably fit three bedrooms in a space that previously had one.*

Getting It Right the Second Time Around

David and Maria Dushkin never liked the addition they had built on their 150-year-old home in Guilford, Connecticut. For 15 years, the couple lived with an addition that didn't do justice to the beautiful Greek Revival-style home, with its mellow orange pine floors and its classical exterior cornices and columns.

Back then, David and Maria found themselves creating a merged family and suddenly needed room for four kids. The newlyweds needed to turn their three-bedroom house into a five-bedroom, and the addition budget was limited. The result was a tacked-on, one-story addition that contained two bedrooms.

"The first guy we had work on this place was really bad," David said. "We went with a low bid in a big hurry, and we lived with the consequences. Money was an issue then. We should have paid twice as much to get what we needed."

David and Marie love their community and the gardens they have created in their yard. Also, David has a large studio building at the back of the property where he pursues a long-time passion for creating metal sculptures.

"We looked at this [house] as sort of our old folks' home," said David, who is retired from his business, Dushkin Publishing Company. "After selling the company, we could have moved anywhere, but this is where we wanted to stay."

So the Dushkins finally decided to tear down the old addition and replace it with one that suited their current needs. By now the budget was considerably larger and priorities had changed. The kids were grown, so five bedrooms were no longer necessary. Maria was more interested in a large, professionally equipped kitchen, while David wanted the luxury of retreating to a comfortable study lined with bookshelves. Most of all, they wanted an addition that would enhance

The original addition at the back of David and Maria Dushkin's Connecticut home ignored the house's Greek Revival style.

The Dushkins' new addition honors the proportions and details of the original house.

their historic home instead of looking like a tacked-on afterthought.

This time, Maria and David did not take bids on the work for their addition, but instead relied on word-of-mouth recommendations to choose their builder and their architect. To build the addition, they chose Ed Flamand of Flamand Builders and Remodelers of Guilford. The architect was Tom Edwards, also of Guilford.

"A close friend recommended Ed," Maria said. "She had Ed remodel her kitchen, and I admired the work. When she was away, I went to her house to water her plants during a monsoon. The skylights didn't leak."

Ed recommended Tom Edwards. David said that he and Tom "clicked" the minute they met. Tom is good at making instant sketches as he talks with clients. The Dushkins told Tom they wanted a kitchen that felt open to their lovely yard and had a place for houseplants. While David and Maria watched, Tom sketched a room filled with windows and skylights.

The biggest challenge Tom faced was to nearly double the size of the house and to create a large modern kitchen. Tom had to accomplished this task while remaining faithful to house's classical style and without overpowering the original house. This problem is not an uncommon one for architects planning large additions in historic areas. Tom's solution was as classic as the house itself. Rather than disturb or try to transform the elegant proportions of the existing house, Tom stepped the main part of the addition away using a small, lower transitional area. The addition repeats the proportions, mass, and exterior details of the original house, although it is slightly smaller.

Drawing 1-9 *A wall of floor-to-ceiling windows plus two skylights brings plenty of sunshine into the Dushkins' new kitchen. The small bedroom is used for overnight guests.*

First Floor—After

Porch

Bath

Living Room

Family Room

Bedroom

Entry

Dining Room

Kitchen

Skylights

Windows

■ = Addition

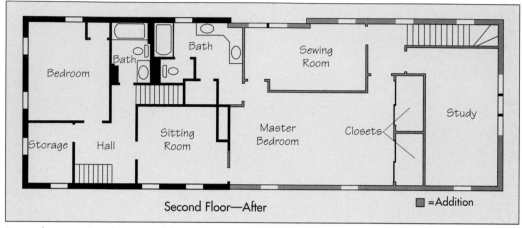

Second Floor—After   ■ =Addition

Drawing 1-10 *The second floor of the Dushkins' addition incorporates a private study for David, a sewing room for Maria, and a master bedroom with ample closet space.*

The Dushkins' kitchen offers modern conveniences without sacrificing classic looks. Windows and skylights fill the room with light and offer a view of the garden.

Upstairs is David Dushkin's cozy office retreat.

The roof ridge is perpendicular to the original one, which makes the entire house more visually interesting from any side.

David and Maria finally have the home they always wanted. The new addition occupies the same footprint as the old one, but because it is two stories high, there was room upstairs to add David's study and to enlarge the master bedroom suite as well. Downstairs, the addition contains a small bedroom, which is nice for overnight guests. Also, the resale value of a house of this size in this neighborhood would be damaged by reducing the bedroom count further. The rest of the addition is, of course, devoted to Maria's dream kitchen. Filled as it is with the warmth of wood and natural light, the kitchen seems as if it had always been there.

David stressed that it really isn't necessary to have a clear picture of what form your addition will take before you meet with an architect. After all, putting form to your needs is the architect's job.

"It doesn't matter what you don't know," David said. "What you do know is how you live and how you want to live. If you come across an architect who wants to tell you what you want, don't hire him."

A Harmonious Dining Room

As you wind your way a quarter of a mile down the rutted dirt drive, you find yourself thinking, "Where could this lead?" Suddenly, the drive spills downhill, and you find yourself in front of Ann Goldberg's white brick house.

The house is 50 years old, but it seems much older with its big fireplaces, classical moldings, and transom windows. As you walk through the house to the back, you are treated to a panoramic view of the Connecticut River.

At one side of the houses is the one-story, dining room addition that Tom Edwards designed and Ed Flamand built for Ann. The walls of this room are mostly glass, consisting of large windows and a pair of french doors, all with transom windows above.

When Ann first considered an addition, she was thinking about a playroom for her two kids. "But

Ann Goldberg's dining room addition continues the rhythm of the main house's windows and pilasters.

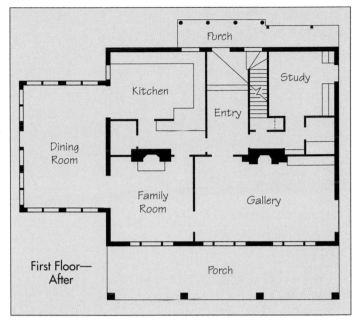

Drawing 1-11   *Ann Goldberg's new dinning room, with windows on three sides, is a transitional space to the outdoors.*

when I began planning, it made more sense to make this [the addition] into the dining room so that the back room of the house became a place for the kids to play."

With its walls of glass and french doors opening to a patio, the dining room creates a graceful transition from the main house to the outdoors. With so much glass, the dining room is a different space from the rest of the house, yet it is in perfect harmony. The reason for this apparent dichotomy is rhythm. The main house has a rhythm created by the consistent size of the windows, the size of the window panes, the spacing of windows, and the use of transom windows. All of these things are continued in the addition.

The addition meets the main house at a brick wall, which adds texture to the room and enhances its role as a transition to the outdoors. The addition has large openings to the kitchen and to the family room.

"I have always liked this house because the rooms flow for entertaining," Ann said. "The dining room really adds to that. I have had 60 to 70 people here with no problem. Most people don't perceive that the dining room is an addition."

That's the idea.

With access to the living room, kitchen, and patio, Goldberg's dining room makes entertaining a large gathering of guests easier.

Cape Cod Transformation

It was a nondescript rambler, the sort of house that sprung up all over the United States during the building boom that followed World War II. This rambler, though, happened to be on a double lot on a street overlooking a creek in Minneapolis, Minnesota.

The lot caught the interest of Dick and Sandy Schoenke, who were living in a neighborhood nearby. The Schoenkes weren't happy with the house in which they had been living. It was too big, too formal, and too dark. And it was on a tiny lot.

Dick and Sandy wanted a sunny house on a big lot where Sandy could garden. The couple also wanted to stay in the same school district so that their kids wouldn't have to transfer. The location of this rambler met these criteria perfectly. But the house—well—it was just another house, and with only two bedrooms, it was smaller than they needed.

The Schoenkes decided to take a look inside anyway, and they brought along Dale Mulfinger, an architect whose kids go to school with the Schoenke kids.

Sandy remembers, "We were looking at the fireplace, and it was so horrible. I said to Dale, 'Can we do do anything about that?' And Dale said, 'Oh you can do anything!' And that's how it all started."

With that, the Schoenkes bought the house and began the process of transforming the one-story rambler into a two-story Cape Cod-style house that would fit in any town on the coast of New England.

"I've just always loved the Cape Cod style," Sandy said. "Dale came over and started asking us lots of questions, and he listened carefully to the answers. He asked how we entertain, and we told him we wanted a more casual space. After our old house, having lots of light was a big thing for us. We wanted space that flowed and a house that is big enough for when we have everyone home but not so big that we feel we are rattling around when no one else is here."

The new second story contains a large master bedroom with a master bath and walk-in closet, as well as two additional bedrooms, a hall bath, and a roomy storage space.

Downstairs, one of the two bedrooms was eliminated to make room for the new dining room. A wall that had separated the old bedroom from the living room was eliminated. A bank of big windows at the front of the house are opposed by French doors topped with transoms at the back. The expanse of glass allows natural light throughout the downstairs, achieving the

Here's a house you've seen before. In some parts of the country, it's called a ranch house; in other places, a rambler. Sandy and Dick Schoenke bought the house because its location was perfect.

After remodeling and additions, the Schoenkes' house sports the Cape Cod style that Sandy has always admired.

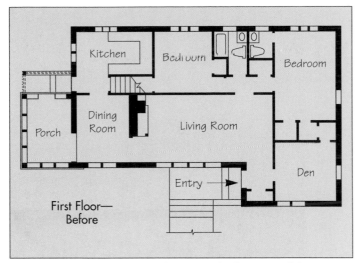

Drawing 1-12 *For the Schoenkes, the location of the rambler was perfect, but the house's layout was uninspiring.*

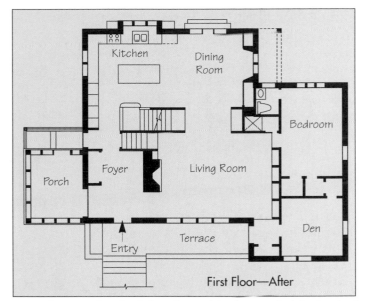

Drawing 1-13 *The Schoenkes' addition extended the back of the house by 10 feet, making room for an expanded kitchen and larger dinning room.*

sunny rooms the Schoenkes wanted so much. To make the dining room larger and to make room for a large kitchen, the back of the house was extended 10 feet. The three-season porch on one side of the house also was extended a few feet.

With its gray cedar shingle siding and roofing offset by white trim and its steep roof with three doghouse dormers, the exterior of the house is pure New England. If the proportion of the windows and transoms look familiar, it's because you saw them in Ann Goldberg's Connecticut house.

The addition was built by John Sylvester Construction, Inc., of Minneapolis. Fortunately, the Schoenkes were able to stay in their own house during construction.

"John did the best presentation, and even showed us a video of his work," Sandy said. "We got along with him 100 percent of the time."

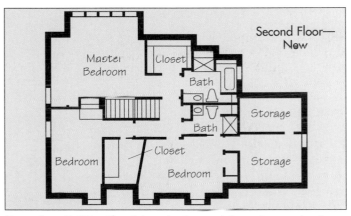

Drawing 1-14 *The Schoenkes' remodeling also involved adding a second story, which included a master bedroom and bath.*

The Schoenkes' living room opens into the dining room, allowing natural light throughout the downstairs.

The naturally finished beadboard on the ceiling in the Schoenkes' kitchen visually lowers it, adding to the cozy Cape Cod effect.

A Cook's Delight

It's just a bump-out, a few feet added to the back of Louis and Lucerna Bocciarelli's kitchen. But it's made a big difference in the usefulness of the kitchen, and it improved the traffic flow in the whole downstairs of this Branford, Connecticut, home. The addition was designed by Doug Denes, a Branford architect.

"Originally, Lou wanted to expand the dining room too, but Doug talked us out of that," Lucerna said.

The old kitchen was designed and built in a time when kitchens were not intended as a social gathering place but solely as a work space. The main work area of the old kitchen was a simple L-shape against two interior walls. The space was too small and too dark, and when Lucerna worked in it, she felt isolated from the rest of the house.

Lucerna loves to cook, and she loves to have company when she cooks. Her new kitchen has a sunny breakfast nook in the shape of half an octagon. The walls of the octagon consist of big windows that fill the kitchen with light and take advantage of the backyard view. Of course, a breakfast nook is a great convenience for a busy family that doesn't want to set up every meal in the formal dining room.

The new kitchen also has a large island that contains the cook top. This way, Lucerna faces into the room while she cooks, so she can enjoy the view or enjoy the company of family and friends who might pull up a stool to the island or sit at the breakfast nook. She can even enjoy the fireplace in the family room. One side of the island has a gradual curve. Doug said that the curve improves traffic by leading you toward the family room and dining room doors.

"This kitchen is great," Lucerna said. "I am never more than two steps away from whatever I need."

The island in Louis and Lucerna Bocciarelli's new kitchen is subtly curved to improve traffic.

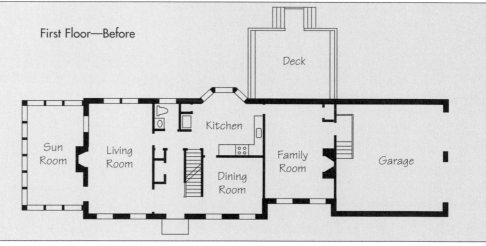

Drawing 1-15   The original L-shaped kitchen in the Bocciarellis' house was cramped and dark.

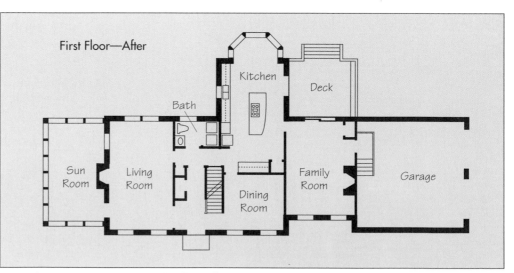

Drawing 1-16   To improve the flow of the kitchen's layout, the Bocciarellis' architect bumped out the space and included a breakfast nook.

Chapter 2

FORMING A PLAN OF ATTACK

You've got lots of thinking to do before you can start sketching your addition on paper. For one thing, do you really want to build an addition at all? And if you do, what should the addition be? Who will design the addition and who will build it? How much will it cost and how will you pay for it? This chapter will help you answer these important preliminary questions.

MOVE OR IMPROVE?

One way to solve your home's space problems is to pull up stakes and buy a house that better meets your needs or can be more easily altered to fill the bill. But relocating even nearby costs—socially, as well as financially. Moving to another town might be logical if you need to relocate for career or other reasons, but moving only to improve your living conditions has to be compared to the cost of improving your existing house. You can't estimate the cost of such a change with any reasonable degree of accuracy until you find a candidate home. Then you can add up the costs of selling your home, moving, closing on a new home, and adapting it to your needs. But even if you come up with a figure, how do you know what to compare it to? The obvious thing to do is to figure out what changes would be necessary to bring your present house up to your present needs and to put a price on the construction. Then weigh the pros and cons of improving and of moving.

How Much to Improve?

You can set a budget for a home-improvement project by asking either "How much will it cost?" or "How much should I spend?" The answer to the first question comes from defining the scope of the project and estimating its cost. This kind of budget might be right for you if you plan to stay in your home long enough to realize the value of the improvements in the form of a better quality of life. But most homeowners eventually move, so it makes for sounder planning to test the cost of the improvements against the added resale value of the house.

"Don't overimprove," warn real estate agents. Though they can't tell you exactly what things constitute overimprovement, they do agree on a few general guidelines. First, know your neighborhood. What are homes selling for? What features do buyers expect any home in the neighborhood to have (two and a half baths, for example)? What items are they most likely to spend a bit extra to get? You probably have a good idea of this already if you have lived in the vicinity for very long. To round out your information, talk to real estate agents and home appraisers who are familiar with your neighborhood.

Here are some other suggestions:

▲ Try to set your budget to keep the total value of your house somewhere between the low and high ends of the selling prices of nearby homes.

▲ Aim to keep your total budget for improvements (including the addition) within 15 to 20 percent of the value of the house as it exists before remodeling.

▲ Don't buck the trend. If home values are generally increasing in the area, you are more likely to recover money invested in an addition than if values are slipping. One indication of the general trend is the number of other homes that are being improved.

▲ When planning your project, remember that the more you customize a feature to your own personality and needs, the less likely that feature will appeal to the unknown future buyer and the less the buyer will want to pay for the amenity.

▲ Keep thorough records of all costs you incur for improvements to reduce any taxable gain on the property when you sell it.

Payback Potential of Various Improvements

Additional space will start paying you back immediately in the form of increased livability. How much payback the improvements yield on the money invested depends

A small, carefully planned addition can go a long way toward improving your home. This addition consists of a bump-out that's just big enough for the dining table yet brings a flood of natural light and a spacious feeling to the entire living room.

on the cost of the improvement and market demand for this type of amenity at the time you sell your house. Predicting demand for even a few years into the future is tricky business. Here are some cost factors to think about early on when considering alternative ways to solve the space problems you identified in Chapter 1.

Living/family rooms. If one area is presently serving all of the household's various social and leisure activities, you can appreciate the need for an extra room. You can expect to at least recoup your investment in additional leisure space. To ensure the greatest potential return, plan the space for easy conversion to another use. If, for example, you live in a neighborhood where home offices are popular, you might plan a family room that can be adapted to this use by including a separate entrance to the outside.

New garage. Adding a garage costs less for each square foot of space than most other kinds of additions. Still, you can expect a return of only 30 to 50 percent of the cost, depending on where you live. Naturally, the

The inside of a garage addition typically isn't finished, so it's usually the least expensive space you can add to your home. Especially in cold climates, a garage can make your life much more convenient, and it adds significantly to the home's resale value.

return will be higher in an area with serious winter weather than it will be in Florida. If you live in an area with mild winters and already have a garage, you might be well ahead by converting the garage to living space rather than adding new space.

New bathroom. Bathroom space is typically the most expensive space you can add. If your addition consists of a bedroom suite that includes bath facilities, expect the bathroom space to cost at least 40 percent more per square foot than the adjacent bedroom. Plumbing fixtures, piping, exhaust fans, special cabinetry and accessories, and finishes such as tile all contribute to this disparity.

Deciding whether to add bathroom space can be tricky. New bath facilities won't necessarily add to the value of your house. In fact, if your house is shy of the neighborhood standard for bathrooms, you may have to add one just to keep pace. On the other hand, if you add a fourth bathroom while the neighborhood houses have only two, you probably won't recoup your expenses. The current demand is for amenity in bathrooms. If you are thinking of additional facilities, don't just duplicate the three-fixture arrangement in the rest of the house. Consider amenities that make the new facilities special, such as a spa, adjacent garden court, or more luxurious vanity.

Bathrooms are expensive to add, so plan carefully. The window seat in this small but elegant bath is an unexpected touch.

New or enlarged kitchen. The same things that make bathroom space expensive apply to kitchens. The main difference is that while adding rooms, such as bedrooms, may require new bathrooms, they don't beget new kitchens. The kitchen may be the most personal room in the house, so knowing how much to spend on improvements—whether as new space or remodeling—means separating your own personal desires for the space from the features that will likely add resale value to your home. Decide early on which features you want for yourself (and are willing to spend extra money on) and which features you want to add to increase the resale value. If your current kitchen lacks counter space, for example, additional counter space means choosing between different lines of cabinets and countertops. The cost of a solid-surface acrylic countertop may be three or four times the cost of one made of laminated plastic.

Do you want to build a kitchen that perfectly suits your own taste? Or are you more concerned with resale value? This kitchen has beautiful wooden details, but open shelving doesn't fit everyone's taste and lifestyle.

You won't recover this difference in resale value, but if you have always craved a solid-surface top and expect to get a few years use out of it, it may be worth the extra cost.

Home office. As hot as the demand is for home office space right now, no one knows what it will be in the future. Fortunately, space for an office is not expensive to add. Unless you build a stand-alone facility with its own toilet and kitchen facilities, the only item for which you may have to spend a little extra is wiring systems. The key to getting the most out of your investment in office space is reconversion. You may plan the space to have a separate entrance to the outside, but plan everything else with an eye to a future buyer who may want to use the room for a bedroom or den. Rather than fluorescent office-type lighting in the ceiling, choose home-type lighting augmented by portable fixtures that can plug in wherever needed. Install demountable shelving and furniture instead of building in items that would lock the space into an office use.

When planning your addition with an eye toward its effect on the home's resale value, don't forget that the condition of the rest of the home completes the picture. A gleaming new wood floor abutting a dull, older one will draw more attention to the condition of the older one than if there had been no addition. The way out of this dilemma is to plan your addition as part of a comprehensive program to bring the whole house up to par. You don't have to do everything at the same time, just list the needed repairs and upgrades and put them on a schedule.

HOW MUCH WILL IT COST?

The total cost of your project, however it is designed and built, will comprise the material and labor that go into it plus any permits, equipment rental, and other costs of doing the work. You stand to save substantially by doing all or part of the work yourself, depending on how you value your own time. Remember, though, not to undertake anything you can't finish—and can't finish well.

You can get an idea of what your project will cost by an estimate made at any stage of the planning. Obviously, the more defined the project is, the more accurately its cost can be pegged. A preliminary estimate made at the concept stage can serve to establish a project budget, help define the extent of the project, and give you an idea of how much you will need to finance the project. The concept should at least define the square footage of each type of area to be added,

such as 150 square feet of bath and 300 square feet of bedroom space. As the project takes shape on paper, the preliminary estimate can be refined to reflect the additional information.

Designers and contractors can make a more exact estimate from completed working drawings and specifications than from preliminary ideas. A contractor's estimate based on the final plan in the form of a bid is, naturally, the most reliable estimate of all.

Ballpark Estimates

Preliminary, or ballpark, estimates project the construction cost by applying a unit cost to the area of the addition. The least reliable ballpark estimate would simply multiply the square footage of the addition by a unit cost. A more reliable method would match different unit costs to different kinds of spaces according to their complexity. A garage, for example, is far less expensive to build than a living room because it normally doesn't require heating and interior finish work. And a living room wouldn't cost the same as a kitchen or bath, with their plumbing fixtures and cabinetry. Your designer should provide an estimate of this type at some point early on in the planning stage.

If you do your own design and planning, you might ask a builder to give you some unit costs to apply to the various kinds of areas in your plan. Many builders will give you a preliminary estimate for free, as an enticement to be considered for the construction phase.

Brick-and-Mortar Estimates

The most reliable cost estimate takes into account the actual construction. This is the type of estimate a contractor would use to prepare a bid. From the final working drawings, the estimator first calculates the quantity of each material, then multiplies this by a unit cost for the material and one for labor to arrive at a line item cost for that material. The contractor draws on a database of unit costs as well as past experience with similar projects. The sum of all line item costs yields a subtotal to which overhead and profit are added to yield a total construction cost.

If you want to attempt your own brick-and-mortar estimate, you can get annually published unit costs (check your library) or use on of the several computer software programs now available. If you manipulate spreadsheets with ease, you might find this route helpful in establishing a budget and comparing alternative design approaches. Be warned, though, that the resulting figures are only as good as the input. Unless you know how each item is constructed, you may make assumptions that don't reflect reality, regardless of how nifty the total comes up on screen. Also, unit costs vary widely from one region to another, and even if area factors take this into account, they may not reflect the costs in your particular location. One further caveat: Estimating costs can be equated to shooting a moving target. Costs change continuously and any database is only as accurate as its most current information.

Finding Financing

An idea of how much the project will cost is the starting point for a financing strategy. You won't know the actual cost of the project until you get bids from contractors or—if you build it yourself—pay for the materials. Even so, you will need a project budget at the outset so that you will be able to seek financing. A target budget can also be one of the parameters that defines the size of the project. After setting a budget, you need to appraise your financial standing. Your assets, your credit history, and maybe even your standing with well-to-do relatives can affect where the money comes from.

Personal and Family Resources

The easiest source of financing may already be within easy reach if your project is small enough: checking and savings accounts. You forsake earned interest by withdrawing funds from these sources, but won't have to pay additional interest for using the money. You may be able to borrow against a savings account at an interest rate only a few percentage points above the rate of return the account is paying. And tapping existing money accounts gets the money fast, without paperwork or encumbering other assets.

If tapping cash accounts won't yield all you'll need, can you round out the extra amount needed by borrowing from credit cards or insurance policies? The amount of ready cash available from credit cards has gone up dramatically in recent years if you are prepared to pay the highest possible interest rates. Before borrowing from a life insurance policy, check with your agent to see how much you can borrow, the repayment interest, and period of repayment.

Investments are another avenue. Drawing funds out of a money-market account is often as simple as writing a check. Shares in individual stocks and mutual funds can usually be liquidated. Liquidating individual bonds before their maturity comes with a penalty, though, as does cashing in any certificates of deposit, IRAs, or annuity funds.

How about borrowing from your parents or other relatives? You'll escape closing costs and other application paperwork and may even be able to flex a bit on the time of repayment if you get into dire straits. But therein lies a pitfall. It may be too easy to slack off, particularly if you don't compulsively pay bills as they become due. If this happens, you risk souring family relationships. Is it worth the risk?

Using Your Home to Finance Your Addition

Many people find the cash they need to finance home improvements and additions by using the equity they have in their homes. Choosing this route allows you to take advantage of your largest single asset—your home—with the additional attraction that interest charged on any mortgage or loan secured against a mortgage is deductible from your income taxes. There are three ways to do this.

Home-equity loan. If you have paid off a good portion of your house, you may get up to 80 percent of the equity amount in a loan secured against your home. A home-equity loan opens a line of credit you can draw on as you need to make payments on the construction. Closing costs are low, but the interest rate is likely variable, so beware. You can get pinched in a time of rising rates. On the other hand, you pay interest only on the funds used. This feature makes a home-equity loan appealing if you don't know the final construction cost at the outset.

Second mortgage. For a second mortgage, you borrow a fixed amount of money that is released in one lump sum and pay it off over a period agreed on with the lender, in much the same way as you do with your first mortgage, except the term will probably not exceed 15 years. The maximum amount loaned will be based on a percentage of the market value of your home less the balance owed on the first mortgage. The second lender then gets second claim to your property, after the primary lender, if you default. Similar to your first mortgage the interest rate can be fixed or variable and is deductible from your income tax. One downside is that after you agree to the amount to be financed and the interest rate, you are stuck with it, regardless of the final cost of the project. Remember, too, that for a second mortgage you will need to do a new title search, have a new appraisal, and pay closing costs.

Refinancing. Refinancing means that you apply for a new mortgage that will pay off any amount owed on your present mortgage and provide you with the funds needed for the addition. The same front-end steps (title search, appraisal, closing costs) are necessary if you decide to refinance, since this option effectively means starting from scratch. You can usually borrow for a longer term than with a second mortgage, generally up to 30 years. This option appeals when interest rates are low or at least lower than your present rate by at least two percentage points. Depending on the lender and the term of the loan, you may be able to get the amount you need without increasing your monthly payments—you may even lower them.

Loans from Lending Institutions

If you have to borrow to finance your addition, you'll probably get what you need at the lowest cost if you use your equity as collateral for the loan. When such a route is not feasible, there are various types of unsecured loans to consider that are offered through banks, savings and loans, and credit unions. The amounts you can get vary, as do repayment periods,

financing costs, and interest rates. (See "Comparing Home-Improvement Loans," below.) If you decide to go after any kind of loan or refinance your home, you should have certain data at hand:

▲ Employment and salary history, including details of other income sources.

▲ List of assets, including real estate, stocks, bonds, mutual funds, pension funds, and life insurance policies.

▲ List of liabilities, including amounts owed on outstanding loans, mortgages, credit cards, and payments automatically deducted from your checking account.

▲ Project data, including when your home was purchased, purchase price, planned improvements, and name of general contractor. (Of course, you won't have all the data required for this last item until your project has been planned, designed, and bid or estimated.)

COMPARING HOME-IMPROVEMENT LOANS

Type of Loan	Pros	Cons
Commercial bank: commercial loan	Arranged on signature Simple interest results in less total interest than a conventional home-improvement loan Negotiable repayment period Faster to arrange; no property appraisal required	Hard to get unless you have a long-standing relationship with bank and an excellent credit record Repayment period means higher monthly payments
Commercial bank: home-improvement loan, line of credit	Low closing costs You pay interest only on the amount actually used Interest is tax deductible if loan is secured against your mortgage	Finances only up to 80% of your equity in your home Interest rates change constantly, so you can be hurt if rates are rising Total interest rate is figured on the repayment period
Savings and loan association: home-improvement line of credit	Finances 100% of loan up to $15,000 Longer repayment period than some other loans Interest is tax deductible if loan is secured against your mortgage	Early repayment is penalized Total interest may be high if repayment period is long Lender may require a second mortgage and property appraisal
Credit union: home-improvement loan	Simple interest with no other financing charges No penalty for early repayment Interest is tax deductible if loan is secured against your mortgage	Must belong to a credit union that offers home-improvement loans Repayment period may be short, with larger payments Lender may require a second mortgage and property appraisal

WHAT TO DO YOURSELF—WHAT TO HIRE OUT

Doing some of the design and construction work yourself can be a satisfying experience and save you money. It can also turn a dream into a nightmare if you get in over your head. Instead of satisfaction with a job well done, you'll suffer frustration at one botched. Rather than savings, you'll end up paying someone else more to rescue the job than if you had hired them for the job in the first place. An even more likely possibility is that you will be perfectly capable of doing the task, begin it with gusto, then have to put it on hold because of other demands on your time. You have probably seen remodeled homes where some things never seem to get finished. Certain rooms still sport drywall that has not been finished past the taping stage. Maybe the owner hasn't gotten around to putting the wood trim around the doors and windows, even though the doors and windows have been in place for two years.

To get the most out of a task you are considering doing and avoid the pitfalls, know what's required to do the job right, then match this against your capabilities. This book can help you with the first part by laying out the basic ways a home addition goes together, from planning to completion. As each material or system is described, an indication of how difficult it might be for a do-it-yourselfer is given along with a recommendation if the task is better left to a specialist. From this information, you can assess your own capabilities—your time, skills, and tools—and weigh these against the demands of the job. Here are some questions to consider.

Do I really want to do this job? Stop here if the answer is no. Digging in to do a job that you loath may save money, but isn't worth it in the long run. Take drywall, for example. Cutting sheets and nailing them to studs is easy to like. Progress is rapid as each piece covers bare studs. Then comes the messy, tedious part: finishing the joints. Embedding tape into dry-wall compound is messy enough, but sanding the dried compound and refilling low spots—done right—tests the mettle of the most avid do-it-yourselfer. The fine dust that fills the room finds its way around your headgear to irritate your eyes and nose. It also sneaks around any barrier you have put up to infiltrate the rest of the house. Is it worth it? Only you can decide.

Am I able to do this task successfully? This question is easy to answer if you have done something similar before. If not, don't automatically think you can't do it—find out what's required. It may be something you can easily learn and get a great deal of satisfaction

from mastering. Today, many resources stand ready to help you. Take plumbing, for example. In the days when water pipes were made of threaded steel and waste piping was heavy cast iron joined with melted lead, plumbers were the only people who had the tools and skills to plumb a house. Today, lightweight copper tubing is the norm for hot- and cold-water piping. Plastic piping is used for waste and vent pipes. Both materials are readily available at home centers and hardware stores.

Do I have the time to complete this task? Jobs, such as installing interior wood trim, can be done piecemeal, so they tend to get left unfinished, pending free time that never seems to be available. Other tasks must be done in one whack. If you are hooking up plumbing fixtures, your household has to go without water until the job is done. Then there are jobs that have to be done in a particular sequence, such as wiring or installing sheathing on the roof or walls. The next step of the construction can't progress until the prior one is complete. So, to plan your time adequately for these kinds of jobs, you have to consider "when" as well as "how much."

What about tools? If you have an electric drill, a portable circular saw, and a standard assortment of hand carpentry tools, you are probably equipped to do 90 percent of the assembly of a home addition. Augmenting this list with the most frequently used tools for wiring and plumbing won't likely break your budget. Expensive tools for special purposes, such as floor sanders, are available at rental agencies almost everywhere. The main limitation about rental tools is time. Renting a tool for as long as it takes to do a job in occasional sessions may cost more than paying a professional to do the entire job.

Can I save enough money to justify doing this job myself? Cost savings may not be the driving issue for you if you regard any work you do on your home as a hobby or a way to relieve the stress of your regular job. If, however, you are taking time off from income-producing work, the time is a cost to be traded off of the savings you may make by going it solo. To reckon the difference you need to rate the hourly cost of your time and know how long it will take you to do the job, then compare this with the cost of paying someone else to do it.

How will it affect my household? If you undertake major parts of the project, you stand to remove yourself from your normal role in the household—okay if you agree beforehand with all affected—but potentially dangerous if some members sense neglect. And if you stretch the project out to complete it, working nights and weekends, your household might get very tired of living in inconvenience. A final source of stress may come from your own frustration and fatigue in trying feel a rapport with, who will interpret your dreams into a reality you will love living with. Above all, the designer must be someone you can trust.

Finding the Right Consultant

If the range of design consultants impresses you, expect at least as much variety in their capabilities and personalities. Finding the perfect designer for your project begins with getting leads. Sources for these include

▲ Friends, relatives, or business associates who have successfully worked with a designer on a project.

▲ Tradesmen you know or who have worked for you (carpenters, electricians, plumbers, roofers, excavators).

▲ Listings in the Yellow Pages of the local telephone directory.

People you know and trust provide the most reliable information. Their experiences working with a designer doesn't necessarily have to have been with their own home. Some of your business associates may have gone through a building project with their business or as a member of a civic board. Ask them how the project turned out and whether the designer kept an open mind and ear to the client's wishes. Was the project completed on schedule and budget? Pump them for anything else that concerns you. Be sure to ask if they would hire this person again.

Listings in the Yellow Pages tell you only that the person has a business number, so regard any leads you turn up there only as a starting point for further research. You may also be able to find raw leads by phoning state professional associations, such as the regional chapter of the American Institute of Architects or Council of Consulting Engineers. While these organizations may list their professional members by specialty (residential design, for example), they won't tell you anything more. You'll have to get that information from the designer.

Call any likely candidates and ask them to meet you at your house. Meeting you on your own turf allows the designer to see the site of the project firsthand, and you may find issues to discuss that might not occur to you in the designer's office. Some designers may charge a fee for the initial meeting if they feel it might not result in a commission. Ask if this is the case, and if the charge can be deducted from the services rendered later if you enter into an agreement. The initial meeting can be worthwhile for you, whether or not you hire the candidate designer. In learning more

about how the building process works, you will be better able to pursue your goals—if not with this designer, then with another.

The interview is a two-way street. While you are obtaining information about the designer, he or she is finding out about you, your house, and the project. Be prepared to answer questions such as

▲ What are your overall aims for this project? Agree beforehand with your spouse or partner on overall goals for the project, even if you disagree on minor points.

▲ Have you fixed a budget for the project? You don't have to at this point, but it will help if you have one.

▲ What factors will determine the schedule for design and construction?

▲ How will decisions be made? If you and your spouse are equally involved, you shouldn't expect the designer to settle disputes when differences occur.

▲ Have you ever been through a design or building project? If so, what pleased you and what disappointed you?

For your part, don't hesitate to ask whatever you want, but include

▲ What similar projects have you designed?

▲ May I talk to clients you have worked for? Sometimes, clients don't want to be bothered. So if the designer can't put you in touch with clients whose projects he shows you, request the names and addresses of past clients.

▲ How will you approach this project and who will be working on it? This is important if the designer has a staff.

▲ What kind of fee arrangement is possible? Don't expect an exact figure at the first meeting; the designer may want time to work up a proposal.

Tell the designer that you are interviewing other candidates as well, and let him or her know when you expect to make a decision. Next, contact the designer's past clients. Tell them you are considering this designer and would like to hear about any experiences they care to share about their own project. Then be prepared for a flood of advice, pro or con. Working with a designer to change something as personal as your home is never a neutral experience.

MATCHING THE EXPERT TO THE TASK

Key:
✓ *Usually Provided*
+ *Sometimes Provided*

Task or Service	Architect	Structural Engineer	Mechanical Engineer	Electrical Engineer	Civil Engineer	Surveyor	Building/Home Designer	Kitchen/Bath Designer	Drafting/Planning Service	Landscape Architect
Evaluate Existing Building or Site										
Survey site, provide site plan of existing conditions					✓	✓				
Overall condition of entire building	✓									
Foundation	+	✓								
Structural condition of floors, walls, roof	+	✓								
Heating, cooling, ventilating systems			✓							
Electrical and lighting systems				✓						
Planning and Design Services										
Overall planning and design, coordinate other designers	✓									
Determine structural members and system layouts		✓								
Plan and design interior spaces	✓						✓	✓	+	
Plan and design kitchens and baths	✓						✓	✓	+	
Prepare construction drawings									✓	
Design landscaping										✓
Lay out heating, cooling, and plumbing systems			✓							
Design electrical and lighting systems				✓						
Possible Fee Arrangements										
Hourly rate	✓	✓	✓	✓	✓	✓	✓	✓	✓	✓
Fixed fee for stipulated work	✓	✓	✓	✓	✓	✓	✓	✓	✓	✓
Percentage of total construction cost	✓									
Percentage of the cost of items specified by consultant								✓		
Fee included in prime professional (by prearrangement)		+	+	+				+		

Design Professional

Negotiating a Contract for Design Services

When you have selected the designer you feel most confident working with, always formalize the terms of your agreement in writing. Architects may use their standard contract form or one customized for residential work. Whatever form of contract the designer suggests should include provisions for the following items

▲ Definition of the project: what it amounts to and where it is.

▲ Definition of the services to be provided by the designer.

▲ Definition your responsibilities, as owner of the project.

▲ List of any constraints (time, for example) to be imposed.

▲ Basis of the designer's compensation (fixed fee, percentage of construction cost, percentage of cost of items specified) and the schedule for payments.

▲ Statement of responsibility for problems. For example, the designer pays for corrections in the work due to his or her negligence; the owner pays for omissions and changes.

It's always a good idea to have an attorney review the draft of any contract before you sign it.

Working with an Architect

Depending on the extent of your project, you may need partial services, such as a layout and cabinet specifications from a kitchen designer, or the full services of a consultant who can help you with every phase from conception through construction. Say you hire architect Adrienne Barnes for full services. Here's what she would likely do at each phase of the project and what you should expect to do to keep the project moving smoothly along.

Predesign. After negotiating the terms of her agreement to mutual satisfaction, Adrienne will need something to start with. She or a member of her staff will come to your house to document the structure, as is, by taking measurements and notes and possibly photographs. She'll go back to her office and use the rough data to make an accurate set of base drawings to use as the starting point for the design phase. But before she actually starts designing, she'll need to define the project in the form of a design program. This information will come from you, so you should have a clear idea of what you aim to achieve and what you can spend.

Schematic design. Adrienne will use the base drawings and design program to work up an initial scheme and rough cost for constructing the job. Her presentation will be your first opportunity to see your project as a concept. Seize the occasion to test the scheme against your goals and note where it falls short. Pass your feelings on to Adrienne. She may revise the scheme and present it again or incorporate the revisions in the next stage of the design.

Design development. Adrienne will likely continue to fine-tune the schematic design to incorporate your suggestions. She may take the design to a more detailed level as "preliminary drawings" that show the plan at a larger scale and add details, such as cabinetry and proposed finishes. Other drawings, such as elevations and cross sections, might also be added. For a simple one-room addition, you might end the architect's involvement at this point, trusting a competent builder to interpret the drawings faithfully in construction.

Construction documents. Construction documents are working drawings that describe in detailed graphic form what a building is to be and how the parts go together. Specifications supplement the drawings in writing, indicating which materials are to be used and how it is to be built. When you finally approve Adrienne's preliminary design drawings, she will prepare construction documents you can use to secure bids from contractors, obtain a building permit, and construct the project. A fuller explanation of construction drawings is in Chapter 9, beginning on page 176.

Bidding and negotiation. With printed sets of the construction documents, you can now solicit bids from building contractors. Adrienne will help you find reliable builders, set a bid date, and receive bids if you have retained her for this phase. While preparing their bids, builders may phone her to ask for interpretations of unclear or conflicting items. If she is playing strictly by the rules, she will answer their questions in the form of written addenda mailed to each bidder before the bids are due, but she may answer informally. The important point is to give the same information to all bidders.

Construction administration. When the bids come in, Adrienne will help you review them and recommend which bid to accept. She'll make her recommendation not just on the prices quoted, but other factors such as the contractor's track record and personality. She will then work with you to prepare a construction contract and schedule. After the work begins, she will visit the site periodically to interpret the documents, help the builder resolve issues that arise, and act as your agent to ensure that the work conforms to the documents. When the builder submits payment requests, the architect will review them for accuracy. As the project moves toward completion, she will make a final inspection and prepare a "punch list" of incomplete or inadequate work, then she'll reinspect the corrections before you finally accept the work and make the last payment.

Chapter 3

DEFINING THE PROJECT

A fter tackling the big
questions—what to
build, how to get it built,
and how to pay for it—you
can get down to the fun
part: planning the actual
project. If you have more
than one possible place
to add on, this chapter
will help you decide the
best location.

LEGAL LIMITATIONS

One of the first things to check out when thinking about expanding your home is whether you can legally add space and, if so, where. Most homeowners live in areas governed by zoning ordinances. Though they often seem overly restrictive, zoning ordinances for the most part do serve the neighborhood's best interest. If a height limitation keeps you from pushing your house up to three stories, a use limitation might restrain your neighbor from setting up a junkyard or pig farm next door.

A municipal zoning ordinance typically carves up the governed area into zones, according to the permitted uses for properties within the zones—residential, institutional, commercial, industrial, or agricultural. A residential zone may be subdivided into areas allowing single-family homes, duplexes, and apartments.

A typical zoning ordinance begins by laying out the permitted uses in each zone, then moves onto the detailed regulations. These regulations define the minimum lot size for each building, maximum size of a building on a lot (typically a percentage), and the area within the lot where the buildings can be built. Setbacks from the property line describe the area on the site where you can build. They often don't leave much wiggle room. If you live in a typical residential subdivision, your house may already be built to the setback lines on the front and sides, and maybe even on the rear. To find where your opportunities for outward expansion are—if any—visit the building inspection department of your city or town. If you don't know which zone you live in, find out by locating your address on the zoning map often displayed in the department. Next get a copy of the zoning ordinance, usually free or for a modest cost, and check out the setback and height requirements for your zone.

Conforming to the local zoning ordinance might not end your legal worries. Some neighborhoods have additional restrictions in the form of "protective" or "restrictive" covenants that were established when the houses were built to ensure buyers that the character of the units would be consistent over time. Look for covenants in your property deed.

Check your deed also for mention of any easements—legal rights of way to some part of your property. An easement may be a narrow strip of land along the side yard for a storm sewer pipe or buried telephone line, or other utility. Or, it may be a guaranteed access to an adjacent property that would otherwise be cut off from the street. Whatever the case, the effect of the easement is to guarantee an area in which no building will occur.

PLANNING FOR THE SITE

The legal constraints that define where you can build may leave few choices on a tight subdivision lot. If you are lucky enough to live on a large lot, such as the one shown in Drawing 3-3, you may be free to build wherever you want. You probably have an idea of where you want the addition, based on your familiarity with the layout of the house, but hold that thought until further on in the chapter. For now, consider how the conditions outside your house can help you determine the best place to add space.

Sun, Wind, Cars, and Neighbors

Unless you aim to build a windowless bunker, the sounds, sights, and constantly changing weather outside play a big role in the mood and comfort inside, and outside influences are not the same for all locations or orientations on the site. Consider, for example, how the sun can enhance or detract from the mood inside.

A place in the sun. Sunlight streaming in from the east can bring a breakfast nook to life in the morning. In winter, any sun penetrating the windows not only

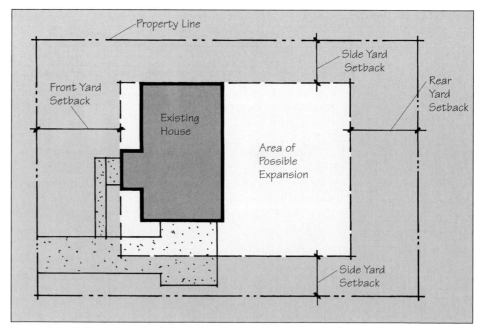

Drawing 3-1 *The setback from the property lines is spelled out in the zoning ordinance. Once it's drawn on the site plan, you can determine the possible areas for expanding the footprint of your house.*

Start with a Site Plan

You will need some kind of plan of the property to help you conceive and build your addition. When you submit a site plan to obtain a building permit, your site plan should include certain minimum data, such as the location of the house on the property, the property lines, the driveway, and the utility lines. An arrow on the plan indicating true north won't be necessary for a building permit, but it will help you in analyzing the effects of the climate on your addition.

This information must be drawn to scale (usually 1 inch = 50 feet, or larger). If you don't already have a site plan with this information, you can have one made by a surveyor, using the legal description on your deed as a starting point. The surveyor may need to take on-site measurements to verify the data or establish data not described in the deed.

If your site is very large, heavily sloped, wooded, or covered by ponds or streams, you might want a more detailed site plan that pegs the locations of these features and shows contours. A "topographical survey," such as this one (right), is made by a surveyor from raw data supplied by a crew at the site.

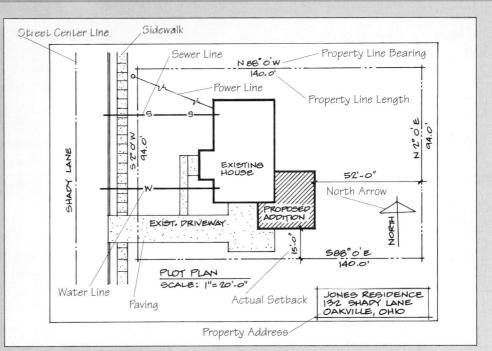

Drawing 3-2 *A site plan often must be submitted for a building permit or zoning variance or exception.*

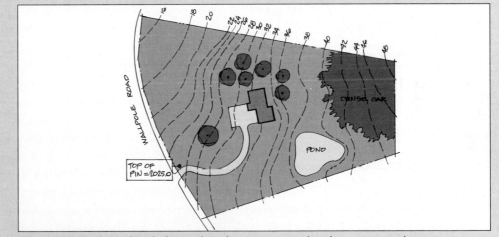

Drawing 3-3 *A detailed site plan shows topographical contours and existing landscaping.*

cheers the spirit but helps heat the house as well. On the other hand, solar rays invading on an August afternoon make you want to pull the drapes and turn on the air conditioner. Knowing how much direct sunlight you want in each new room—and when you want it—can help decide where the addition should go.

In the northern hemisphere, the sun's daily path cuts mostly through the southern sky. The sun tracks highest in the summer when it begins its daily journey on the northeast horizon, veers south as it rises to its noontime zenith, and descends toward the northwest where it sets. If your house has rooms with west-facing windows, you know that the hottest time of the year in these rooms is during summer afternoons.

As we approach winter, the sun's path moves more toward the south. Get in touch with the daily and seasonal pattern of sunlight on your house, then think about how much sunlight you want in your new spaces, when you want it, and when you want to block it out. If your new room is a sun space, its location and orientation are very important for maximum solar exposure. A room planned mainly for video entertainment may need to exclude sunlight.

North-side rooms get direct sunlight only during early morning and late afternoon in summer. This might suit a room where windows don't matter, such as storage or an entertainment room used mostly for listening to music or watching video media. Maybe even for a

Appealing Your Case

Don't despair if your proposed addition seems to conflict with a provision of the local zoning ordinance. Depending on the conflict, you may be able to get permission anyway by appealing for a variance or exception. Variances are typically granted if the petitioner will incur hardship because the project is not allowed. If you suddenly face caring for an elderly parent, for example, you may appeal for a variance to add an apartment onto your house, even though apartments are not allowed in your zone. An exception may be granted for a "permitted use" if the project fits the intended spirit of the ordinance and does not harm the interests of abutting property owners. Ironically, "permitted use" in this case really means "permitted if you secure an exception." A home office might fall in this category.

To appeal for an exception or variance, you will need to apply in writing—usually on a form available at the building department. The application may ask for a list of names and addresses of each neighbor within a certain distance from your property. You can get these from an area map at the building, planning, or zoning department. The municipality will then mail each of these neighbors a copy of your request and inform them of the date of your hearing. You'll also need a plot plan of your property, drawn to scale, showing the existing house, property lines, setbacks, and proposed addition.

You present your case at the hearing and hope that any neighbors with a long-held grudge won't show up and try to scuttle your project. It may help to get the support of your neighbors well ahead of time and urge them to show up to speak in favor of your appeal.

Windows and reflective white walls take full advantage of this breakfast nook's southern exposure.

bedroom. But isn't it nicer to wake up to sunlight streaming in through the windows? If you agree, you will want to position your bedroom to have at least one window on the east. A dining nook facing east also benefits from morning sunlight, while dodging the heat of the afternoon.

In winter, the sun tracks lower in the southern sky. Rooms you want to capture the most solar light or heat should be positioned to have windows facing as close to due south as possible. Sitting rooms make good candidates. Sun spaces must be sited facing south to capture solar heat.

Avoiding unwanted solar heat is just as important when locating rooms to take advantage of solar energy. The early morning sun streaming through east-facing windows is welcome for most of the year. Even in summer, the sun's morning debut usually comes on the heels of a cool or cold night. But by the

time the sun tracks around to the west, the house has had several hours to warm up. Any additional heat in the late afternoon is most unwelcome. This heat comes in through west-facing windows because the sun is in the western sky in the afternoon. In Chapter 8, we'll look into ways to block unwanted solar light and heat with blinds and drapes, but the more you do by placing the rooms wisely, the less you'll have to depend on inside fixes. If there are large trees near your house, you probably know where their shade falls in summer afternoons. Can you locate your addition to take advantage of the shade?

Winds. The breezes that help cool your addition in summer turn into enemies in the winter. Cold winter winds come mostly from the north, so consider planting a group of tall evergreen trees north of the house to buffer their impact. Deciduous trees don't help once they drop their leaves.

Other factors. Views and proximity to the street and neighboring houses also weigh into intelligent siting of the addition. When these factors are added to the other criteria—setbacks, solar orientation, winds—it is quite likely that compromises will be necessary. Should you put the new dining room on the east where it can trap morning sunlight, or will the view into the neighbor's messy side yard steer you away from this location? Should the new living room go on the west where the views to the distant hills are

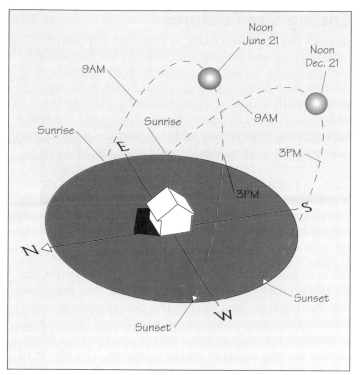

Drawing 3-4 *Here are the solar paths in the northern hemisphere. Note that the sun is always in the southern sky at noon.*

magnificent, even though the afternoon sun will cook the occupants in the summer? Consider how people will use the space, and use this consideration to find the best fit between inside and outside.

Dealing with Slopes

The shape of the land around your house greatly affects where you add on and the physical form of the addition. Ideally, the ground adjacent to your house should slope away from the house on all sides

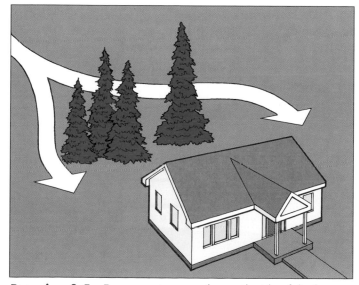

Drawing 3-5 *Evergreen trees on the north side of the house can reduce the impact of winter winds.*

to divert rainwater away from the foundation. If it doesn't, planning for the addition should also include regrading the site next to the house. You can build an addition over steeply sloping ground, regardless of the direction of the pitch. One approach is to shape the addition the way you want it to relate to the house and adjust the slope by scooping out some portions and filling in others. Or you might leave the site alone and tailor the addition to fit the existing slope. A third tactic is to consider both the site's slope and the new building as a unified problem and work back and forth between them, conceiving the building and reshaping the site. Let's see how these approaches might affect the design of an addition uphill or down-hill from a single-story house with a basement.

Uphill additions. The cross sections in Drawing 3-6 show three ways to add uphill from a house. The main-floor addition simply expands outward into the hill in the two top examples. In this way, the main floor of the house aligns with the floor of the addition, which could be an important requirement. In the top example, the site is gouged out to just below the floor line. But the deep cut yields a steep bank beyond, which might require a retaining wall

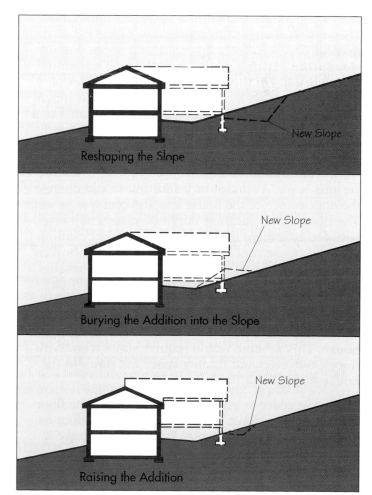

Drawing 3-6 *Here are three ways to build onto the uphill side of a house.*

Bearing Walls

Some of the walls of your house are there only to separate one space from another or to enclose the interior from the outside. These walls do not support any structure above them, so they can be removed or altered in any way you wish. Other walls—bearing walls—do support a floor or roof above. You can pierce them to make new openings into your addition only after providing alternative means for supporting their imposed loads. This is usually done by installing a header beam over the length of the new opening. The first task is to identify which walls are bearing walls.

To be a bearing wall, the wall must both support part of the structure above it and itself be supported from below by a structural member, such as a beam, wall, post, or the foundation—something heftier than mere joists. Let's look at how a homeowner, we'll call him Randy Johnson, might determine which walls are bearing walls. Randy began his quest by poking his head up into the attic, through an access panel located in the ceiling. He saw a series of 2x8 rafters that extended from the eaves up to meet at the roof ridge. At the ridge, each pair of rafters perched on a strut that disappeared into the insulation at the attic floor. When Randy lifted up a length of insulation, he could see that the struts sat on a flat 2x4 nailed to the bottom of the ceiling joists. He knew there was a hallway wall that ran along the center of the house. Measuring from the 2x4 to the eaves and from the hallway wall to the outside walls confirmed that the 2x4 was the top plate of the hallway wall. A visit to the basement revealed a beam below this wall, supported by steel columns. Randy concluded that the roof was supported at the eaves by the north and south outside walls and at the center by a wall.

But the structural system of the garage was different. Randy could easily observe the garage's roof supports by standing on the floor below because there was no ceiling. Trusses spanned across from the outer walls, leaving the floor uncluttered by posts. For more information about roof structures, see "Framing the Roof," beginning on page 93.

Randy marked the house's north and south exterior walls on the floor plan to remind him that these were the walls that required alternative support above any new openings. The east and west walls were not marked because they support no loads. Randy also marked the interior wall that supports the attic floor joists.

Of course, not all houses have a structural system as simple and easy to grasp as the Johnsons'. Yours might come closer to the two-story house shown in the cross section in Drawing 3-12. Here, the best starting point for a structural sleuth might be the basement. Concrete-filled steel columns (often referred to by the brand name Lally columns) near the center of the floor support a beam, upon which the first-floor joists bear. From the floor above, a wall appears to coincide with the beam below. Measurements from the side walls confirm this location. This—along with the fact that the wall continues the full length of the house, unbroken except for door openings on the first floor—gives evidence that it is a bearing wall. You can't know for sure without cutting into the ceiling to see if the floor joists above it are discontinuous and overlap the wall top plate as drawn here. The walls on the

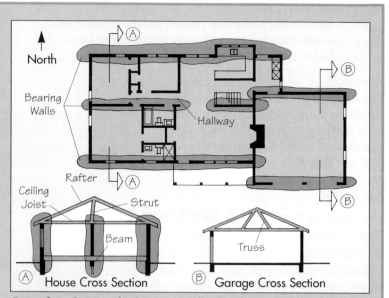

Drawing 3-11   *The bearing walls shown on the floor plan and cross section of the Johnson house are circled. Steel posts in the basement support a beam that runs down near the center of the house. A wall on the main level sits above this beam and supports, in turn, a strut in the attic.*

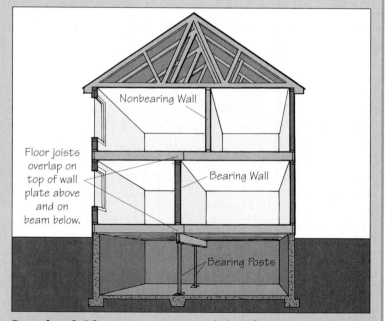

Drawing 3-12   *A cross section can help define the main structural supports of the house. The middle wall on the second floor carries no weight since it lies under trusses designed to span the full width of the house. But the middle wall on the first floor carries the floor above. This weight passes, in turn, onto the beam and posts in the basement.*

second floor aren't directly above the first-floor bearing wall. The roof framing consists of trusses that span the outer walls and don't require intermediate support. This setup indicates that no interior walls on the second floor are bearing walls.

If you plan to do your own design, you can use techniques such as these to find the bearing walls. But do get expert advice to verify your conclusions and to learn the best way to provide alternative support.

Bumping Out

The simplest addition requires no foundation of any kind. Instead, the outer wall of the room to be enlarged simply gets bumped out a few feet to hang off the house. The smallest versions of this approach are available as mini-greenhouses you can install over a kitchen window opening. Available as glazed kits that poke out a foot or so beyond the outside wall, these add-on bay windows contain adjustable shelves inside for housing plants and knickknacks.

A bump-out bay window can turn a mundane kitchen window into a sunlit niche, but the kitchen doesn't gain any additional floor space. For that, you'll need to enlarge the room. You may be able to gain an additional 3 feet or so of width in the room using the bump-out idea. A few extra feet of width may be all you need to transform a too-tight dining nook into an area that seats more people with better comfort (Drawing 3-13). The key to poking out the wall without adding supports below lies in extending the floor joists outward over the foundation (or bearing wall if it is a second story) with "sister" joists. Naturally, this works only when the existing joists run perpendicular to the wall to be bumped out. After removing the band joist (rim joist or sill beam) from the outer edge of the floor framing, sister joists are attached to the main floor joists, with the ends extending out from the wall, as shown in cross section in Drawing 3-14. For every foot of free end

A simple bump-out may be all you need to alleviate a cramped dinning area. In this case, joists couldn't be sistered so the bump-out has its own foundation instead of being cantilevered.

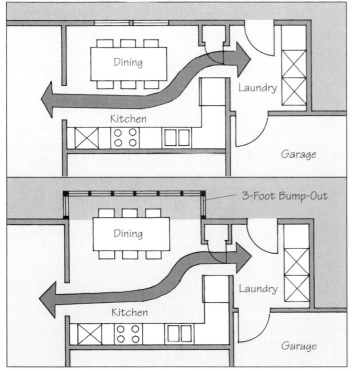

Drawing 3-13 *The kitchen-dining area at the top was congested and plagued with traffic passing from the back door through the kitchen. Bumping out the dining room wall just 3 ft. (bottom) alleviated this congestion while providing better isolation of the dining area and a better view to the outside.*

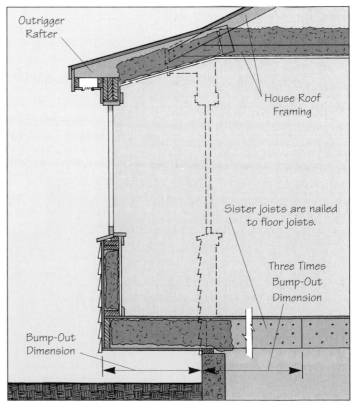

Drawing 3-14 *A bump-out addition requires removing the original wall and extending the roof/ceiling and floor. Sister joists attached to the original floor joists support the addition.*

beyond the foundation, you should provide 3 feet inside for stability. A 3-foot cantilever, for example, needs 9 feet of attachment inside the house. If the wall to be removed is itself a bearing wall, it will require alternate support with a beam. (See "Bearing Walls," page 44.)

Adding over Open Ground

If your addition requires more than the few feet gained by a bump-out, it can extend out as far out as necessary, but it will have to sit on its own supports. Supports can be intermittent posts or piers, a shallow crawl-space foundation, or a full basement, as described in the next chapter. The important thing is that building an addition onto the side of the house is building from scratch—with the costs per square foot equaling or exceeding those of a new house.

But planning a successful outward addition is not like planning a new house because you don't start with an empty lot. Whatever you add on is sure to affect the appearance of the house, for better or worse. And even if the addition sits on its own supports, it has to join the house somehow. On successful additions the intersection is not noticeable—it looks as if the house was planned that way from the beginning. Other books have suggested ways to blend old to new harmoniously, such as matching forms inherent in the house or continuing materials and colors of the exterior. Some of these work, but aesthetic design is more art than science, and skillful designers know how to break the rules successfully. There is likely just the right form to blend to your house, whatever its shape.

A designer will explore several forms for the addition once the plan is set. Having arrived at a form that works, the designer may tweak the plan as necessary to better suit the house. Working back and forth eventually leads to a plan that solves all of the design objectives. If you care to try your hand at designing, the guidelines in the next chapter tell you how to proceed.

Expanding an Attic

Adding upward, rather than sideways, may be your best bet, particularly if you can't add to the side of the house without encroaching too far into a required setback or sacrificing a view or privacy. If you have an attic, the easiest way to add vertical space is to make it

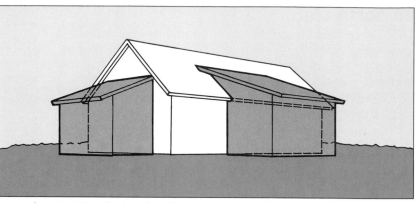

Drawing 3-15   *Shed-roof additions are hard to blend to a gable-roof house, regardless of where they are built.*

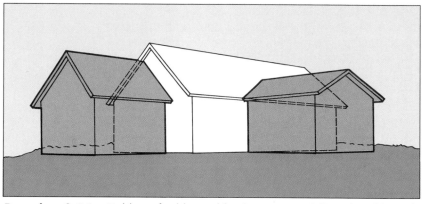

Drawing 3-16   *Gable-roof additions blend more gracefully with gable-roof houses, especially if the roof pitches match.*

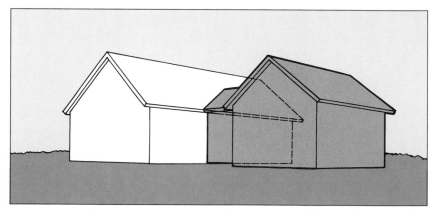

Drawing 3-17   *A T-shaped addition allows you to add a lot of space without overwhelming the house.*

habitable by poking the roof up in certain places with dormers to gain adequate headroom. (See "Solving the Headroom Problem," page 52.) This approach will probably save money by skipping the need for a new foundation and most of the walls and roof. The project should also move faster than a footing-to-roof addition, and think of the possibilities for better views that a top-side addition can offer. Designed skillfully, a dormer or two can also enhance the appearance of your house.

The transition between main house and a T-shaped addition often takes the form of a breezeway.

The interior of the breezeway is the perfect place for a wetbar because it is situated between the kitchen addition and the house's main entertainment area. The big windows and skylights bring light and air into both the addition and the main house.

Still not convinced? Your attitude toward attics might be traced to unpleasant memories of the past. Maybe you had an attic bedroom when you were a child, and it always seemed too small and cramped. You couldn't walk very far without bumping your head. You froze in January and roasted in July, even with the windows open. Each of these drawbacks can be overcome by expanding the attic and insulating it to current standards.

Dormers are the forms that result from poking the roof up in only some spots. In addition to increasing the headroom below, dormers also offer a vertical surface for windows. (The advantages of dormer windows are weighed against roof windows in Chapter 6, beginning on page 123.) There are two basic types of dormers: shed and gable.

Shed dormers. This simpler of the two dormer types, shown in Drawing 3-18, takes its name from the shed-like form it projects out from the main roof. The simpler form also means easier framing—something to bear in mind if you are building your own. Another advantage is headroom. Because a shed dormer's width isn't limited by a double-pitched gable roof, it can be as wide as the attic, with as much usable headroom to match. This can be a pitfall, however, because the wide shed dormer alters the appearance of the house. If overdone, it can overwhelm the original roof form.

Another fact to bear in mind is that the maximum height under a shed dormer occurs where it meets the main roof. If the height here is already marginal—say, less than 90 inches—it will be even lower beyond this point, as the roof slopes downward. If you want to roof your dormer with asphalt (fiberglass) shingles, allow a minimum slope of

Drawing 3-18   *A simple shed dormer can be as wide as needed to gain headroom below. Try to hold the sides of the dormer back from the gable of the main roof so that the original roof form won't be lost.*

Drawing 3-19   *Doghouse dormers have their own little gables and side walls. They can be added in groups to provide small areas of greater headroom or joined together by a shed dormer to provide a large high area in the room while maintaining the gable form.*

3 in 12. (This means the roof travels 3 inches vertically for every 12 inches horizontally and is expressed as 3/12.) Wood shingles aren't practical on slopes shallower than 4/12. Test the usable space inside by drawing a cross section, to scale, through the attic and shed dormer, before committing yourself. As a rule of thumb, you won't get much headroom from a shed dormer if the main roof slope is less than 6/12, unless the roof begins on top of a kneewall at the eaves.

Gable dormers. Gable dormers have two-way pitched roofs that jut out perpendicular to the main roof, making them tricky to frame since each piece has to be accurately cut on an angle. The most common gable dormers, shown in Drawing 3-19, have side walls that make them look like large doghouses sitting on top of the roof. (Another name for them is "doghouse dormers.") The side walls can be eliminated in favor of a triangular form where the gable roof reaches down to join the house roof, as shown in Drawings 3-20 and 3-21. There are even gambrel roof dormers that mimic the roof forms of Dutch colonial houses. In all cases, the pitch of the dormer roof determines its width and the amount of floor space inside with usable headroom. To see just how much headroom the dormer adds, you'll need an accurate drawing of the cross section through the dormer.

The size, number, and location of the dormers have a major effect on the space they shelter. If you are thinking of small gable dormers, think in multiples. Groups of two or more small dormers look better on the outside than one, and the more you deploy, the more usable space you'll get inside.

Drawing 3-20   *A gable dormer without side walls yields more headroom than a doghouse dormer and blends well with the main roof. In this example, the dormer sits on top of the main roof and extends above the ridge line.*

Drawing 3-21   *Many variations of dormers are possible. Here, the gable dormer extends up from the outer wall, and the ridge matches that of the garage.*

From the inside, you would never think that this soaring, sunlit space is a dormer.

From the outside, you can see how the dormer addition on this gambrel roof picks up the pattern of the windows below.

Attic ceilings. If you use cross-sectional drawings to determine the size, type, and location of the dormers needed to expand your attic upward, you'll soon see that the space inside is not like that of the first-floor rooms. Instead of monotonous, flat ceilings, the new attic room will be a dynamic space with a ceiling that slopes in many directions. This, combined with the views from on high, will surely create a room that lifts the spirits. Though some of the ceiling at the center may be flat with a small attic space above, much of the sloping surface will be a cathedral ceiling. Exciting as this can be, a cathedral ceiling can be challenging to design and build. The cavities between the joists may be too shallow for the amount of insulation you need and still afford an air space between the top of the insulation and bottom of the roof deck. Chapter 6 suggests some viable ways to insulate and ventilate a cathedral ceiling. (See "Insulation," beginning on page 110.)

Attic floors. If the attic floor started out as merely the ceiling of the rooms below, it might not be stiff enough to serve as a floor. Code commonly sets the minimum floor load capacity at 40 pounds per square foot. A design professional can help you determine whether your attic floor is up to the task; if it's not, he or she can suggest ways to beef it up. You can get an idea of what to expect by measuring the joist size, spacing (center to center), and clear span, and comparing these data with the those shown below in the table "Attic Floor Joists."

If the floor structure falls short, you'll need to strengthen it for the proposed greater load. The most common way to do this is by adding joists sized to the proper capacity between the existing joists.

Adding a Story

If adding dormers to your attic won't yield enough headroom for the space you need, consider raising the entire roof. You might extend the walls out beyond the walls below for even more space. First, make sure you can legally expand upward by checking out the height restrictions of your zoning ordinance. You can safely assume that you can match the height of the highest part of your home by extending another portion upward, but increasing the height beyond that may not be possible.

Any upper-floor addition offers the advantages of views and privacy. The cost will probably be less than that of building new space on the ground. (If the ground-floor addition is not built over a full base-

Varied ceiling angles make this attic bedroom into a cozy retreat. A balcony takes full advantage of the views from on high.

ment.) If you keep the addition within the footprint of the house, it will cost more than a simple attic expansion with one or two dormers but less than refitting an attic with several dormers. When thinking of costs, though, don't forget that replacing the old roof with a new higher one not only shelters the added space, but also the original house. If the new roof is better insulated than the previous one, the improvements in comfort and energy savings benefit the whole house. Offsetting this plus is the added cost you'll probably incur by upgrading the former ceiling to make a floor, as with expanding the attic.

ATTIC FLOOR JOISTS

Nominal Size of Floor Joists	Maximum Span for 16" Joist Spacing	Maximum Span for 24" Joist Spacing
2x6	8'–7"	7'–6"
2x8	11'–4"	9'–6"
2x10	14'–3"	11'–8"
2x12	16'–6"	13'–2"

Solving the Headroom Problem

If your attic is unused or used only for storage, you may wonder if you can turn it into usable space. You might be able to, but doing so will depend on increasing the headroom. Likely as not, the space inside is shaped like a triangle, and the only area high enough to walk in is an aisle down the center. A scale drawing of the cross section is a good way to see what your options are. Measure the width of the space at the floor and the height at the ridge. If the outer edges of the roof sits atop kneewalls instead of the attic floor, measure the height of these as well. Sketch the section to scale, as shown in Drawing 3-22.

For rooms to be occupied, most codes require a clear height of at least 90 inches over half of the floor space. Draw a horizontal line that will indicate 90 inches above the attic floor, and determine how wide the line is before it runs into rafters at the sides. This is the clear floor area with minimum head height. To get the resulting room width, double this width. The leftover spaces at the outer edges can be enclosed for storage.

If you find that the resulting room is still too narrow for a usable room, you can get more headroom with dormers added to the roof or raising an entire portion of the roof.

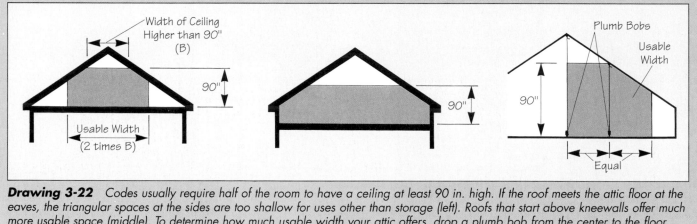

Drawing 3-22   *Codes usually require half of the room to have a ceiling at least 90 in. high. If the roof meets the attic floor at the eaves, the triangular spaces at the sides are too shallow for uses other than storage (left). Roofs that start above kneewalls offer much more usable space (middle). To determine how much usable width your attic offers, drop a plumb bob from the center to the floor and mark the position on the floor. Then find the point on the roof that lies 90 in. above the floor and use a plumb bob to mark its position on the floor. Measure the distance between the two marks. The total usable width will be four times that measure (right).*

Building over the existing house walls by extending them higher up is the simplest way to build an upper-floor addition. Because this approach imposes no new loads on the walls below except for the new outer walls themselves, it is very likely that the supporting walls and foundation can carry the load safely. An upper-story addition can also poke out beyond the walls below. The lower walls might be able to carry a wider load, but they might need some kind of reinforcing. It may be simpler to bear the overhanging addition on posts. If you contemplate an addition wider than the structure below, get advice from a design professional on how best to support it.

You may have a flat-roofed garage abutting your two-story house just begging for a second story. Why not? The same rules apply here as already mentioned for an upper-floor addition with one more quirk: the garage roof. The good news is that the roof was probably designed to carry snow loads, which means it is probably adequate for its new use as a floor for living space. The bad news is a possible slope. Converting the former roof to a floor will require leveling the surface. One way to do this is with a gridwork of light subframing called sleepers. A roof 20 feet wide with a slope of 5/12, for

example, is easily leveled by laying 2x4 sleepers flat and supporting them on the roof with shims. If the roof slopes more than this, it probably makes better sense to tear it off and install new floor framing.

Converting Roofed Areas

When considering sites for an addition, don't overlook underused roofed areas outside the house, such as porches and carports. Maybe you have a double carport but only one car. Closing in half of the space can yield a room large enough to suit many uses. Now that people spend more leisure time inside, the generous porches that wrap around many old houses go largely unused. Some or all of this space might be better used for current space needs. On the other hand, your porch may be a fundamental part of the home's character. Closing it in risks destroying a valued asset. Such a concern is justified. Even so, a skilled designer might see ways to enclose the porch without destroying its appearance. You might even want to consider adding on a porch to enhance your house.

Porches are often too narrow to make usable rooms. A porch 6 feet wide or less might serve certain uses,

Drawing 3-23 *A second story can be added within the footprint of the house or be extended beyond, as in this example, where the extension out to the front improves a ranch house by breaking up its length.*

such as a sun space or vestibule entry, but is just too narrow to accommodate most furniture. Don't write off the porch, though, until you're sure you can't expand it outward. Look at the porch shown in Drawing 3-24. In this example, bumping the wall out just 2 feet yielded a space wide enough for a home office.

Enclosing a carport or porch usually counts as re-modeling existing space rather than adding on. But this is wishful thinking as far as costs go. Sure, you begin with a roof and floor surface, but the roof needs insulation and a ceiling. The floor may need reinforce-ment, particularly if it is presently a porch. Old porches rarely have foundations that can adequately support an enclosed room above. The cost of this work, combined with the new exterior walls and interior finishes may easily amount to 80 to 90 percent of the cost of entirely new space.

Of course, other advantages might make enclosing a carport or porch attractive even if the cost savings aren't great. Unless the new walls are to bump out beyond the foundation, the addition won't consume any ground outside the house's footprint, thereby avoiding encroachment into zoning setbacks. And if you do your own construction, you'll be able to do it under continu-ous shelter, which will allow you to work on the project as your time allows, independent of weather conditions.

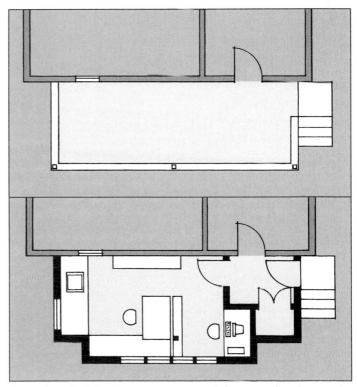

Drawing 3-24 *Bumping out a porch by just a few feet might make the difference between a space too narrow to enclose for a room and one that's usable. In this example, a porch finds new life as an airlock entry vestibule and home office.*

Providing a Way Up

One of the first hurdles when planning an attic addition is vertical access. Chances are that your current attic has no stairway or one that's not suited to regular use. A stairway can eat up a lot of area on both levels served. If you can't gain enough space from an existing area, consider building a stairway outside the house. The square footage needed depends on the height between floors and the type of stairway.

Rise and run are used to indicate the steepness of stairs. The unit rise is the number of inches in height of each step. The unit run is the step's horizontal dimension in inches, measured from the back of one tread to the back of the step below (thus not including the overhanging nosing, if any). All steps in a stairway should have the same unit rise and run. To fit our stride as we climb stairs, a higher rise necessitates a lesser run. The table "Stair Rise and Run Dimensions" gives some workable rise to run ratios for stairs.

STAIR RISE AND RUN DIMENSIONS

Rise (inches)	Run (inches)
6	13½
6¼	12⅞
6½	12¼
6¾	11⅝
7	11
7¼	10½
7½	10
7¾	9½
8	9
8¼	8½

A stairway with a unit rise of 8¼ inches and a unit run of 8½ inches, the steepest allowed by most building codes for residences, saves horizontal space but is not the most comfortable to climb, particularly for people who walk with difficulty. Stairs with a 7:11 ratio are more convenient. The clear width of a stairway should be at least 36 inches. Landings of the same width as the stairway are required at the top and bottom of each run of stairs. Allow 36 inches for the length landing.

A straight run from floor to floor is the most economical stairway and easiest to negotiate. Finding a location with enough horizontal distance for the stairs and two landings can be a problem, though. Say you have 8 feet 10 inches (106 inches) floor to floor, and want the rise of each step to be close to 7 inches. This means you'll need 15.14 risers, which is rounded to 15. Dividing the total height of 106 inches by 15, we get the rise of each step to be 7.06 inches, or 7¹⁄₁₆ inch. The 15 risers require 14 treads, which at 10 inches each, add up to a combined length of 140 inches or 11 feet 8 inches. Add two landings at 36 inches each, and you end up with a total stairway of 17 feet 8 inches. If you can't find a place for a stairway this long, how about a scissors stairway—one that doubles back on itself after meeting a mid-height landing? The

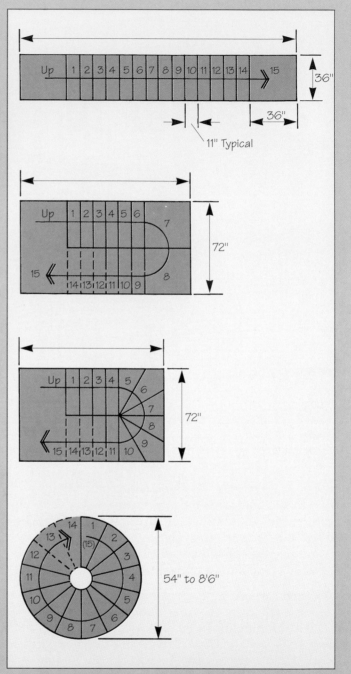

Drawing 3-25 *Each of these four stairways contains 15 risers. The straight-run stairway (top) is the easiest to climb and to carry bulky items up. Each successive arrangement saves more floor space but becomes harder to negotiate.*

total length of this type of stairway can be reduced to 11 feet, if the landing makes one step in itself, and 9 feet 4 inches if the landing is subdivided into six pie-shaped treads, as shown in Drawing 3-25. Making all of the treads pie shaped and arranging them into a circle yields the most space-conserving stairway of all. Prefabricated circular stairways are available in diameters of 54 inches to 90 inches, with steel center poles and wood or metal treads. The smaller-diameter stairs are not as easy to climb as straight stairs, though, and can make it impossible to move large furniture up and down.

Chapter 4

FROM DREAM TO DESIGN

The skeleton of your project should be apparent by now, if you are planning according to the sequence of this book. With an idea of its size, location, cost, and financing, you can now move from planning the project to thinking about its design. If you engage a designer, your role will be to communicate your aims and make decisions about the design as it progresses from rough concept to final working drawings. This chapter describes what you'll need to know to do your own design and the general approach a designer might follow in creating a design concept. You'll learn how to document your house before

A New Bathroom

Fixtures, cabinetry, plumbing, and floor and wall finishes combine to make baths and kitchens the costliest space to construct on a square-foot basis. To get the most out of your investment, consider getting some expert advice. You can engage an architect or interior designer to do the overall design or hire one to review your own scheme and make suggestions. Another option is to engage a bath or kitchen designer that you can find by visiting a kitchen or bath specialty store. The visit will be worthwhile, in any case, giving you a chance to check out the latest upscale fixtures and cabinets. Even if the fixtures are beyond your budget, learning what's available makes you a better-informed consumer, and information is your best tool, whether you employ a designer or do it yourself.

If you do your own design, first get up to speed on the planning basics from kitchen and bath how-to books. You'll also find the latest trends and many exciting ideas by scanning through recent home magazines at your library.

Bathroom facilities can vary from a tightly planned half-bath squeezed into a 38-by-72-inch space to elaborate suites that offer luxury amenities (and costs to match). Here are some general tips to keep in mind when planning any bath space:

▲ Consider how the existing waste piping can be extended to serve the proposed fixtures. Waste piping is fat and must follow a continuously sloping path to drain properly. Routing hot- and cold-water supply pipes is less demanding since they are smaller and can bend around other construction.

▲ Locate bath facilities in the public part of the house close to the rooms they serve but not directly adjacent. A half bath serving a living room, for example, might be located off a small hallway, rather than entered from the living room directly.

▲ Locate bath facilities in the private parts of the house close to the rooms they serve, which are usually bedrooms.

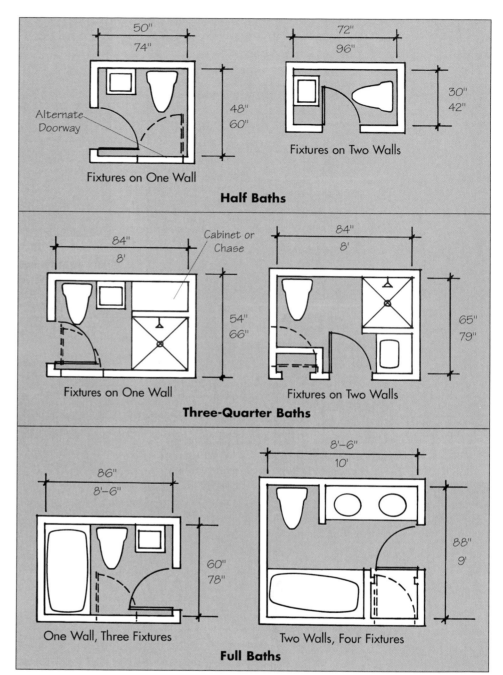

Drawing 4-17 *These designs are the most efficient bathroom layouts. Each dimension contains the range of usual clearances; the smaller dimension is the smallest practical size for the bathroom layout.*

▲ Don't strand new bathroom space too far from its supplies—towels, toilet paper, cleaning, and maintenance items.

▲ Make sure bath facilities added for a person with special needs (for example, a wheelchair user) really do meet those needs.

▲ When planning windows in your bath, consider privacy. Frosted windows are one option. If windows are not an option, adequate light can come from a skylight or electric lighting, and ventilation can be provided by an exhaust fan to the exterior.

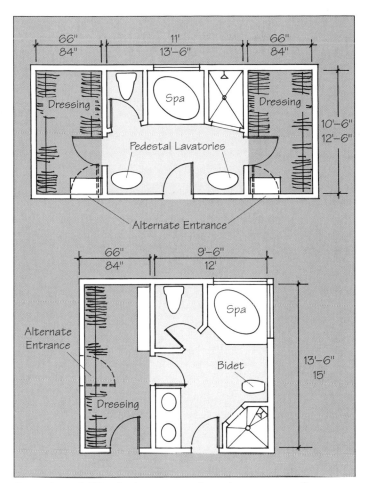

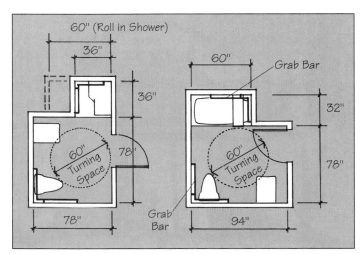

The Shakers called it "borrowed light." This bathroom uses high interior windows across from exterior windows to allow light to come through the bathroom into the entertainment area.

Drawing 4-18 *Bath suites combine the necessary fixtures with amenities, such as spas and bidets, and may connect to the bedroom through walk-in dressing rooms. The bath suite at top opens on both sides into separate dressing rooms, which could also connect to the bedroom. At the bottom, a shared dressing room abuts the bath and two door locations are shown.*

Drawing 4-19 *Wheelchair-accessible bathrooms require a 60-in. diameter clear turning space inside and doorways with at least 32 in. clear width (net width clear of the door stops). The bathing fixture may be a shower (left) or tub with a seat (right). The type of shower must suit the needs of the occupant. A shower with a seat works for an occupant capable of moving out of the wheelchair. Otherwise, a roll-in shower should be provided.*

This is the interior of the bathroom shown above. Because the bathroom windows are set high, there is lots of light with no loss of privacy.

Kitchen Additions

Kitchens are no longer rooms designed for Mother to spend endless hours whomping bread dough into loaves and canning peaches. Today's smaller families, diverse households, and changing food habits call for new ideas. The solutions should match the needs and lifestyle of the users. A working couple with no children, for example, may want a place to microwave take-out food during the week quickly, but with the capability to work side by side to prepare an elaborate dinner for guests on a Saturday night. They may even want the guests to join in the preparation.

Still, the management and preparation of food remains the linchpin of all kitchen design. Food must come in, be stored, be prepared, and be served. Cleanup must be convenient. A good design allows all this to happen smoothly and efficiently. A great design also creates a space people want to be in.

The flow of food, from an assortment of ingredients on the counter to entrées on the plate, has been analyzed to death. Home economists in the 1950s contrived the "work triangle" concept, which aimed to organize kitchen planning for an efficient flow of food. The concept comprised three basic nodes:

preparation (sink and adjacent work surfaces), storage (refrigerator), and cooking (range and oven). The concept assumed one person would be the main user. In today's kitchens the triangle should be disregarded or adjusted to the actual ways the kitchen will be used. With this in mind, consider the following when thinking about your own kitchen addition:

▲ Try to locate your kitchen addition close to an outside door (for bringing in groceries and taking out the garbage) and with easy access to the dining area.

▲ To make your kitchen addition a cheery, delightful place, try to locate it where you can have a window offering a pleasant view to the outdoors and natural light.

▲ Instead of following conventional "wisdom" such as the work triangle, consider how you and your family really use the kitchen: How and what do you cook, how many people will be working in the space at the same time, do you entertain frequently, do you want the kitchen to be formal or casual?

▲ Remember to include space for noncooking activities, such as a writing desk, telephone area, and shelves for cookbooks.

A plant-filled sunroom addition makes a graceful transition from indoors to outdoors. The brick floor adds to the outdoorsy feel. It also has a lot of thermal mass that absorbs the sun's heat during the day and releases it at night.

This is an exterior view of the sunroom addition shown at left. While its use of skylights and passive solar design are thoroughly modern, its interior and exterior detailing blend effortlessly with the home's Victorian architecture.

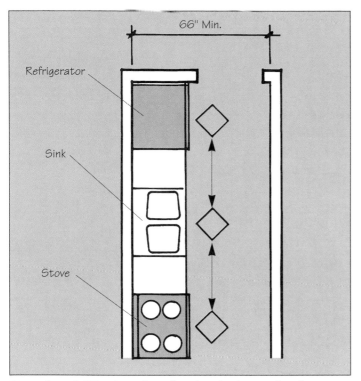

Drawing 4-20 *A single-wall, in-line kitchen makes the most use of the least space. This arrangement may suffice for a single person's needs, but may not provide enough storage space for a multiperson household. Furthermore, the layout does not suit more than a single cook.*

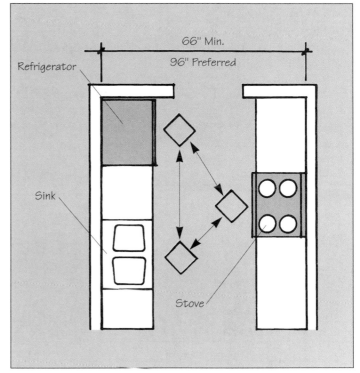

Drawing 4-21 *A two-wall galley kitchen adds a second work area opposite the primary one. One drawback is that through-traffic uses the work space as a passage. Compact and efficient for a single cook, this plan can adapt to a two-cook mode by adding a sink on the other side.*

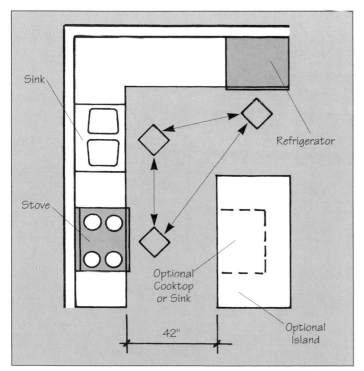

Drawing 4-22 *The L-shaped kitchen plan offers the most flexibility. Work surfaces are easily reached, and the plan can be adapted for a two-cook operation by tailoring the island with the appropriate fixtures, such as a second cooking surface or sink. The outer edge of the island can also be designed as a quick-meal dining surface.*

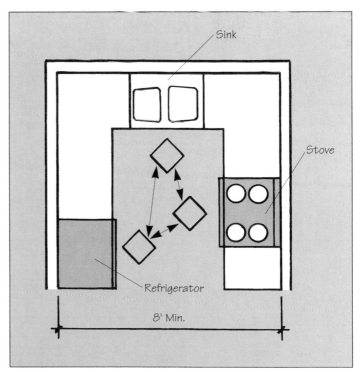

Drawing 4-23 *The U-shaped plan, perhaps the most common kitchen plan of all, uses limited space efficiently while avoiding through traffic. If one side of the U is open to the adjacent room, it can be fitted with a dining surface that is similar to an island. The downside of a U-plan is that it does not readily adapt to more than one cook at a time.*

This large modern kitchen reflects the way kitchens are used today. No longer a place just to prepare food, today's kitchen is a gathering place for family and friends. Big windows bring in lots of light.

Those big arch-top windows don't repeat the window pattern of the existing house. They don't have to: The stucco siding and ornate exposed rafter tails do the job of blending the addition into the architectural style of the house.

Adding a Bedroom

Your present bedrooms were likely designed for an unknown, average occupant. When you add new bedroom space, you'll have an opportunity to tailor the space to the specific needs of a known user. Do you need a place to exercise, do yoga, sew? Any of these activity spaces can be built into a bedroom addition. Maybe your ideal bedroom is a master suite that includes generous walk-in closets and a master bath. Here are some points to help you tailor the space to your lifestyle:

▲ If the bedroom addition will not include new bath facilities, locate it close enough to existing bathrooms to ensure easy access.

▲ Start the layout by locating the bed(s): Make in-scale templates and experiment with different layouts. For a two-person room, consider how each occupant travels in and out of his or her bed space, and provide a smooth pathway that does not conflict with the other person's pathways.

▲ Consider bedside accessories—tables, book and magazine racks, television—and decide how you would like to organize them in relation to the bed(s).

▲ Make a list of every function/use to be accommodated, such as sewing, ironing, sitting, putting on makeup, exercise or yoga, and meditation. Make templates for any needed equipment or furniture.

▲ Provide enough of the right kind of storage space for clothing and accessories, then make sure it is easily accessible. Walk-in closets, while more luxurious, are less efficient than shallow closets along a wall. The current trend favors storage in movable furniture, such as armoires and chests of drawers, over fixed closets, with an eye toward keeping the room flexible for another future use. Portable storage devices also use space more efficiently than do closets with 4½-inch-thick walls.

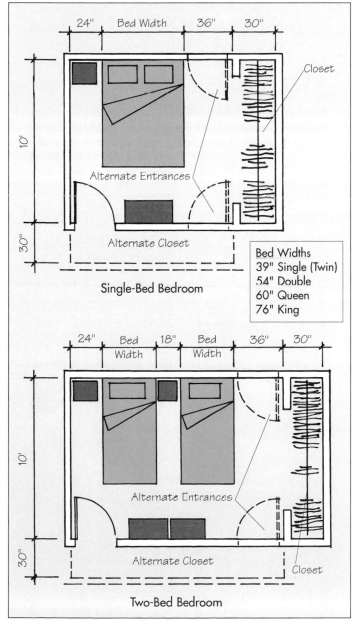

Bed Widths
39" Single (Twin)
54" Double
60" Queen
76" King

Single-Bed Bedroom

Two-Bed Bedroom

Drawing 4-24 *Here are minimum clearances for single- and double-bed bedrooms.*

Here's a bedroom addition that makes you feel like you are waking up in a tree house. The glass block at right allows light into a master bath while preserving privacy.

▲ If you want the sun space to contribute meaning-
fully to your home's heating, provide hinged or
sliding doors to close it off from the house on
cold nights.

▲ Heavy materials, such as brick, stone, and concrete, store heat well. The darker the color, the
better able it is to absorb solar energy. Using these
heavy materials on the floor or on an interior wall
exposed to the sun will help keep the space from
overheating during the day and getting too cold
on winter nights.

This sun-room addition, made with bent laminations, is available
as a manufactured kit.

Drawing 4-27 *The author's sun-space addition rises two
stories, abutting the kitchen and dining rooms on the ground
level and master bedroom on the second floor. Cold air from the
house enters the sun space through a vent in the bottom of the
kitchen door, and, after being warmed, rises to reenter the house
through another vent above the plant shelf. Plastic flaps over the
vents allow air to freely circulate when the temperature in the sun
space is warmer than that of the house, but automatically close at
night, as the sun space cools, preventing heat loss from the house.*

This sun-room addition is not large but features leaded windows
that blend elegantly with the home's architecture. The wicker furniture, birdcage, and Chinese-style plant stand add to the ambiance
that evokes an earlier, graceful period.

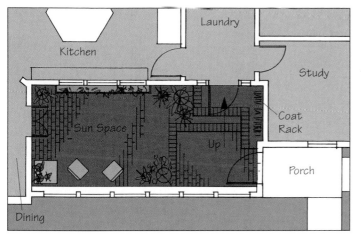

Drawing 4-28 *A layer of brick pavers set in sand provides the heat-storing surface in the author's sun space. Besides helping to heat the home, the addition serves as a transitional space between indoors and out. The near end acts as an airlock vestibule, and the coat rack near the door includes a shelf for hats and gloves and space for footwear storage. The far end provides a pleasant, sun-filled place to sit on a cold winter day.*

SHAPING THE EXTERIOR

So far, to break the design process into manageable bits, we've been concentrating only on the plan. The next phase involves stretching the two-dimensional plan upward in space to create a third dimension. We'll do this with overlay drawings, as we did earlier in this chapter when we developed a floor plan, using the Frankel addition as an example (see Drawing 4-12). Start by taping your base plan down to your drawing board. Position the plan on the board so that the side you want to study in elevation is facing the bottom of the board. Next, mount the corresponding base elevation above this plan so that it aligns with the plan, as shown by the Frankel example in Drawing 4-29.

Drawing on tracing paper, explore design solutions for the elevation. You may be surprised to see what the features on the floor plan actually look like on the wall they correspond to. If you don't like the look, change the plan. Pros do this, constantly working back and forth between plan and elevation until they find a concept that works in three dimensions.

When you are satisfied with the first facade, rotate the plan to position the adjacent wall toward the bottom of the board and mount the corresponding elevation above, and repeat the process for this facade.

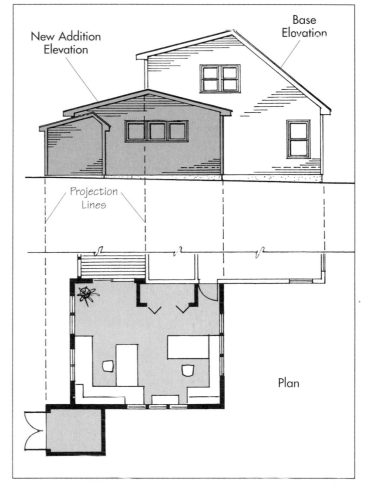

Drawing 4-29 *Position the elevation above the portion of the plan containing the addition. Project vertical lines up from the plan to create the elevation of the addition, then rotate the plan and repeat the process for adjacent sides.*

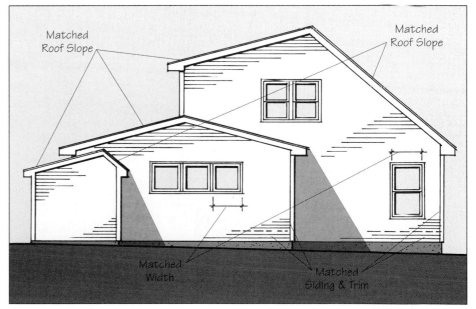

Drawing 4-30 *Designers use many means to make an addition look like it belongs to the house. The Frankels' addition blends primarily through matching roof slopes and similar trim and siding. A subtler link is in the windows. Even though the windows are horizontal, rather than vertical, their individual pane widths echo those of the main house.*

There is no magic formula or set rules for shaping an addition that fits both the plan and the house elegantly. Every design rule has probably been broken, with good results. A good place to begin is with the roof. For your first facade, choose the elevation that shows the roof slope. Try sketching in a few roof lines for the addition, using the same roof slope as that of the house. Note in Drawing 4-30 how the Frankels matched the less-steep slope of their house for the addition, and again—lower still—in the storage shed.

Another trick for blending the addition to the house is to echo the horizontal lines of the house. In the Frankels' addition, this was done by matching the windows and eaves. You can do even more to make the addition feel as if it belongs to the house by repeating exterior finish materials and colors. The Frankels did this by simply using the existing house's siding and trim on the addition.

But what if the Frankels' house had been mainly brick, and they didn't want to go to the expense of brick for the addition? They might find another way to relate the addition to the house, using the same colors or matching the trim. Maybe wood siding occurred above the brick on dormers or gable ends. Even these incidental occurrences can provide the precedent for cladding the addition with wood siding.

Some houses are harder than others to add to with an addition that looks like it belongs. Say, for example, you have an eighteenth-century house built of stone with elegant proportions and detailing—all of which would be very costly, if even possible, to replicate today. The way out might be to pull the addition away from the main house with a smaller connecting element. Separating the addition this distinctly allows more freedom in both form and materials than if you attach the addition directly. If you find yourself in a similar bind, consider hiring some professional design help.

When you land on the three-dimensional solution that clicks with the existing house, you can use your design sketches to make preliminary drawings or, after deciding on materials for your addition, go directly to working drawings. It will help you see what the project will look like, though, if you take the time and effort to make preliminary drawings similar to the plan and elevation you made to document the existing house. Overlay a clean sheet of tracing paper on the sketches and draw the outlines of the elevations with a soft pencil or fine-tipped marking pen. Draw the important lines, such as the outer edges of the building and roof, with heavy lines; use light lines for features of lesser importance, such as siding lines or window muntins. You can use copies of the completed originals to experiment with different color schemes, using colored pencils or markers. Now you are ready to consider the materials and equipment that will make your design real.

Repeating the siding treatment of the existing house is not the only way to create a harmonious addition. This addition departs from the house's brick but picks up the curved central form. The addition also is true to the architectural style and period of the house—it could have been an original feature.

Chapter 5

DEFINING THE SUPERSTRUCTURE

Even if an architect designs your addition and prepares the construction documents, you will be called on to choose between various materials. The more you know, the better able you will be to decide among the available options. If you are considering doing some of the work yourself, knowing the options will help you determine which tasks you can undertake successfully. If you design the project yourself and hire a contractor, you'll need to tell the contractor what to build. The next four chapters lay out the choices you face, from digging the hole in the ground to painting the trim. In this chapter we'll focus on the bones of the project: the foundation, walls, floors, and roof.

Proper materials are the starting point for a successful wood foundation. Most wood species deteriorate when exposed to moisture and must be chemically treated to withstand constant contact with the soil. The most used treatments to date have been chromated copper arsenate (CCA) and ammoniacal copper arsenate (ACA), which is injected under pressure into the pores of the wood. Wood foundations thus treated and held together by stainless-steel nails will resist rot and decay for 70 years, according to studies by the National Forest Products Laboratory. These preservative treatments contain arsenic, a poison, so be prepared to wear a respirator to avoid breathing the sawdust and gloves to protect your skin.

Keeping Your Foundation Dry

Water is the bane of any structure below the ground, as you already know if you have ever had to evacuate standing water from your basement. Just as insidious as the visible water trickling through cracks in the foundation is the unseen moisture that seeps through the pores of the walls or floor. This is the culprit that

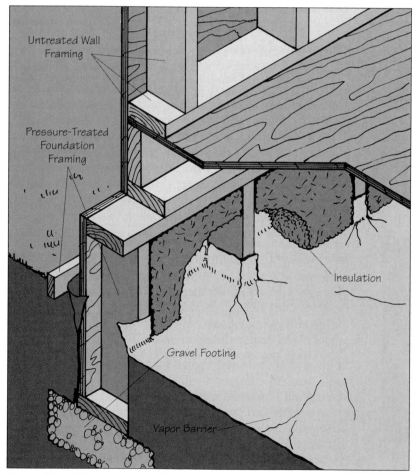

Drawing 5-7 *An all-wood foundation consists of a pressure-treated wood stud wall perched on a gravel footing. Cavities between the studs provide a natural site for insulation. A plastic sheet should be carefully installed over the soil to keep moisture out of the crawl space above.*

makes basements damp, musty places unsuited to anything but the furnace and old bicycle parts. Dampness—actually water vapor—affects the health of your household, too, by promoting the growth of microorganisms. Water vapor also affects the well-being of the house by condensing and reducing the effectiveness of thermal insulation. It provides fertile conditions for mildew and dry rot.

Keeping moisture out of your new foundation requires a three-pronged approach. Starting at the bottom, water is drained away from the bottom of the foundation, the foundation is sealed with a damp-proof or waterproof barrier, and the ground is sloped down from the foundation to conduct surface water away.

Footing drains. A drainage channel next to the bottom of the foundation prevents water pressure from building up against the wall by collecting it at the base and carrying it away. A common way to do this is to surround the outer perimeter of the footing with a 4-inch-diameter perforated pipe, as shown in Drawing 5-8. The pipe sits just outside the bottom of the footing and eventually leads to a drainage site. If possible, this is a point on the site where the leader pipe meets the grade, or "daylight." This drainage is easy to accomplish if your site slopes but may not be possible for a dead-level lot. If you face this prospect, you may be able to drain into a storm sewer line in the street or into a dry well or sump pit—a hole lined with concrete block and filled with gravel.

To get water down to the footing drain, a granular material such as sand or gravel must be placed next to the wall for the first foot or so during backfilling. A layer of filter fabric over the drainpipe keeps fine particles from clogging it. Instead of gravel next to the foundation, you can install one of several types of drainage boards or mats now available.

Damp proof or waterproof? The next defense against water is an appropriate moisture barrier on the outer face of the foundation. A damp-proof barrier will bar water vapor, or dampness, from wicking through the pores of the masonry, but it won't stop water under pressure. At a higher cost, a waterproof membrane will stop both water and dampness. Which is right for your addition? It won't pay to do any more than necessary to meet the needs of your foundation.

Consider damp proofing for full basements in low water table areas if the space inside is to be used only for heating equipment and storage. Also consider damp proofing crawl spaces. The most economical damp proofing consists of one or two coats of a water-emulsion bituminous

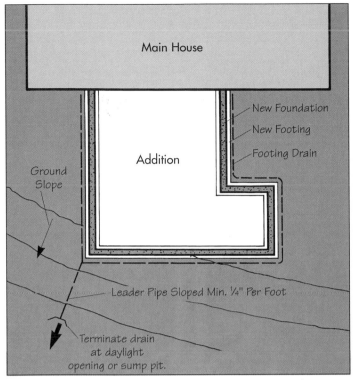

Drawing 5-8 *A footing drainage system consists of a 1-in.-diameter perforated pipe running around the outside edge of the footing and connected to a leader pipe that surfaces downhill or drains into a sump pit.*

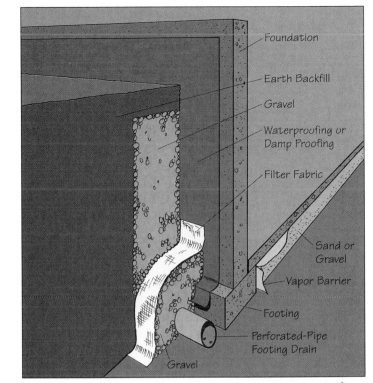

Drawing 5-9 *The traditional way to keep moisture out of a foundation begins with a damp-proof or waterproof coating on the outside. Gravel backfill conducts surface water down to a footing drain. Filter fabric above the pipe keeps small particles out of the pipe. A vapor barrier below the floor slab prevents entry of ground water from below.*

coating applied to the foundation with a roller or brush. Cementitious coatings can also be damp proof, but they don't flex to bridge cracks, as do bituminous coatings. Most damp-proofing products can be easily applied by a homeowner.

In general, consider waterproofing in a full basement if the water table rises seasonally above the footing line or if the basement will be finished. Installing waterproofing materials usually requires special expertise or equipment and is best left to a contractor. Most systems are made up of several layers of hot- or cold-applied liquids combined with sheet membranes. The waterproofing part of the system may be a liquid polymer, elastic sheet, or even cardboard panels that contain bentonite (a kind of clay that expands when wet to prevent water from passing through). Bentonite clay is the only option completely free of petrochemical-based derivatives.

Choosing the waterproofing membrane is daunting enough—but that's only part of the challenge. The membrane can be part of a multilayer system that includes insulation (as we'll see in the next chapter) and/or a layer to drain water to the footing drain (instead of gravel). Your architect can help steer you toward the right choice. If you are flying solo, ask the advice of builders familiar with basement damp proofing and waterproofing (don't pursue the matter with anyone who doesn't know the difference).

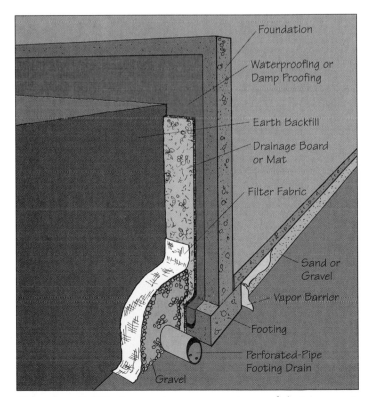

Drawing 5-10 *In recent years, many types of drainage mats have been developed to replace gravel backfill. The type shown is a ½ in.-thick mat of woven polypropylene, which allows water to flow down to the footing drain.*

Draining the surface. Diverting surface water away from the foundation before it can seep down to wreak havoc below should be your first line of defense, even if it is the last item to be built. You can do this by making sure the final grade slopes away from the foundation for a distance of 10 feet or so. Even an uphill-facing side can drain into a downward-sloping swale before the grade resumes its uphill climb. Gutters and downspouts on the eaves divert drainage off the roof, but you'll have to remember to clean out the dead leaves and debris regularly.

Attaching the Foundation to the House

The joint between the new and existing foundations can be the Achilles' heel of the new foundation. Without proper support, the free end of the new foundation can settle, causing the floors to become offset. And any movement invites water to leak through the joint. If your new foundation wraps entirely around the addition, including a parallel wall adjacent to the house, the structural and water problems are less critical. But if the foundation of the addition connects directly to the house, you will need secure anchorage and a well-sealed joint.

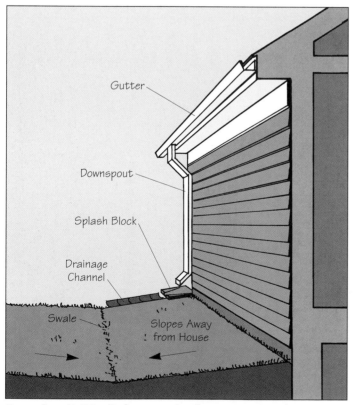

Drawing 5-11 Defense against basement water begins at the eaves, with a gutter and downspout that leads roof water away from the foundation. Sloping the grade away from the foundation about 10 ft. prevents ground water from seeping down next to the foundation where it can build up pressure and enter through cracks.

Steel brackets attached to expansion bolts drilled into the house's foundation provide support for a new abutting block wall foundation, as shown in Drawing 5-12. If the new foundation is to be concrete, a solid structural connection results from drilling steel dowels into the house's foundation, as shown in Drawing 5-13. You won't need to make the joint between the foundation of the addition and house watertight unless the addition tops a full basement. In that case, the joint needs to be sealed with a flexible sealant placed in a vertical groove between old and new constructions.

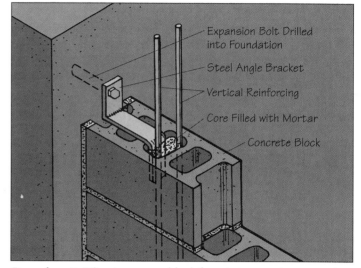

Drawing 5-12 A concrete-block foundation can be secured to the abutting house foundation with steel angle brackets at every third course. The core containing the turned-down leg of the angle should be grouted full as each course is laid. Vertical rebar set in this core ties the blocks together.

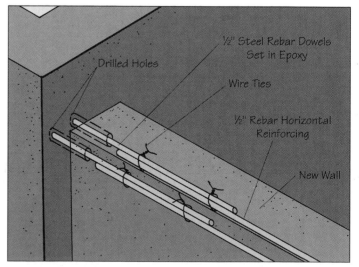

Drawing 5-13 A new concrete foundation is securely anchored to the house by steel dowels set into drilled holes at the top and bottom of the wall and held firm by epoxy. The dowels should extend into the new wall at least 24 bar diameters (12 in. for ½-in.-diameter bars, designated as #4). Horizontal rebar of the same diameter is then wired to the dowels.

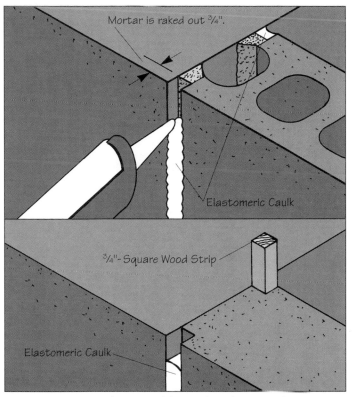

Drawing 5-14 *The inevitable crack in the vertical joint between the old and new foundations is a natural gateway for leakage. Careful sealing with an elastomeric caulking compound can keep water outside. The caulk is injected into a raked-out joint in a concrete-block foundation (top) or into a vertical joint formed by a square wood strip in a concrete foundation (bottom).*

FLOOR STRUCTURES

The first floor of your addition may be a heavyweight masonry material that sits directly on the ground or a lightweight assembly of wood or steel members that floats above a crawl space or basement. Unless you are building atop an existing floor, you can choose the type of floor for the first level based on the use of the space above, cost, comfort, the floor's ability to accommodate mechanical and electrical systems, and how much of the work you can do yourself. Second- and third-level floors will most likely be framed because constructing raised concrete slabs is costly.

Heavyweight Floors

If a concrete slab makes a good floor for a basement, why can't it suit a first floor if there is no basement? It can if the soil is stable and dry. But you should know the limitations of a slab poured directly on grade. Remember all those ducts, pipes, and wires that snake through the ceiling of your basement? You'll have to provide for them somehow. Heating ducts encased in concrete pipes can run below a slab, but this is expensive and puts them permanently out of reach. It usually

makes more sense to route them in the ceiling above if they can snake around the ceiling framing. You'll also have to insulate the topside of any ducts exposed to a cold attic.

Sewer piping can be run below a slab on grade, but it's not a good idea to locate hot- and cold-water pipes under pressure where they will be inaccessible if they leak or need to be changed. The water pipes, too, can run in a ceiling above the space, as long as they are well insulated from a cold attic above. Electrical wiring can be safely run below a slab, but it must be contained within a metal conduit.

A concrete floor slab is usually reinforced with wire mesh to control cracking under temperature changes. A plastic sheet below the slab keeps soil moisture from wicking up through the concrete into the space above. If the space above is to be occupied, a slab in a cold climate area should be insulated by rigid foam sheets below the slab or on the outside of the foundation.

If you subcontract the construction of your slab, the contractor will have all of the ingredients in place and a crew of two or more on hand to help pour, distribute, float, and finish the slab by the time the ready-mix concrete truck arrives. Concrete is unforgiving, so don't undertake the work yourself unless you have the experience, tools, and helpers.

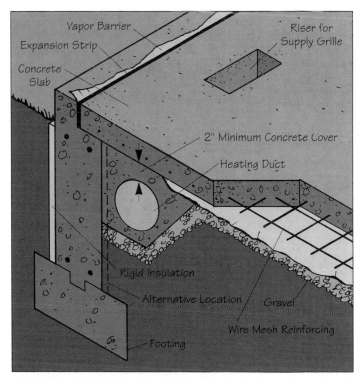

Drawing 5-15 *A concrete slab floor can rest on a stem-wall foundation, as shown here, or terminate in a thickened grade beam, as required by the frost line or local code. Ductwork can run in concrete-encased channels below the slab or through the ceiling above. Water-supply piping should not be routed below the slab.*

Heavyweight floors make particularly good sense for sun spaces because of their unsurpassed ability to absorb and store solar heat. You can start with a concrete slab and top it with a stone or tile finish (or leave the concrete exposed) or omit the slab completely in favor of brick or stone loosely laid over sand. In any case, the floor should be protected from the weather by a layer of insulation outside the foundation or under the floor.

A Wood-Framed Floor

A wood-framed floor may be a better choice than a slab on grade, even for a one-story addition. Why? First, you are more likely to be able to put up a wood floor by yourself than a concrete one. Second, a wood floor always spans an open space—crawl space or full basement—which is usually the handiest place to run pipes, wires, and ducts.

Like a living organism, a wood-framed floor consists of skin and bones. The subfloor—or skin—provides a support for the flooring underlayment and/or flooring. Plywood has mostly replaced the 1-inch-thick boards once used as subfloors. Some plywood is sanded on the top side for use as a combined subfloor/underlayment (more about underlayments in Chapter 7). Just below the skin are the supporting ribs, the floor joists.

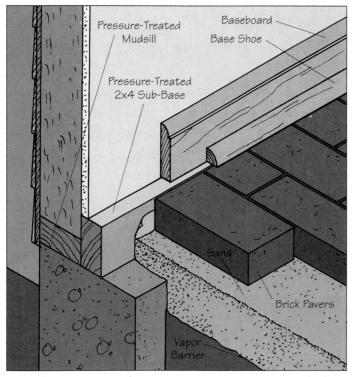

Drawing 5-16 *Brick pavers set over a 3 in.- or 4 in.-thick sand base make a good floor for sun spaces. A plastic vapor barrier below the sand keeps ground water from wicking up through the brick. Installed as shown, the edge of the brick is concealed by the wood base shoe.*

Most joists with a span of 12 feet or less are made from 1½-inch-thick lumber (nominal 2-inch thickness). But the rising cost and declining quality of lumber are now making joists of other materials more popular. Manufactured lumber, sheet steel, and steel-and-wood composite joists outperform sawn lumber joists and are becoming competitive in price. These alternatives are usually the most practical choice for spans of 20 feet or more.

Joists spaced 12, 16, or 24 inches on center pass their load onto a column (post), wall, or beam (girder). If you think of a joist as a rib, its supporting beam is akin to a spine. Beams transfer the accumulated load of everything bearing on them to walls or columns. A single piece of two-by lumber on edge may be all that is required to support a light load on a short span. Additional strength to support a heavier load or longer span can come from sandwiching several two-bys together or using a larger single member or another material, such as manufactured lumber or steel.

Sizing Wood Floor Members

Sizing the members for a wood-framed floor is as much art as science, requiring choices not only in the materials to be used for the components but also in their size and layout. A designer would probably start a framing plan by selecting a joist spacing— 12, 16, or 24 inches on center. Close spacing means thinner subfloor and smaller joists, since each joist has to carry less load. Of course, this means you'll need more joists. Homing in on the most economical combination usually comes from totaling up the costs of various combinations. Architects, structural engineers, and builders who regularly lay out framing develop a kind of sixth sense for the most economical framing layouts, so hiring one to prepare or check yours may save you money as well as ensure that the layout can safely carry the anticipated loads.

Wood is an elastic material, which means it bends under stress and returns to its original shape when the stress is removed. For that reason, wood floors yield with each relocation of the weight above. If you are tired of walking on squeaky floors, you are probably anxious to make sure the floors of your addition bear their burdens in silence. A floor that won't bounce requires a degree of stiffness beyond that needed to just support the load without collapsing. Designers use span tables and formulas to size members to meet both objectives. Formulas take into account the strength of the wood species, size of the member, span, loading conditions, and allowable deflection under the maximum load. Span tables for species of lumber used in various parts of the United States are published by regional trade associations. If you live in the south and use southern pine, for

Manufactured Lumber

The cost of joists and beams sawn directly from logs has been erratic over the past several years, while the quality of this lumber has steadily declined. Even though wood is a renewable resource, it isn't being renewed at the rate it is being consumed. Younger trees cut to meet the demand yield smaller pieces at the lumberyard. These pieces are plagued with checks, warps, and knots.

If forests won't meet the need for structural wood, why not use something else? That's exactly what's happening in more and more new homes today. One alternative is joists and beams made of wood fibers glued together under high pressure, drawing on the technologies long used to make plywood. These products outperform their sawn lumber counterparts in many ways:

▲ Longer lengths. By making beams and joists in a continuous process, lengths are limited only by the means of shipping. If your floor is 30 feet wide, you can order 30-foot-long joists to span the gap without intermediate supports.

▲ Less moisture. About one-half the moisture content of yard lumber. You won't have squeaky floors when the heat is turned on and dries out the inside of the new construction.

▲ Consistent sizes and shapes. Unlike yard lumber, manufactured boards won't check, warp, and split.

▲ Randomized defects. A knot in a 2x12 joist goes completely thorough, reducing its strength. Engineered lumber contains mere slices of knots only as thick as the layer in which they occur.

▲ Lighter weight. Engineered lumber is manufactured in shapes that get the most for the least, with the result that they support the same loads with less lumber than yard lumber.

▲ Holes for ducts and pipes. Larger diameter holes can be cut through manufactured joists than through standard lumber.

Manufactured lumber is made by several processes. In one, plywood veneers are glued together, called laminated-veneer lumber (LVL).

LVL beams look like long pieces of thick plywood, except that the grain in each veneer layer runs parallel to the length, rather than alternating crosswise, as in plywood panels. Another process glues 2x4s or 2x6s together into beams, called glue-laminated beams. Wood fibers are bonded in yet another process to form structural framing members and sheathing panels under the heading of oriented-strand board (OSB). Wood I-joists are I-shaped with LVL or 2x4s making the serifs of the I, connected by a thin plywood or OSB center piece.

Manufactured joists and beams go up much the same as standard lumber, secured with nails or screws. Some tasks, such as drilling holes for wiring or piping are even easier, thanks to prescored knockout holes in the web (midsection) of joists. But you can't hack holes through manufactured joists with the same freedom as with standard lumber. More careful planning is required because of the composition of the joists. Thin webs of I-joists can be perforated only in certain locations. Joists with trussed-metal webs cannot be altered on site at all. They can be built to accommodate special needs but must be ordered that way. Always follow the manufacturer's recommendations for cutting and joining manufactured joists.

Manufactured lumber framing members include from left, I-joists; oriented-strand boards for use as rim joists, headers, and studs; laminated-veneer lumber used for headers and beams; and larger oriented-strand lumber used for beams. At back are three sizes of parallel-strand lumber used for beams, columns, headers, and posts.

example, you could request a copy of "Maximum Spans, Southern Pine Joists & Rafters," from the Southern Pine Marketing Council. The Western Wood Products Association publishes similar data for fir and hemlock (used in the west). Homeowners in the east can get data from the Northeast Lumber Manufacturers Association. Even if you determine your own framing layout and sizes of members, you can assure yourself that your

scheme is the most economical way to meet the structural requirements by having it reviewed by an architect, engineer, or builder.

A final note to anyone concerned with avoiding squeaky floors: The best insurance is a framing system designed not merely to meet but to exceed minimum standards. This might mean, for example, sizing the joists to deflect a maximum of ¹⁄₃₆₀ of the span rather than ¹⁄₁₈₀ and using ¾-inch plywood subfloor nailed and glued to the joists rather than ⅝-inch plywood, nailed only.

Beams, Posts, and Columns

Is it better to select joists that span the full distance or to use smaller joists supported midway by a beam? Answering this typical question involves balancing functional and economic factors. Spanning the full distance leaves a clear space below—a plus if the space is used for certain functions, such as playing table tennis or pool, but of no particular advantage in a crawl space or basement used for storage. In economic terms, clear spanning saves the cost of intermediate supporting members but requires stronger joists. Joists of standard lumber, in any case, likely won't span more than 20 feet, and this assumes the better grades of 2x12 joists. The most cost-effective solution is arrived at by comparing the alternatives.

Manufactured joists provide one answer to spans greater than 20 feet. For example, I-joists, 16 inches deep and spaced 16 inches on center, can span up to 30 feet under normal floor loading. If a clear span isn't high on your list of priorities, consider using smaller joists with one or more beam lines to provide intermediate supports. A beam can be located below the joists with the joists sitting on top if there is space. If the space is needed for headroom, the beam can be installed so that its top is flush with the tops of the joists, as shown at the bottom of Drawing 5-19.

You can use a smaller beam to carry a heavier given load if the beam is manufactured than you can if the beam is standard lumber. Say, for example, you have a 16-foot-long beam that runs down the center of a 16-foot-wide basement. Here are some of the options:

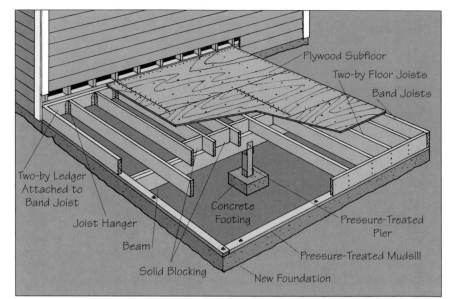

Drawing 5-17 *A floor framed conventionally with dimensioned lumber requires one or more beams, unless the width spanned by the joists is less than about 17 ft. Plywood subflooring should be laid across the joists in a staggered pattern and secured with both nails and construction adhesive for best results.*

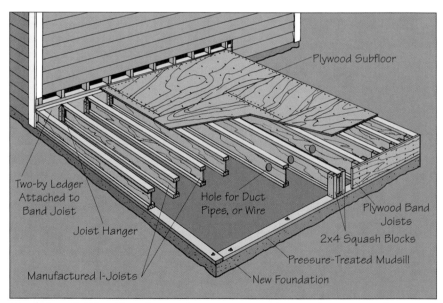

Drawing 5-18 *Manufactured joists can span longer distances without intermediate supports than can joists of conventional lumber. The I-joists shown here consist of a ½-in.-thick plywood web sandwiched between a 2x4 flange top and bottom. Holes can be cut in the web for ducts, pipes, and wires (except near the bearing ends). Large holes in lumber joists can result in structural failure.*

Option	Actual Size
Four 2 x 12s (standard lumber)	6" x 11¼"
One 3⅛" x 13½" glue-laminated beam	3⅛" x 13½"
One 1¾" x 16" LVL beam	1¾" x 16"
Two 1¾" x 14" LVL beams	3½" x 14"
Three 1¾" x 11⅞" LVL beams	5¼" x 11⅞"

The most economical choice is probably one 1¾ by 16-inch LVL beam, but 16 inches of depth may require more vertical space than you want to allow, so two 1¾ by 14-inch LVL beams might be more practical.

Wood posts and concrete-filled steel columns are commonly used in basements to support beams at intermediate points. Wood posts, usually 4x4s or 6x6s, can be joined to beams with post cap connectors made of

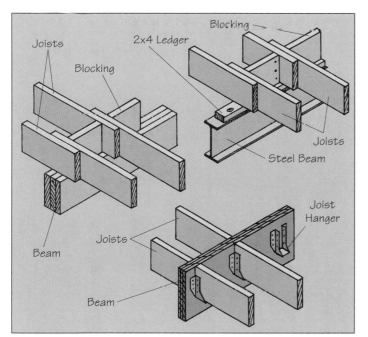

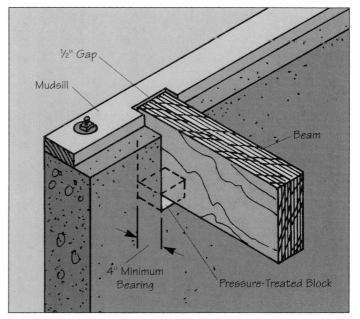

Drawing 5-19 *Floor joists can run over the top of the beam (top left, top right) or be attached to the face of the beam (bottom) to preserve headroom. When joists run above a beam, blocking must be provided for lateral stability.*

Drawing 5-20 *A pocket in the foundation wall provides support for a beam that is below the joists. A ½-in. space around three sides of the beam and a treated wood block below prevent moisture in the concrete from deteriorating the beam.*

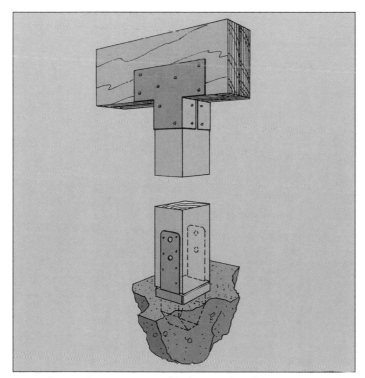

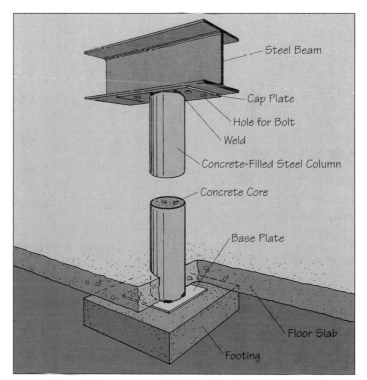

Drawing 5-21 *A variety of galvanized-steel connectors are available to secure wood beams to posts and posts to a concrete base. At the top is a common post-to-beam connector. The base connector shown at the bottom is cast into the concrete. The post sits on a raised plate that isolates it from moisture in the concrete.*

Drawing 5-22 *Concrete-filled steel columns come with the cap and base plates welded on. The column is mounted to a footing before the slab is poured. The cap plate can be bolted to a steel beam, as shown, or secured to a wood beam with lag screws.*

galvanized sheet metal. Another special connector, called a post base, anchors the post to the footing by bolts set in the concrete. The post base should be shaped to keep the wood from contact with concrete.

Concrete-filled steel columns (often called by the tradename Lally columns) are 4 inches in diameter and come in standard lengths with metal cap and base plates already attached.

Tying the New Floor to the House

The easiest way to join the new wood-framed floor to the existing house is to run the floor joists parallel to the ones in the house. The first joist is nailed through the sheathing to the house's band joist. Its ends bear on the mudsill that will support the other joists for the addition. If your layout works better with the addition's joists running perpendicular to the house's joists, you can support them at the house with a separate foundation wall or beam or simply attach them with joist hangers to a ledger joist bolted to the house's own band joist.

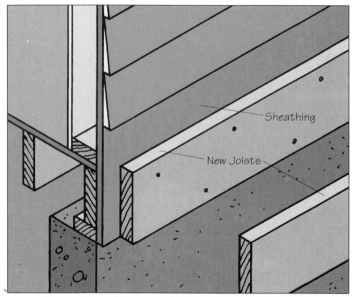

Drawing 5-23 *If the joists for the addition run parallel to the abutting house wall, simply nail the first joist through the existing sheathing into the band joist.*

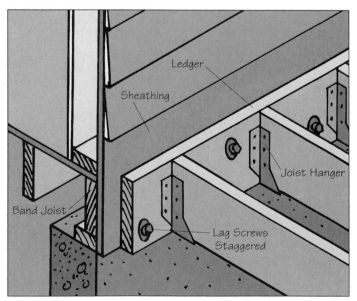

Drawing 5-24 *Joists running perpendicular to the abutting house wall can be supported by joist hangers attached to a ledger joist that is bolted through the sheathing to the band joist.*

Because a wood-framed floor spans an open crawl space or basement, you will need some way of getting into the enclosed area for repair or maintenance. An existing basement window in the house wall may be large enough for access to a crawl space. If not, you can cut out an opening in the foundation with a diamond-blade masonry saw from a rental agency or hire a specialized contractor to do the job. (Look under "Concrete Cutting" in the Yellow Pages.) You may be able to get into the crawl space only from the addition. If so, consider locating a hinged access panel, at least 24 inches square, somewhere in the floor, such as in a closet.

If your addition tops a full basement, you'll need a normal access doorway from either the house or the outside. As with a crawl space, you can cut a connecting doorway with a concrete-cutting saw if you must have direct access from the house. If you need to get into the addition basement only from the outside, you can save money and effort by forming a door to the outside in the new foundation wall. If the grade near the new doorway slopes away from the addition, you may be able to open onto the site directly or with only one or two steps. But if the only way onto grade is up, consider enclosing the steps with a hatchway to avoid trapping water at the base.

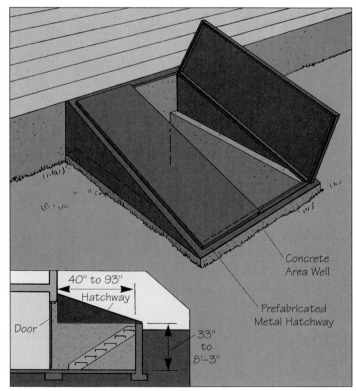

Drawing 5-25 *Stairs set into a well provide a way into and out of a below-grade basement addition. A metal hatchway above the well keeps out water, snow, and ice—a necessity in most regions. The length and height of the well depend on the number of stairs inside. The size ranges indicated in the inset are based on available standard hatchways.*

STRUCTURAL WALLS

The structural walls of your addition must not only support the weight of the subsequent floors and roof but also resist the horizontal forces of winds and earthquakes. Because these horizontal forces vary from place to place, the building codes in your area define the type and extent of horizontal bracing required. Your house may have been built before a code was formulated, so local regulations may require a higher degree of lateral stability for the addition than exists in the original structure. An architect hired to design your addition will constantly weigh the horizontal bracing method required for any system under consideration. Other factors that affect the choice for the best type of system include the following:

▲ The type of substructure—foundation or existing walls.

▲ The type of construction of the adjoining house.

▲ Energy performance.

▲ Cost relative to other alternatives.

▲ The structural system—exposed or concealed.

▲ The exterior finish.

If you will do the work yourself, that also bears consideration. Let's see how some of the major building systems measure up.

Stud Walls

Wood studs. The reasons that have made wood studs so popular for new houses over the last 50 years may make them the right choice for your addition. Stud construction is often the most economical option. One moderately skilled person can put up stud walls quickly with only a few hand tools and a good 7-inch-diameter portable electrical saw. If your addition is above an existing wood-framed wall—a second story, for example—the light weight of wood studs makes them a natural choice.

The cavities between the studs make natural pockets for thermal insulation. When higher levels of insulation are required than a 2x4 wall accommodates, increasing stud depth to 2x6 often fits the bill. Foam insulation can easily be tacked onto the inside or outside for even more insulation.

Stud walls not only provide a fitting backup for a lightweight siding or stucco finish but also provide

Steel Floor Joists

Steel has recently joined manufactured lumber as an increasingly used alternative to sawn lumber. Cold-formed from galvanized sheet stock, steel joists and studs are formed into C-shaped channels for structural efficiency and made in lengths up to 40 feet. Other advantages over sawn lumber are as follows:

▲ Steel joists cost less than two-by sawn lumber.

▲ Steel is much stronger than wood.

▲ Steel contains no checks, warps, or knots.

▲ Moisture does not cause steel to swell or move.

▲ Because steel joists come in various thicknesses (gauges), they offer various strengths for the same depths, resulting in more flexibility for layouts.

Installing steel joists requires a combination of sheet-metal techniques along with standard wood carpentry. Cutting the material is dangerous, requiring protection for hands and eyes. Because steel readily conducts heat, you must use wood framing or insulation between the steel and the outside of the house to prevent winter heat loss and summer heat gain. Steel joists come with prepunched cutouts in their webs to allow wiring and piping to pass through. Plastic grommets must be snapped into wiring holes to prevent the sheet metal from cutting into the wiring insulation.

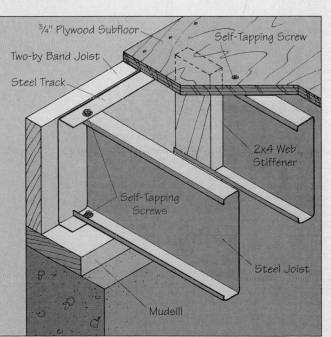

Drawing 5-26 *Steel joists frame into a C-shaped track mounted inside the wood band joist. The thin web of the joists are stiffened by 2x4 blocking at the bearing points. Self-tapping galvanized screws attach the plywood subfloor to the flanges of each joist.*

the kind of structural support needed for brick or stone veneer.

Steel studs. Handy as they are, wood studs are slipping in popularity because of falling quality and rising prices. Studs made of light-gauge formed steel, long used in commercial buildings, have steadily gained favor in home construction. Like wood studs, steel studs are lightweight and make a good backup for surface finish materials or brick veneer. But they have a few disadvantages as well.

Though the cavities between steel studs—like wood—can be stuffed with thermal insulation, steel conducts heat so much better than wood (400 times better) that many designers prefer not to use steel studs in exterior walls of homes where winters are cold. Besides the heat lost to the outside through the studs, the cold inner flange invites condensation of moisture, which can ruin wall finishes. One way around this problem is to apply rigid insulation to the exterior side of the studs, in addition to any insulation that will fill the cavities in the wall.

Another disadvantage is the installation itself, at least for people used to carpentry methods. Sheet-metal skills, not carpentry, are required to cut and join steel studs. Installing steel studs may require specialized tools, such as a metal-cutting electrical saw and electrical or pneumatic drill. Goggles and gloves are a must to prevent injury from ragged cuts and flying bits of metal. Finding a pro to install steel studs isn't hard. Home builders are increasingly using steel studs. But don't forget that if you subcontract someone else to put in your kitchen or bath cabinets or even to install wood trim, they will have to attach their work with self-tapping metal screws, rather than with nails or drywall screws.

Steel studs come in gauges (thicknesses) of 12, 14, 16, 18, 20, and 25—the lower the number, the heavier the material. All gauges except 25 are suitable for supporting vertical loads, leaving 25-gauge studs for interior walls or exterior walls that carry no vertical

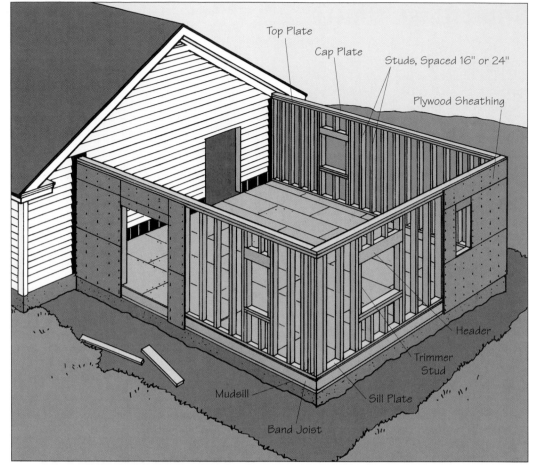

Drawing 5-27 *Wall framing consists of a sill plate, vertical studs, and a double top plate. Double studs frame the sides of window and door openings. Header beams sized for the width support the wall above the openings. Walls are usually framed in sections on the floor with the top plate, then tilted up into place. The cap plate then goes on, tying the sections together.*

loads. Studs are C-shaped, with the flanges typically 1½ inches wide and with depths of 1⅝, 2, 2½, 3½, 4, and 6 inches. Installation typically follows a one-two-three sequence. A C-shaped track is first screwed to the floor, then another one is screwed to the ceiling. Studs are fitted into the tracks, one at a time, and secured by driving a self-tapping sheet metal screw through the flange of the track into the flange of the stud at the top and the bottom. If the studs feel flimsy at this point, don't worry. They gain stiffness when the wall finish is screwed to them.

Masonry Walls

Most people have warm feelings toward brick. It is undeniably durable and evokes quality. But be prepared to pay extra for these advantages. Considered a nonstructural material, brick must be backed by a structural wall, either studs or structural masonry, such as concrete block. The combined brick and structural backing is called brick veneer. If you are choosing brick for your addition because your house is brick, keep in mind that you probably won't be able

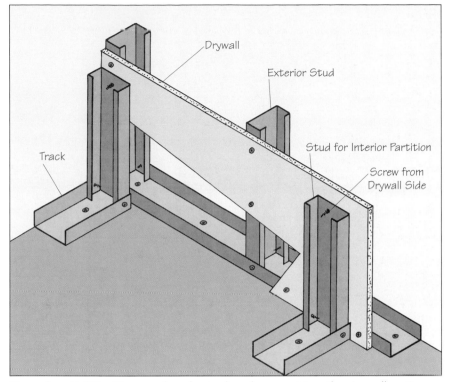

Drawing 5-28 *Like wood studs, steel studs are put together in wall sections while lying flat on the floor and then tilted up into position. After track channels are screwed to the floor deck, drywall is screwed to the flanges of the studs. Note that the screws attach to the backside of intersecting wall studs.*

to the concrete block. Another way is to build a stud wall inside the block wall. Furring out creates a 1½-inch-deep cavity that can be filled with rigid foam insulation. A 2x4 stud wall will provide enough space for fiberglass-batt insulation, which is less expensive than rigid foam.

From the standpoint of energy conservation, masonry materials are poor insulators—a definite drawback in any area where insulation is necessary. The backup stud wall needed for brick creates natural cavities for insulation. However, the small amount of insulation that fits into the cores of concrete blocks won't be adequate for cold climates; more insulation would have to be added inside or outside the block.

Solid masonry walls do have one advantage that offsets their meager ability to insulate: They are terrific heat storers. This storage capability works well in areas with large temperature swings from day to night, such as in the Southwest. Heavy masonry construction will absorb heat during the day and release it slowly at night, helping to even out temperature swings.

to match the existing brick exactly. Even a minor variation in color or texture can look poor. You may get a better job by selecting a contrasting material, such as wood siding. If you do use brick, entrust the work to a seasoned mason. Bricklaying is a demanding craft that tolerates few errors.

Concrete block doesn't exude the same glamour as brick, yet it can still make a reasonable wall material for some additions, particularly if the main house is made of block. Block is relatively economical and can be laid up by most people willing to acquire the skill and a few masonry tools. It easily serves as support for vertical loads. Block accepts masonry surface treatments like stucco and polymer-based masonry coatings, but it is not a good candidate for siding. Paint and plaster can be applied directly inside, but running pipes and electrical wiring through block is a nightmare. In garages and utility sheds, this is no problem—these utilities can simply be left exposed on the inside wall surface. For living areas, though, it's more common to use two-by lumber to create a cavity for wiring and plumbing. This can be done by "furring out" the wall—that is, attaching the wide side of two-by lumber directly

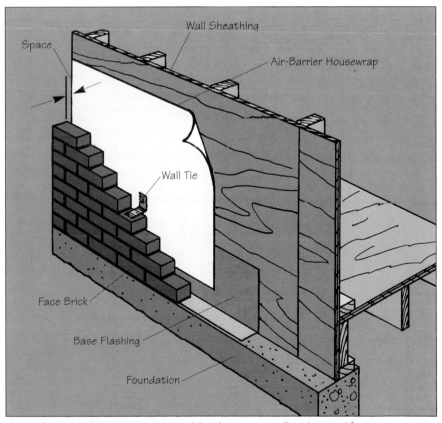

Drawing 5-29 *Here is a typical brick veneer wall with wood-frame construction. Galvanized-metal wall ties hold the brick to the stud wall. The ties are typically mortared into the horizontal joints at every sixth brick course and nailed through the sheathing into every other stud.*

Post-and-Beam Framing

Both solid masonry walls and stud walls support the weight of floors and roofs in a continuous line, but there's another way: Use fewer supports, spaced widely, with beams above to pick up the load. Lateral bracing can come from sheathing on the exterior or diagonal members within the frame. This approach has a long history and was used in most houses from colonial times up to the 1940s, when framing with studs began to dominate housing construction. In traditional post-and-beam construction, members connect to each other by mortise-and-tenon joinery held together by wood pegs. Posts are spaced in a regular grid of 8-, 10-, or 12-feet square, which limits the flexibility of the floor plan somewhat but results in a simple yet elegant system that is left exposed and finished naturally on the interior.

Traditional post-and-beam houses were clad with boards on the outside, making them hot in the summer and cold in the winter. Today, the outer skin most often consists of a thermally tight sandwich panel. A core of foam insulation is enclosed within plywood or a similar panel, outside and inside. Siding can be applied to the outside. The inside face of the panels can be finished with plaster or drywall, and the structural members are left exposed inside.

A post-and-beam addition probably makes the best fit for a similarly constructed house. Designing and planning such an addition are anything but simple, and erecting it with traditional joinery requires special skills and tools. If you are considering this type of addition, make early contact with a post-and-beam supplier (who may be listed under "timber frame" in the phone book). These suppliers provide assistance with layout, then prepare detailed shop drawings for the various parts of the structural system. When foundations are ready, the supplier will send a crew out to your site to erect the members or hire a local contractor skilled in putting up their system.

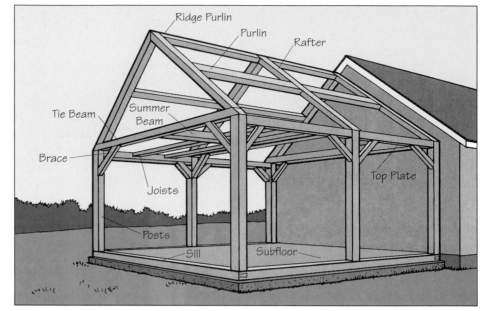

Drawing 5-30 *A post-and-beam structure can bear on a timber sill (as shown) or a wide mudsill, such as a 2x8. The posts, beams, rafters, and purlins that comprise the frame are held together by round wood pegs drilled through the precisely cut joints. Triangular braces at each joint hold the frame rigid. Stress-skin panels often clad the exterior, but conventional stud framing may also be used.*

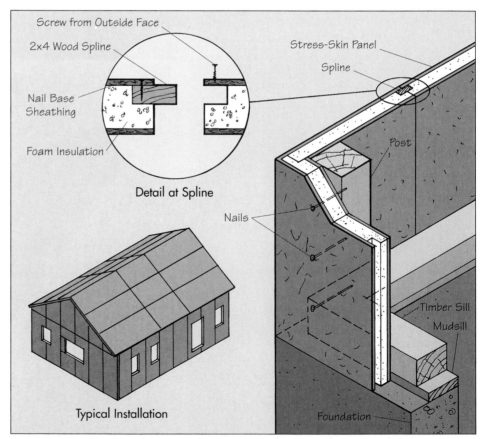

Drawing 5-31 *Stress-skin panels often enclose post-and-beam houses. Panels are prefabricated, weathertight, energy-efficient sandwiches of foam insulation between a nailable sheathing, such as ½-in. waferboard. There are several methods of joining panels together. The one shown here uses a wood spline, which allows the insulation to be continuous at the joint. Panels are attached to the frame by galvanized ring-shank nails long enough to penetrate the frame by 1½ in. Shingles and siding can be nailed directly to the outer sheathing.*

Post-and-beam framing is often left exposed on the interior and is sometimes embellished with carved details

FRAMING THE ROOF

The shape of the roof usually suggests a logical way to frame it. A roof containing an attic can be framed with rafters or trusses. Framing a roof above a cathedral ceiling is more challenging. If the slope of the ceiling parallels the roof, the obvious choice—rafters—will need to be deep enough for the thickness of insulation. The way the roof of the addition meets the house also enters into the equation. Framing a new roof to end at a flat wall is simple enough, but tying into the house roof requires careful layout and skill to cut and fit pieces on tricky angles.

Site-Framed Rafter Roofs

Shed roofs (roofs with a single slope) are the easiest to frame with rafters spaced at 16 or 24 inches on center. The high end can bear on a ledger joist secured to a wall of the house or on the top plate of a side with a sloped roof.

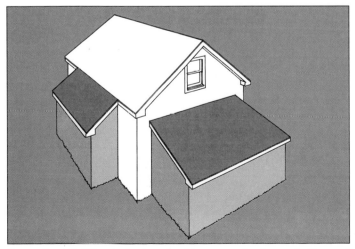

Drawing 5-32 A shed-roof addition can be framed off a wall of the main house or from the eaves of the main roof.

The Common Wall

The wall of the house that abuts the addition will lose its role as an exterior wall after the addition is built. Your plans may call for a separate new wall parallel to the house wall to support a floor or roof, in which case the house wall can simply remain in place. If you don't need a new separate wall, you'll have to do something about the existing siding or brick.

If the former outer wall is brick, block, or stone, the mass of the wall will act as a good sound barrier between the house and the addition, a boon for a home office or recreation room. The insulation in a frame wall helps bar sound as well, so try to keep it intact. Rather than tearing off the siding and ripping out the insulation to run new pipes and wiring, consider building a 2x4 stud wall to provide a chase for utilities and a nailing surface for drywall.

Before you bury an attractive brick or stone wall under a new interior wall finish, ask yourself if leaving it exposed in the addition might yield a more attractive result. Existing windows will have to be dealt with. You may be able to match the brick and plug them up. Plugging them with another material might look like patchwork, though. How about turning them into bookshelves or display cases?

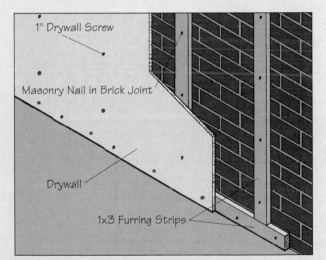

Drawing 5-33 A furred (strapped) wall finish can be applied to a common wall of masonry by attaching 1x3 furring strips to the wall with masonry nails driven through the joints, then screwing drywall to the strips. Building a new stud wall next to the existing masonry wall may be easier, though, and will give you a space wide enough to run electrical wiring and pipes.

Framing double-sloped roofs is more complicated, because they must resist an outward force, or thrust, in addition to the vertical load of the roof. You can get a feel for this by doing a simple experiment. Sit at a table or desk, clasp your hands together, and rest your elbows on the desk some distance apart from each other. Now push down on your clasped hands with your chin. Notice your elbows wanting to slide apart?

You can prevent this by either placing a sling between your elbows or by supporting your chin on a stack of books.

Tying rafters together. Just as the sling kept your elbows from sliding apart, horizontal members between two sloping rafters can prevent them from spreading apart under the load of a roof. The tie triangulates a pair of rafters into a kind of a truss. The lower the tie, the better it works. The tie can be the attic floor if the floor framing is tied to the rafters and continuously tied together across its span.

If you want to increase the amount of attic space that is tall enough to use, you can achieve this by raising the roof on kneewalls at the outside walls. Since triangulating the roof at the floor is no longer possible, collar ties between rafters might do the trick, if properly designed. They must be adequately connected to the rafters and placed as low as is feasible to maintain head room.

Ridge supports. Just as a stack of books could hold your chin up in the experiment, a continuous wall or beam under the ridge can keep rafters from spreading. A beam used in this way can be fit into the plane of the rafters or sit below them, as shown Drawing 5-35. A beam used to support rafters at the roof ridge is itself supported by columns or a wall that carries the load to ground. If your rafters are tied together with collar ties or floor joists, you might see a two-by board running along the ridge. Most likely, this is not a structural ridge beam. Rather it is a nonstructural ridgeboard that the carpenters used as a convenient way to raise the rafters and accurately space them. You can tell for sure that the ridgeboard is nonstructural if there is nothing stronger than a stud supporting it at the gable ends. Codes in some parts of the United States require ridgeboards or blocking between the framing to help the roof act as a diaphragm in resisting wind or seismic forces.

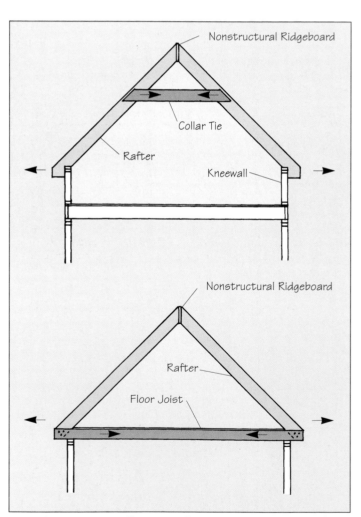

Drawing 5-34 *Collar ties or floor joists between the rafters can resist outward thrust of a gable roof. To be effective, collar ties must be properly located, sized, and connected to the rafters. In shallow-pitched roofs, collar ties may not leave enough head-room below. Floor joists, if used as ties, must be continuous unbroken members or members tied together between the bearing walls. They must also be sufficiently connected to rafters.*

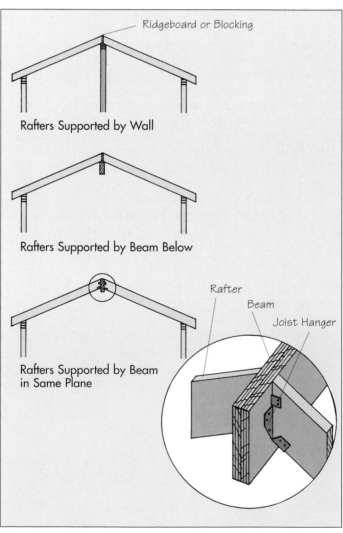

Drawing 5-35 *If ties are not used to resist outward thrust, rafters must be supported vertically by a wall or beam. The beam can be below the rafters or in the same plane (bottom). Many special metal connectors are available for connecting the rafters to the face of the beam, as shown in the detail.*

Trussed Roofs

Most people know that a diagonal brace is a quick fix for a teetering frame. The brace makes the rectangle rigid by changing it to a triangle, putting each of the three sides into pure compression or tension, relieving the joints from having to keep the frame rigid. Trusses use this same principle to carry a roof above an open space efficiently. Trusses of steel or heavy timbers have been supporting the roofs of large buildings for centuries. In recent years, a breed of lightweight trusses have gained popularity for homes. These factory-made trusses consist of 2x4 and/or 2x6 members connected to each other by sheet-metal plates (gussets). Though trusses cost more in material than site framing, they save enormously in labor. The more trusses, the more economical they become. (If the roof requires fewer than, say, six trusses, site framing will probably be cheaper.) Another big advantage of trusses over framing with trusses is that the bottom chords of trusses can span greater distances than usual ceiling joists without intermediate supports, leaving the layout of the space below completely flexible. Trusses can be made to handle any span, but their practical length is limited to around 40 feet, the length of a truck trailer. If the slope is steep, the height of the truss may also be a limiting factor. Also be aware that trusses greatly reduce the usable space in an attic.

Factories scattered all over the country prefabricate trusses to meet the specifications of the job. An order for prefab trusses must include the following data:

▲ The quantity of each type of truss needed.

▲ The dimensions and profile of each type of truss, including a sketch of the truss that indicates the clear span, slope, and length of overhangs at the eaves but not the web members.

▲ The loads to be supported by the trusses.

Roof structures must support two types of weights or loads: loads produced intermittently by snow and wind (live loads) and those due to the weight of the structure itself (dead loads). If you are designing your own addition, you can obtain the live loads from your local building department. Most light construction produces dead loads weighing 5 to 10 pounds per square foot.

The engineers at the truss plant will use the supplied data to engineer the trusses,

including the configuration of the interior, or web, members. The fabrication shop then turns the design into jigs, from which the trusses are produced. After delivery, trusses should be covered and stored vertically until time for installation.

Trusses are usually spaced 24 inches on center. If you install your own trusses, have an assistant on hand to help lift them into position and hold them steady while you nail a 2x4 brace across the tops. Bracing must be sufficient to keep all trusses from tipping over until all trusses are in final position and the sheathing is nailed to them. Trusses can take almost any shape as long as they can be triangulated.

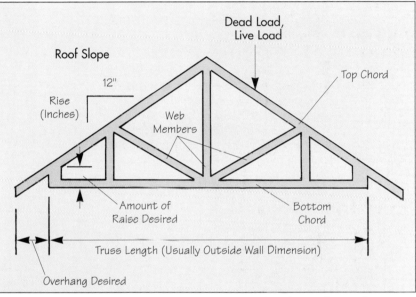

Drawing 5-36 Engineered trusses are designed and manufactured to your specifications. The web members are usually left up to the manufacturer unless there are special requirements.

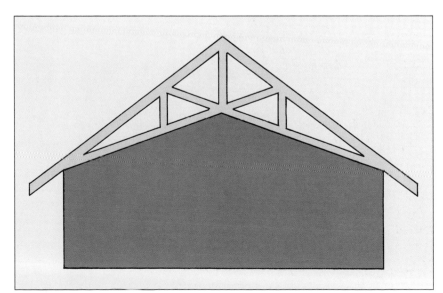

Drawing 5-37 Trusses can be shaped to fit almost any roof and ceiling need. Scissors trusses, such as these, would suit a cathedral ceiling.

Trusses are so versatile that they can even be shaped to fit a hipped roof. Each truss on a hip has a different shape. The truss nearest the peak looks like the other roof trusses with its top lopped off slightly. Each succeeding truss has a longer lopped portion. The last truss near the outside wall supports the intersecting jack trusses that support the eaves.

Joining the Roof to the House

The roof of the addition can meet the house in many ways, depending on shape, roof slope, materials, and construction of new and existing parts. A shed roof can hang off an eave or wall, as shown in Drawing 5-32. The intersection of a gable roof with the house is relatively simple if the new roof abuts the gable end of the house, particularly if the new slope matches the old. The joint is a bit more challenging if the new roof blends into the slope of the house roof. Drawings 5-39 and 5-40 show typical framing for each of these conditions.

Joining a truss roof to gable-end rafters or walls is usually as simple as nailing the last truss to the wall or rafters. Joining a trussed roof to the slope of the roof usually requires you to order trusses that get smaller as they step up the roof. Alternately, the transition can be site framed.

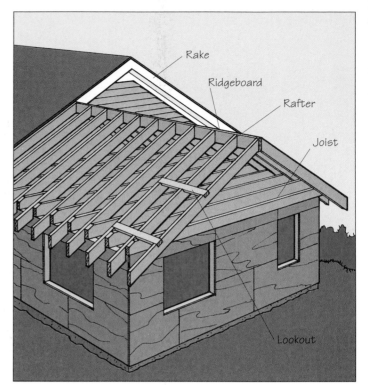

Drawing 5-39 *Ceiling joists go up first to serve as a platform when framing a new gable roof that is parallel to the house's existing gable end. The ridgeboard is then positioned and temporarily supported. Rafters go up next. If the gable end of the addition overhangs, the last rafter can be supported by lookouts affixed to two or more main rafters.*

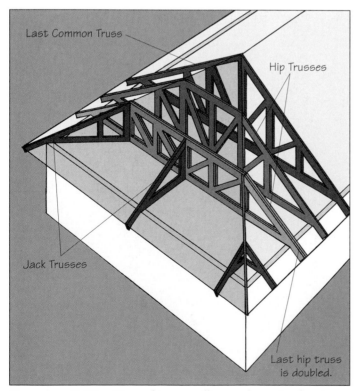

Drawing 5-38 *Hip-roof trusses offer an alternative framing system to rafter systems. The flat-topped trusses begin at the hip after the last common truss and step down in sequence to meet jack trusses, which frame the shallow outer width of the hip.*

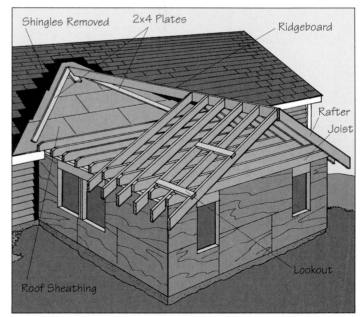

Drawing 5-40 *Joining a gable roof to the sloped side of a pitched house also begins with the ceiling joists. Next, the roofing at the area of the intersection is stripped away and 2x4 plates are nailed to the sheathing to serve as nailers for the addition's roof sheathing. The ridgeboard goes into position and is temporarily supported in place until the main rafters secure it permanently. The pie-shaped area atop the house's roof, must be framed with jack rafters, each cut to a different length and on an angle to fit the sloping nailer plate.*

Dormers

As we saw in Chapter 3, adding one or more dormers to the roof is a good way to increase the headroom in an otherwise unusable attic. Framing a dormer begins by cutting out the opening and nailing a double header and trimmer rafters around the edges to support the walls and roof of the dormer. A shed dormer with a single-sloped roof that springs out from the main roof gains the most headroom and is the easiest to frame. It may not suit the style of the home, however, as well as a gable (doghouse) dormer. Small dormers look better if there is more than one unit.

Framing the roof completes the structural shell of your addition. Now comes putting flesh on the bones. We'll review the decisions you'll face in selecting the right kind of envelope in the next chapter.

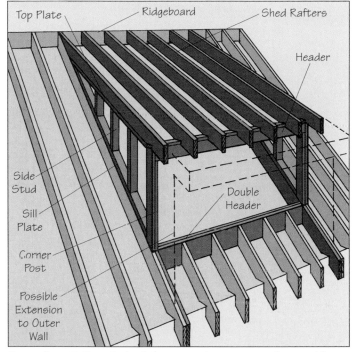

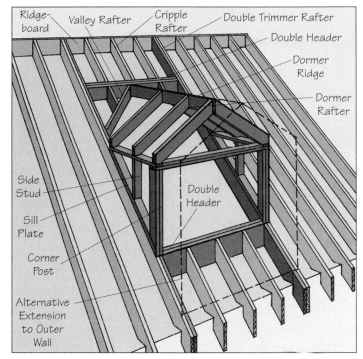

Drawing 5-41 *A shed dormer is the easiest to frame. After creating an opening and installing the header at the bottom, the joists forming the perimeter of the shed roof are erected on corner posts. Next, studs fill in the sloping side walls and vertical front walls with header and edge framing around the desired opening. Rafters go in last and are connected to the roof ridge if the dormer starts at the ridge. If the dormer starts below the ridge, a double header must be installed at the spring point from the roof.*

Drawing 5-42 *Framing a gable dormer also begins by creating an opening and installing headers at the top and bottom. (Bottom headers are eliminated if the front of the dormer extends out to bear on the wall below.) Corner posts and a top plate go in next, followed by the ridgeboard and main rafters. Valley rafters angle out from the top header rafter to create a valley from which the double-pitched gable roof springs.*

Shed dormers are the most efficient way to add space to the attic. This shed dormer balances harmoniously with the heavy horizontal frieze board on this house.

Gable dormers are more complicated to frame than shed dormers and they add less usable space, but they do bring in light and air and may be the only type of dormer that will look right.

Chapter 6

ENVELOPE DECISIONS

The last chapter talked about the bones of your addition. Now it's time to focus on the skin and underlying tissue. The materials you see on the walls and roof are important not only for their appearance but also for keeping out the weather. Just as important is what you can't see—the thermal insulation. It's what will make the inside of your home comfortable.

THE SKIN

The addition can be covered to match the outside facing material of your house or it can be covered with a contrasting material. Matching can be tough. The brick or siding may no longer be available or at least not in the original color and style. If your old siding is in poor condition, now may be the time to replace it with the same exterior finish you use on the addition. Or perhaps a contrasting material is the answer. Each type of roofing and siding poses a different set of questions, as we'll discuss here.

Brick

Brick makes classy cladding, with unsurpassed durability and low maintenance. If your house is brick, you may want to continue with brick on the addition. To do this successfully you'll need to match closely the current brick's size, texture, color, and bond pattern. Size and bond won't usually be the hang-up. Face brick has been available in standard-size units of 2¼ by 7⅝ by 3⅝ inches for many years and can be laid up to match the bond of the adjacent brickwork. Finding a convincing color and texture match is harder. Bricks vary in color with every batch fired. The older the house, the less likely you are to find a good match. Have your mason obtain candidate bricks and lay them up into a sample panel at least 2 feet square. When you view the panel next to the existing brickwork, you'll be able to judge whether the new brick is close enough to the old to proceed. If the new brick is even slightly off, it can look worse than an entirely different material. You may be better off contrasting with stucco or another siding.

Brick is an expensive facing material. Part of its high cost is in the way it goes up—brick by brick, with little room for error. You could probably obtain the few tools required to lay brick cheaply enough, but the skills required to lay up a wall true and plumb come only with years of experience. Unless you already have them, you will be better off hiring a skilled mason.

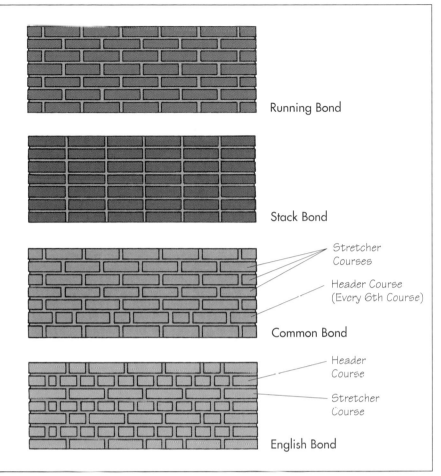

Running Bond

Stack Bond

Stretcher Courses

Header Course (Every 6th Course)

Common Bond

Header Course

Stretcher Course

English Bond

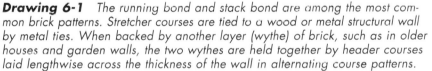

Drawing 6-1   The running bond and stack bond are among the most common brick patterns. Stretcher courses are tied to a wood or metal structural wall by metal ties. When backed by another layer (wythe) of brick, such as in older houses and garden walls, the two wythes are held together by header courses laid lengthwise across the thickness of the wall in alternating course patterns.

If your home is clad with brick, it's usually impossible to match. The designer of this sunroom addition solved that problem by using brick sparingly. By replicating the distinctive existing bond pattern, the new low brick wall effectively ties the addition to the house.

Wood siding comes in various profiles that can go up horizontally or vertically. The style of your house can suggest the appropriate siding style and pattern. You might want to go rustic with rough-sawn knotty cedar or redwood, naturally stained. A more formal house, on the other hand, demands painted clapboard siding.

Horizontal siding is installed like fish scales: Each board overlaps the one below. If careful attention is paid to sealing around trim and joints, the siding resists moisture penetration superbly. Proper nailing is imperative. Stainless-steel nails are the best and most expensive fasteners, hot-dipped galvanized nails are a less expensive second choice. Nail through each board and the underlying sheathing into a stud. Avoid nailing the board to the one it overlaps; the lower board may shrink and split at the nail.

Vertical wood siding evokes rusticity. Instead of different profiles shaped to overlap the adjacent board, vertical siding boards are plain cut and installed quickly by simply nailing up one set of boards (underboards) with spaces between them, then capping the spaces with outer boards. Board and batten is the most common pattern, but others result from varying the size of the under and outer boards, as shown in Drawing 6-6. Choices of surface texture and finish yield further variations.

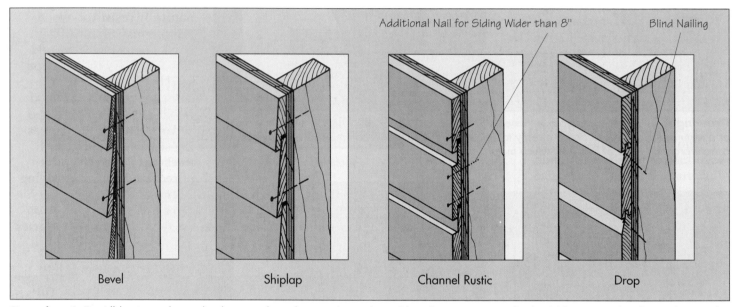

Drawing 6-5 *All horizontal wood siding overlaps the next lower board by about 1 in. Boards should be secured with stainless-steel or hot-dipped galvanized nails that extend at least 1½ in. into the studs. To prevent splitting when the wood shrinks, boards should not be nailed into each other. An air-infiltration barrier is recommended under the siding. (See "Blocking Infiltration," page 117.)*

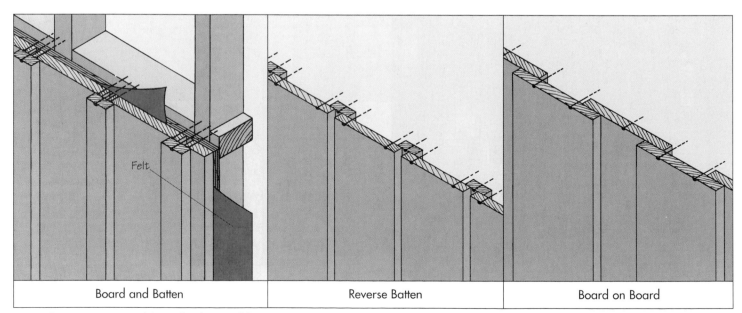

Drawing 6-6 *Vertical board siding yields various patterns, according to the relative width of the boards that make up the outer and inner layers. Because vertical siding does not shed water like horizontal siding, felt is recommended over the sheathing.*

The addition at the right of this photo is virtually a separate structure. Yet the strong horizontal lines of the drop-pattern wood siding, combined with similar roof slopes, makes the addition relate strongly to the main house.

Vertical siding may be easier to install than horizontal, but it is also less watertight. Water crawling down the vertical joints can eventually find its way sideways into the joint. Minimizing penetration requires care in nailing and sealing at joints with trim and other materials.

Wood-composition siding. As the best quality wood siding gets increasingly scarce, other materials come along to take up the slack. All try to imitate the appearance of real wood, some more convincingly than others. The best imitators are themselves made of wood chips or fibers bonded under heat and pressure with chemical resins and formed into boards or panels.

Oriented-strand-board (OSB) and hardboard siding are the

Cedar siding applied in a reverse-batten pattern and left natural lends a contemporary yet rustic look to this home and its kitchen/sun-room addition.

This hardboard siding with a vertical groove pattern is available in panels ½ in. thick by 8 or 9 ft. wide.

two most common wood-composition siding types made in board stock. Both come in 16-foot lengths of uniform consistency and are overlaid, with no knots. Primed at the factory, the boards must be painted or stained after installation. The surface of OSB siding may be embossed to resemble rough cedar. Hardboard, made of much finer fibers, is smooth. The reputation of wood-composition materials has been tarnished in recent years by claims that it deteriorates under exposure to moisture, a particular concern in humid regions. OSB and hardboard are installed with the same tools and nailing techniques used for real wood siding.

Plywood panel siding. Plywood, the versatile material used for sheathing, subfloors, beams, and joists, is also made into siding. But instead of boards, plywood siding comes in panels of 4 by 8 feet, ⅜ or ⅝ inch thick. Grooves cut partway through the surface create the impression of boards. Plywood panel siding is usually installed vertically. The panel edges are shaped to overlap each other at the sides. The horizontal joints between the butt ends of panels must be

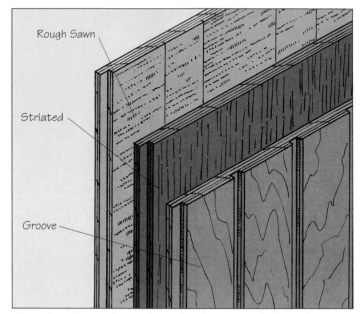

Drawing 6-7 *Plywood panel siding is available with pine, fir, cedar, and redwood surface veneers in various textures. Pine and fir must be painted or coated with preservative. Redwood and cedar may be left to weather or can be stained or painted.*

Rough-sawn plywood siding is combined with a carefully conceived pattern of solid-wood battens to give this home a distinctive and elegant look.

Board-and-batten siding was commonly applied to Gothic Revival homes built before the turn of the 20th century. In this modern interpretation of the style, battens are applied over rough-sawn plywood siding.

flashed to prevent leaks. Redwood- and cedar-faced plywood siding can be painted, stained, or left unfinished. Fir- or pine-faced panels must be painted or stained. Panels go up quickly and easily, but if you do it yourself, have a helper handy to position the panels and hold them for nailing.

Vinyl siding. Plastic will probably permeate your addition—from foam insulation to paints, carpets, and furniture. While you may accept nylon carpeting instead of wool, you may not be ready for plastic-based siding. Does it somehow say "fake" to you? If so, it probably stems from the nature of the material. Vinyl siding is extruded from polyvinyl chloride (PVC) plastic in thin profiles and embossed to look like wood. Unlike wood, vinyl siding expands and contracts significantly along its length. So instead of meeting a solid trim, as does wood, vinyl siding must run behind the trim piece so that it can move. The inevitable gap between trim and siding reveals that this material is thin, not solid like wood.

Nonetheless, vinyl siding is increasingly popular, accounting for about half of all residential re-siding jobs and 16 percent of new houses. People who re-side with vinyl are usually tired of years of repainting wood. Those who choose it for new work do so largely to avoid having to repaint in the future. Is it really as permanent as the guy who calls you at dinnertime claims? The color may chalk with age, but it won't come off because it's embedded into the material. But how well vinyl siding resists bowing and impact damage depends on the thickness of the vinyl and the installation. A quality job starts with siding that's at least 0.044 inch thick. Vinyl siding comes in many colors and patterns, including wood board siding, shingles, and shakes. Lighter colors fare better than dark ones, which may fade in time.

If the main house is clad in cedar shingles or shakes, it will be easy to clad the addition to match. Natural cedar siding with white trim is a classic style, especially in New England.

You can get vinyl siding at the lumberyard if you want to put up your own. Nailing the siding itself is easy enough, but the devil lurks in the details—trim and eaves. Doing these competently requires the special skill and tools of a seasoned tradesman.

Metal siding. Aluminum and steel siding are stronger than vinyl and about twice as expensive. The extra cost comes with a few advantages, though. The prefinished coatings hold dark colors better than does vinyl, and metal siding expands much less than does plastic, making for more pleasing trim details. Steel, the most expensive, is also the strongest. The extra strength might be important in areas such as the Midwest, to resist pounding by golf-ball-size hailstones, and in the South, where flying debris from hurricanes poses a frequent threat. If environmental responsibility figures into your decision, aluminum is among the most energy-intensive materials to produce. And though much aluminum is recycled these days, none of it finds its way back into aluminum siding, which is made entirely of raw ore. Both steel and aluminum siding require special skills and tools to install. Then there's the danger of being cut or injured. For these reasons, you will be ahead by hiring a pro.

Shingles and shakes. Shingles are the cladding of choice for certain traditional styles, such as Cape Cod. It's not uncommon to come across shingled farmhouses in New England that have withstood the elements for a hundred years or more. Of the species available, quality and price are highest for #1 red cedar shingles. All come in random widths of 16 or 18 inches long and taper from about ½ inch at the butt end to ¹⁄₁₆ inch. They are installed to overlap in a similar way to fish scales, leaving a choice of exposure (4½ or 5 inches is common). Installing shingles is slow and tedious, so labor accounts for part of their high total cost. Nailing up your own shingle siding can be a pleasurable, Zen-like experience if you have the time. If you use paneled shingles, you'll pay a bit more for materials but save on labor. Panels come in multiple-coursed units, 8 feet long.

Wood shakes are similar to shingles but are thicker and more irregularly shaped. The exposed face of most shakes sold for residential construction are split for a rustic look. The smoother back side is sawn. Shingles and shakes are combustible, making them a poor choice for areas prone to fire, such as the foothills above certain California cities.

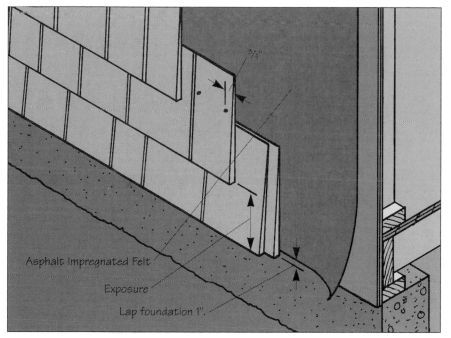

Drawing 6-8 *Wood shingle siding begins with a double starting course that laps the foundation by at least 1 in. Shingles should lap each other enough to provide a thickness of two shingles at any given point. Courses should be determined to yield an equal exposure over the entire height of the wall. Allow ¼-in. vertical joints between shingles and a 1½-in. minimum offset between the vertical joints of successive courses. Use hot-dipped galvanized nails placed 2 in. above the butt line of the previous course.*

Trimming the Exterior

The right trimwork is just as important as the right siding. Good detailing at corners, roof edges, windows, and doors not only affects the addition's appearance but is crucial to keeping water and weather outside. The cladding material and style of the house together suggest the appropriate trim material and how it should be installed. If you pay a premium price for the best bevel cedar siding, you won't want to blow your investment by using anything less than quality woodwork for the trim. A brick or stucco exterior, on the other hand, could be trimmed with wood, vinyl, or aluminum.

Most homeowners who opt for vinyl or metal siding do so because they value low maintenance. To keep the addition's exterior consistent, they would trim the job with the same material as the siding instead of wood, which requires periodic repainting.

Turning corners. Brick and stone turn corners without another trim material. Wood and shingle siding can be mitered

COMPARING SIDING AT A GLANCE

Siding	Cost	Finish	Pros	Cons	DIY[1]
Wood Boards	Medium to high	Paint or stain	Attractive, durable	Periodic refinishing, can weather unevenly	Yes
OSB	Low	Preprimed for top coat or prefinished	Uniform lengths, knot free, stiffer than hardboard	Periodic refinishing, limited textures available	Yes
Hardboard	Low	Preprimed for top coat or prefinished	Uniform lengths, knot free, wide range of textures and patterns	Periodic refinishing	Yes
Plywood Panels*	Low to medium	Paint or stain, cedar and redwood can remain unfinished	Fast installation	Limited patterns, needs flashing at butt ends	Yes
Vinyl	Low	No finish needed	Fast installation, no finish, long warranty	Vulnerable to impact damage, poor appearance at joints	No
Aluminum	High	Prefinished	Durable, needs no finish	Dents under impact and needs professional installation	No
Steel	High	Prefinished	Durable, needs no finish, resists impact better than aluminum	Needs professional installation	No
Shingles	High	Leave unfinished or stain	Good appearance, durable, choice of exposure widths	Weathers unevenly if unfinished, slow to install	Yes

[1] **Do-it-yourself: A Yes indicates that those familiar with simple carpentry can probably install the siding; a No indicates that special tools or skills are required, and a pro should install the siding.**

***The cost of plywood panel siding varies with the surface species: Pine is the least expensive, and redwood is the most.**

at the outside corners and made to die into vertical trim at inside corners or abut vertical trim at all corners. The outer corners of mitered bevel siding can also be capped with special aluminum trim. Vinyl, aluminum, and steel siding terminate in trim of the same material, shaped to turn corners and angles.

Cornices and gables. The roof can meet the wall below with nothing more than a simple trim board, called a rake board, or the roof can overhang the wall with an elaborate cornice. The existing cornices and gables of your house should provide your starting point if you want the addition to look as if it belongs the original building. Of course, matching the convoluted trimwork of a grand old Victorian home today can be very costly, even if you can find a carpenter up to the task. In that case, you may be better off with a design that emulates the spirit of the existing eaves economically rather than one that slavishly copies the original.

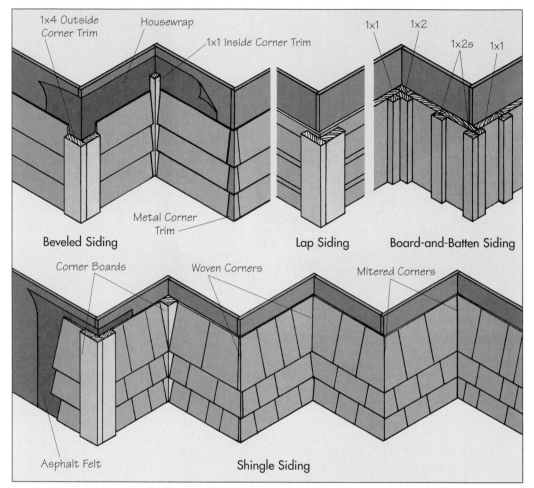

Drawing 6-9 Corners for board siding may be trimmed with vertical boards or metal corner pieces. Shingle siding can meet at woven or mitered corners or at vertical corner boards.

There's no formula for how to blend in the new roof, but the two most important features that relate the new roof's edge to the existing one are the angle of the slope and the extent of the overhang. If you match these on the addition, you will be halfway there. Then look for stock moldings and trim that either match or recall the shapes of the ones on the house. Wood moldings come in a wide variety of prismatic shapes (shapes with a constant profile over their length). For more complicated shapes, such as dentils, check out plastic moldings. Catalogs that cater to old-house restoration are a good place to begin your search for special stock shapes. Also, some carpenters and cabinetmakers can reproduce existing moldings.

Trimming doors and windows. The trimwork you select for the exterior affects your window selection because windows and doors often come with exterior trim attached. If you want a genuine traditional look, choose wood windows surrounded on the outside by a wood casing. The most common exterior trim is brick mold, 2 inches wide by 1¾ inches thick. The more tra-

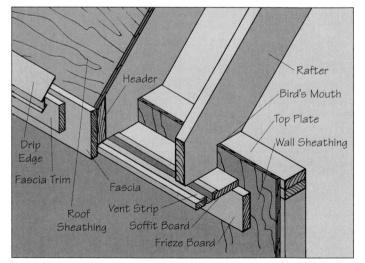

Drawing 6-10 A narrow box cornice is framed by simply cutting a bird's mouth out of each rafter and using the overhanging ends to support fascia and soffit trimwork.

ditional option is a flat casing, 3½ inches wide by ¾ inches thick. Wood windows are installed with the exterior trim snug to the sheathing. The siding simply butts into the trim, as shown in Drawing 6-13.

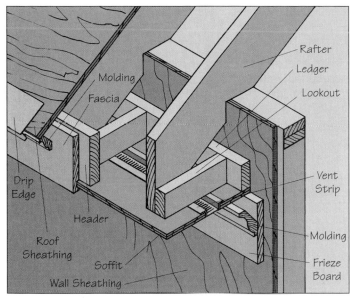

Drawing 6-11 *A wide box cornice detail requires horizontal pieces (lookouts) to support the soffit.*

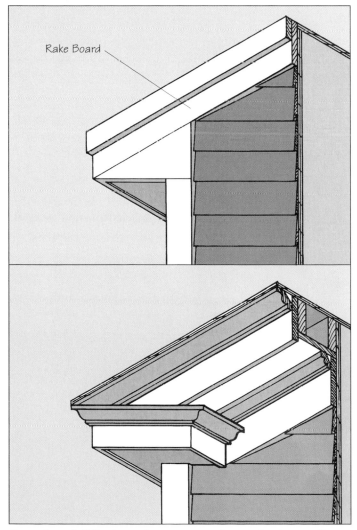

Drawing 6-12 *A cornice return can be as simple as a flat trim that wraps around the corner at the gable end (top) or as elaborate as an assembly of trim and moldings that typify colonial, Cape Cod, and other traditional styles (bottom).*

Wood windows are also available with vinyl and aluminum cladding on the parts exposed to the weather. Clad windows and windows made entirely of vinyl or aluminum do not have casing on the outside. Instead, the cladding material protrudes out beyond the siding in a narrow profile. With these windows you can either run the siding up to the window with no casing, as shown in Drawing 6-13, or nail the casing over the integral nailing flange and butt the siding to the casing, which gives a more traditional look.

Accessory trim. Your addition may call for other types of exterior carpentry to help it blend with the main house. Detailing this kind of work to get the appearance you seek and still have it fit together properly is hard enough. But outside finish carpentry must also resist weather. Good design, flashing, and connections are needed to meet this challenge. Use a naturally decay-resistant species, such as cypress, cedar, redwood, or mahogany, or a pressure-treated pine for decks and railings. Other trim can be any species that accepts paint well, but it should be free of knots, which eventually show through the paint. How much of the exterior finish carpentry you can do yourself depends on your skills and the complexity of the work. Most people who have done any carpentry can put up a simple deck with rustic detailing. But cutting and fitting shaped moldings around a Victorian cornice tests the mettle of even skilled carpenters.

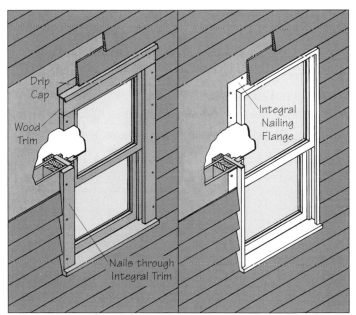

Drawing 6-13 *Here are two ways to trim a wood window in a wood frame wall. Unclad (all-wood windows) come with a brick mold or flat trim piece attached to the outside of the frame. Nail through the trim to secure the window to the opening. Wood windows clad with vinyl or aluminum on the outside (as well as all-vinyl and all-aluminum windows) have an integral nailing flange.*

Insulation

Your addition needs some amount of thermal insulation in the walls and roof, no matter where you live. A well-insulated envelope will save on the cost of fuel and keep you more comfortable throughout the year. If the weather extremes of the last few summers and winters portend more erratic weather ahead, as many believe, good insulation will become even more important.

How much insulation is enough? Don't use your house as a standard for the new addition; if it is currently under-insulated, you'll do well to consider upgrading. The proper amount depends on the severity of your climate. The ability of a material to insulate against the passage of heat by conduction is measured in R-value. The higher the R-value number, the better the insulator. Drawing 6-14 and the table "Recommended Minimum Total R-Values," on page 111, will give you an idea of the minimum R-value for your location, but check with your building department to see if local codes call for different levels.

Insulation Materials

Choosing the right type of insulation from the wide variety available requires matching the insulation to the application, balancing R-values with cost, and—if you install it yourself—weighing the ease or difficulty of installation. The table "Comparing Types of Insulation," on page 112, can serve as a quick guide for comparing some of the common options.

Blanket and batt. Fiberglass and mineral wool blanket and batt insulation are the most common forms installed by do-it-yourselfers. Thicknesses range between 3½ and 12 inches and widths between 13 and 23 inches, for a snug fit into stud or joist cavities spaced 16 or 24 inches on center. The insulation is packed into bundles containing 4-foot-long batts or into rolled blankets. Fiberglass consists of glass fibers held together with a binding substance. If you have worked with fiberglass insulation before, you know how it makes your skin itch and eyes and nose run, even when you wear long-sleeved shirts, a dust mask, and goggles. You'll be happy to learn that the binder has been improved in some brands to lessen the scratching and to keep the fibers from breaking off and becoming airborne so that they won't get into your nose and eyes. You can even buy fiberglass that is completely encased in plastic to further reduce contact with the fibers.

Among other recent improvements in fiberglass is a denser insulation. Instead of the R-11 you used to get for blankets made to fit into a 2x4 stud wall, you can now get R-14. Denser insulation in a 2x6 wall yields R-21 instead of the former R-19. Fiberglass comes unfaced to friction fit between framing, or faced with Kraft paper or foil that you staple to the face of the framing. The foil facing can do double-duty as a vapor barrier, but only if the edges are thoroughly sealed with tape or caulk. It's usually easier to apply a layer of polyethylene sheet over the insulation after installing it. Kraft paper facing is only a marginal vapor barrier.

Mineral wool, sometimes called rock wool, is similar to fiberglass in facings and installation. It costs a bit more and irritates skin, eyes, and nose.

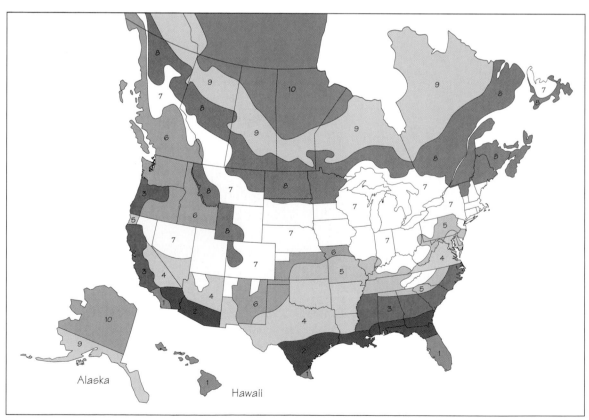

Alaska

Hawaii

Drawing 6-14 *Use this map and the table "Recommended Minimum Total R-Values," on page 111, to help you determine how much installation to install in your area.*

RECOMMENDED MINIMUM TOTAL R-VALUES

Insulation Zone[2]	Ceilings[1]		Floors[3] (all fuels)	Walls (all fuels)	Foundations[4] (all fuels)
	Oil, Gas, Heat Pump	Electric Resistance			
1	19	30	0	19	11
2	30	30	0	19	19
3	30	38	0	19	19
4	30	38	19	19	19
5	38	38	19	19	19
6	38	38	19	19	19
7	38	49	19	19	19
8	49	49	19	19	19
9	49	49	19	19	19
10	55	55	19	19	19

[1] *Cathedral ceilings and ceilings below ventilated attics.*
[2] *See Drawing 6-14, on page 110.*
[3] *Recommended levels for floors above crawl spaces or basements if the foundation walls are not insulated.*
[4] *Recommended levels for foundation walls if the floors are not insulated.*

Rigid sheet. Various plastics are foamed into sheets 2 or 4 feet wide, 8 feet long, and from ½ to 4 inches thick. Many parts of your addition may be good candidates for rigid foam sheets. If your floor is a slab-on-grade and you live in a cold climate, 1½ or 2 inches of rigid foam under the slab will ensure warmth underfoot. A preferred way to insulate a foundation is with rigid foam applied outside the wall before backfilling. You may want to increase the R-value of a stud wall or cathedral ceiling by adding rigid foam to one side.

Foil-faced foam on the inside face of the studs can even serve as a vapor barrier if you seal the edges with tape.

Putting up rigid foam is very easy. After marking the foam, you cut through it with a sharp knife, using a straightedge as a guide. Then nail it to the framing, using washers to keep the nails from puncturing the surface. You can also glue the foam to the substrate with adhesive applied from a caulking gun. (Make sure to get adhesive recommended for foam plastics.)

Fiberglass blankets now come encased in plastic, which takes most of the itchiness out of installation work.

Rigid foam insulation is easy to work with. A sharp knife is all you need to cut it.

Comparing Types of Insulation

Key:
U - Usually
S - Sometimes
L - Low
M - Medium
O - Outside
I - Inside

Type of Insulation	R-Value (per inch thickness)	Relative Cost per R-Value	Vapor Barrier is Integral with Material	Can be Installed by Homeowner	Can Fill Cavities between Studs, Joists & Rafters	Applied to Inside or Outside of Walls or Cathedral Ceilings	Applied to Outside or Inside of the Foundation	Applied under Concrete Floors	Common Widths & Lengths
Blanket and Batt Insulation									
Fiberglass	3.3	L	S[1]	U	U	I	I		15"x various 23"x various
Mineral wool batts	3.6	L	S[1]	U	U	I	I		15"x various 23"x various
Ridge Sheet Insulation									
Phenolic foam	8.5	H	U[2]	U		O,I	O,I	U	4'x8'
Polyurethane isocyanurate	7.2	M	U[2]	U		O,I	O,I	U	4'x8'
Extruded polystryene	5.0	M		U		O,I	O,I	U	4'x8', 2'x8'
Expanded polystyrene (beadboard)	4.0	M		U		O,I	O,I	U	4'x8', 2'x8'
Loose Fill Insulation									
Cellulose, blown in	3.7	M			U				
Cellulose, bagged	3.7	L		U	U				
Perlite pellets	2.7	L		U	U				
Fiberglass, blown in	2.2	M			U				
Mineral Wool, blown in	2.9	M			U				
Sprayed Insulation									
Cellulose	3.5	M			U[3]				
Urethane	6.2	H		U	U				

[1] The foil facing on some batt and blanket insulations can serve as a vapor barrier, but only if the joints are taped adequately.

[2] Applies if the boards are faced with aluminum foil and all joints are taped or caulked.

[3] Spray cellulose is limited to wall cavities.

Loose fill and sprayed. Cellulose, perlite, fiberglass, and mineral wool are available as loose fibers or pellets and bagged for pouring by hand or blowing by pneumatic equipment. You may need some loose insulation for nooks or crannies that are hard to fill with other types. More likely, loose cellulose or fiberglass will be a heavy contender for blowing into the attic floor of your addition (if the attic is to be unoccupied). Cellulose insulation is made from recycled newspapers treated with a fire-retardant chemical. Cellulose's R-value is slightly lower than those of fiberglass and mineral wool, but its slightly greater density makes it less susceptible to being blown about by sudden gusts whipping through the attic. The main drawback of cellulose is its tendency to attract and hold moisture, so make sure you have a good vapor barrier on the ceiling.

Radiant barrier. Thermal insulation is made more effective in roofs and attics in hot weather by a class of materials grouped under the name of radiant barriers. All radiant barriers contain a shiny metallic surface that reflects radiant heat. (Thermal insulation blocks conduction.) Radiant barrier materials come as rigid sheets of foil-faced foam or plywood and rolls of flexible sheet. Radiant barriers benefit homes south of the Mason-Dixon line more than homes in northern locations. To work best, the barrier material must be installed with an air space separating the reflective surface from the adjacent material. The radiant barrier is commonly placed just below the roof sheathing. (Some plywood comes with a foil face to double as sheathing and radiant barrier.)

Where to Insulate

The ideal position for insulation in the addition depends on the type of construction and the use of the space inside. Let's look at the options from the top down.

Roofs and ceilings. Two factors argue in favor of the attic floor in an unoccupied attic as the best site for overhead insulation. First, it is easier and more economical to install insulation on the attic floor than between the roof rafters; second, this will allow you to ventilate the attic. Ventilation will keep the roof cooler, year round. In warm climates (and in summer in cold climates), a cooler roof will inhibit deterioration of the roofing. In winter, a cold roof won't allow ice to thaw and refreeze, creating ice dams that cause water to penetrate the roof. You don't have to go too far north to find a homeowner with a horror story of rotting eaves and dripping ceilings.

If the attic is to be occupied or if the ceiling occurs just under the roof (cathedral ceiling), the insulation has to go somewhere within the roof-ceiling assembly, either above the roof deck (sheathing), between the rafters, or in some combination of both. The air space to prevent roof damage must occur above the insulation. But

The quickest way to install loose fill insulation is to blow it in with pneumatic equipment.

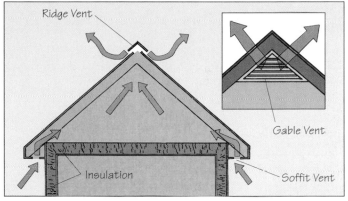

Drawing 6-15 *An unheated attic is easily ventilated by allowing outside air to enter through soffit vents and escape through a ridge or gable vent.*

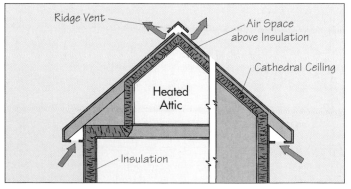

Drawing 6-16 *To ventilate a heated attic or cathedral ceiling, provide a point of entry through a soffit vent, an unobstructed air path above the insulation at least 2 in. wide, and an escape port through a continuous ridge vent.*

instead of a large, open attic, the ventilation channel shrinks to a narrow gap. For between-rafter insulation, the 2-inch minimum for air to circulate can be achieved by using foam-plastic insulation baffles stapled to the underside of the roof sheathing. An air space above rigid insulation placed atop the roof sheathing can be achieved by attaching 2x2 strapping vertically to the insulation at the points where rafters occur.

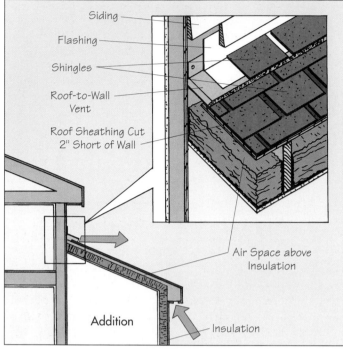

Drawing 6-17   *If your addition abuts a higher house wall, you can use a special roof-to-wall vent to ventilate its roof.*

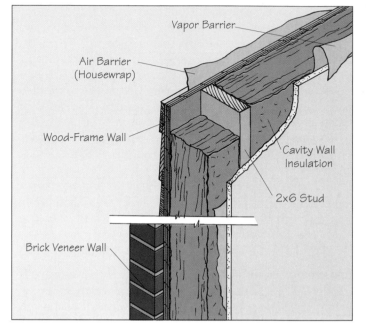

Drawing 6-18   *Cavities created by 2x6 studs are thick enough for R-19 insulation or better.*

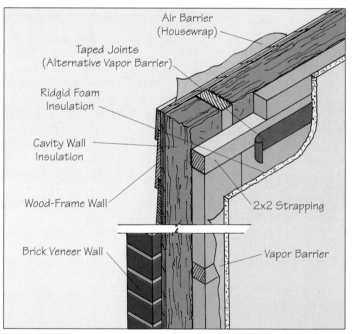

Drawing 6-19   *Cavity insulation can be combined with rigid foam to achieve the desired R-value. In this detail, 2x2 strapping, placed horizontally across the studs every 24 in., creates a cavity for the rigid foam and a nail base for the interior wall finish. A vapor barrier can be achieved by applying a sheet of poly-ethylene over the foam or by simply taping the joints.*

If your addition abuts a vertical wall on the high side, the overhead insulation can also go in the attic floor or within the rafters, but you'll need something other than a standard ridge vent to let the air escape. Special roof-to-wall vents are made for this purpose.

Walls. R-11 fiberglass stuffed between 2x4 studs no longer meets current standards. The R-value can be beefed up by using deeper studs (2x6, usually) or by adding another layer of insulation to the inside or outside face of the wall. Select a system that contains a means for blocking vapor and air as well as heat. (See "Controlling Indoor Moisture," page 116.)

Insulating below. Use the table "Recommended Minimum Total R-values," on page 111, and Drawing 6-14 to figure out how much insulation you might need below the main level of your addition. Where you put the insulation depends on what's down there. If it's just dirt under a slab-on-grade floor, you won't need the rec-ommended minimum (R-19) because the heat lost from the conditioned space above will be less to the ground in contact with the slab than to the air below a free-standing floor. You may need no insulation at all below a slab if you live in insulation zones 1 through 4. Other colder climes do require insulation, particularly near the slab edges; 1 or 2 inches of rigid foam below the slab or on the foundation will stem this loss, making for a warmer floor.

There are two ways to insulate living areas that sit above a crawl space or basement. We'll call these two ways "cold basement" and "warm basement" (or cold and warm crawl spaces).

Insulating the floor between the basement and living space above results in a cold basement. If you insulate the foundation walls instead, you get a warm basement.

It's easier and likely cheaper to insulate the floor than the perimeter walls, but these initial advantages come with some drawbacks. First, by linking the basement temperature to the outside, you get a space that will

Vertical Strapping
Sheathing
Siding
Ridgid Foam Insulation
Vapor Barrier
Cavity Insulation

Drawing 6-20 *Rigid foam can be applied outside the wall sheathing. Vertical strapping at the studs serves as a nail base for the siding and provides an air space to allow moisture to escape from the back of the siding.*

may be used, installed from below by stapling the Kraft-paper tabs to the bottom edges of the floor joists or using insulation retainers. Insulation for a warm basement can go on either side of the foundation wall. In the coldest climates, insulating the outside of the foundation couples the wall to the inside temperature. The wall stays warmer, so it isn't as likely to crack in freezing weather. This tactic also yields benefits in the summer if the day-to-night temperature difference is great in your climate because the mass of the foundation walls evens out the temperature swings, keeping the space cooler during the day.

Rigid foam is used on the outside of foundations because the backfill around the foundation would crush fiberglass, making it useless. You can also apply rigid foam to the inside of the foundation wall by using adhesive or nailing it to furring strips. Another method is to erect a stud wall just inside the foundation and insulate it with batts or blankets. The studs also afford a space in which to run wiring and a substrate for a finish-wall material. A crawl space can be insulated with foam sheets inside or out, or by simply hanging batts or blankets from the mudsill and draping them down over the wall and onto the earth.

be cold in winter. That's okay if you use the basement only for housing the furnace and bicycles, but it is a real problem if you intend to finish the space for occupancy. Even if you don't, you'll have to make sure any ducts and pipes are insulated to keep them from freezing when temperatures dive. The extra effort of wrapping pipes and ducts may soon eat up any savings you'll make over insulating the walls for a warm basement. A warm basement, in addition to being more comfortable in winter, saves energy. Furnaces and water heaters give off heat anyway, and a warm basement conserves this heat. A cold basement wastes it to the outside.

If you opt for a cold basement, you can insulate between the floor joists in much the same way as for a cathedral ceiling. Kraft-faced or unfaced insulation

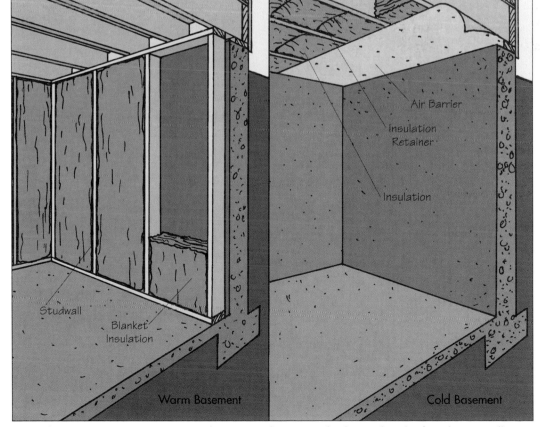

Studwall
Blanket Insulation
Air Barrier
Insulation Retainer
Insulation
Warm Basement
Cold Basement

Drawing 6-21 *Basement or crawl-space insulation can be located in the foundation walls (left) or ceiling (right). Insulating the ceiling leaves the basement cold, requiring protection against freezing for pipes and ducts.*

Controlling Indoor Moisture

People tend to feel most comfortable when the air they breath contains 40- to 60-percent relative humidity. A tea kettle kept steaming away atop a wood stove compensates for the drier winter air for some homeowners; a humidifier does the job for others. But while additional moisture may have been necessary in the days when outside air infiltrated unchecked through windows and cracks, it isn't needed if you build your addition to today's tighter standards. It might even damage the house. Warm, moist air migrates to the colder outdoors. As it wends its way through the cracks and crannies in walls and ceilings, it condenses at some point. If enough moisture collects, it can cause insulation to lose efficiency, wood to decay, and outside paint to peel.

Does this potential moisture problem mean you should not seal your addition so tightly? Not at all. Good sealing is a primary way to conserve heating and cooling energy, which will only get more important in future years. Here are some ways to protect your new addition against damage from indoor moisture:

▲ Don't intentionally add moisture to the air.

▲ Don't store green firewood inside the conditioned space.

▲ Duct clothes dryers to the outside, never to an attic or basement.

▲ Provide controlled ventilation in the form of individual exhaust fans in kitchens and baths or a centralized ventilation system. (See "Ventilation," beginning on page 163.)

▲ Consider installing a mechanical dehumidifier or air-conditioning system.

▲ Install a vapor barrier.

A vapor barrier is a material that bars the passage of moist air. Polyethylene sheets and aluminum foil are the most commonly used vapor barriers in new construction. Even oil-base paint or shellac can be used. Vapor barriers are always recommended in cold climates to keep moisture out of the walls and other structural cavities in winter. The barrier always goes between the insulation and the heated space, usually just under the wall finish material. In warm climates, the reverse is true—the barrier goes near the outer surface to keep the more humid outside air from entering the air-conditioned interior.

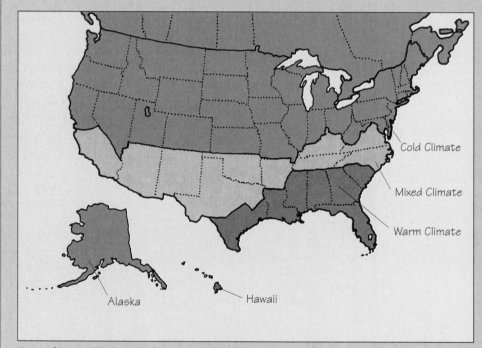

Drawing 6-22   *Vapor barriers are necessary in cold and mixed climates and recommended in warm climates if the house is air conditioned.*

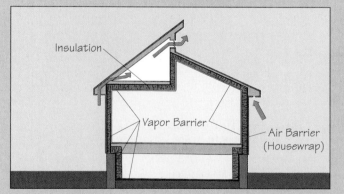

Drawing 6-23   *In cold climates, the vapor barrier goes inside the insulated shell. The outside is wrapped with a vapor-permeable air barrier. Roofs are ventilated, and crawl spaces may be sealed (as shown) or ventilated if the floor is insulated.*

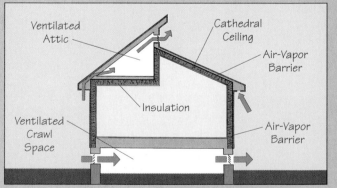

Drawing 6-24   *Air-conditioned houses in warm climates should have an air-vapor barrier, such as polyethylene or aluminum foil, installed outside the insulated shell. The roof is ventilated, as is the crawl space or basement.*

Blocking Infiltration

Installed with care, the right kind of thermal insulation in the right place will go far toward keeping your new addition toasty in winter and cool in summer. But for all that, insulation only addresses one method by which heat travels: conduction—heat transfer from a warmer material in contact with a cooler material.

Heat also travels by air movement, called convection. You will appreciate just how much convection counts if you have ever sat near leaky windows in an old, poorly sealed house on a winter's eve. Blocking convective heat loss starts with well-weatherstripped windows and doors with their frames sealed to the abutting construction, both inside and out. Other cracks in the building shell must also be sealed. But rather than chasing each crack down with a caulking gun, a faster, better way is to wrap the exterior with an air-barrier sheet, also called "housewrap." Housewrap materials let moisture escape but check air movement. Installation is as simple as unrolling the sheet and stapling it to the sheathing before the siding goes on. Finally, cracks and holes around gas pipes, phone wires, and window and door trim are caulked tight.

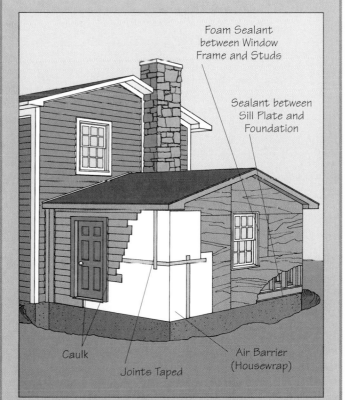

Foam Sealant between Window Frame and Studs

Sealant between Sill Plate and Foundation

Caulk

Joints Taped

Air Barrier (Housewrap)

Drawing 6-25 *Preventing infiltration begins with sealing the sill plate to the foundation. The gaps between window and door frames and structural framing can be sealed by injecting foam from a pressure can. The many cracks and crannies in the framed shell are blocked off by air-barrier housewrap, with joints taped. After siding and trim are installed, all joints between abutting materials are sealed with a suitable caulk.*

DOORS

You go through doors many times every day without ever thinking about them, so selecting doors for your addition should be easy, right? Maybe, but your choice for each door should be carefully thought out as to function, hardware, and appearance. Add weather resistance if it is an outside door.

What's the Door for, Anyway?

A door is a barrier that controls access between two areas, so a good way to begin making your choice is by asking yourself what kind of control you want. A door between the kitchen and dining room gets used a lot. Much of the traffic is people going to or from each room with their hands full. One solution is a door that swings both ways (double acting), fitted with spring hinges and a push plate on either side. How about a pocket door that can be parked in the wall for most of the time and closed only when necessary to keep cooking smells or noise out of the dining area. Or if you don't mind the aroma of cooking and want a more open, informal approach, why not leave the opening without any door?

Along with controlling people traffic, doors should also hint as to what's on the other side—major entrance, minor room, closet, public area, private sanctuary. To clue people clearly, the design of the door must fit its status. The unadorned flush-face door you use between interior rooms won't work as well for the new outside entrance. This location needs visual clues in the design of the door itself—ornamentation, glazing, hardware, or accessory features such as sidelights or transoms.

Door Types

You can narrow your choice when you know how you want the door to function. Here are some common door types, along with the types of hardware appropriate to their operation.

Single acting. The most common door is single acting. It is hinged on one side and opens only in one direction. It can close into a latch or be fitted with a push plate.

Double acting. If you want the door to swing in and out, choose a double-acting door fitted with a push plate on both sides and spring hinges that automatically close the door. Double-acting doors work well between the kitchen and dining room.

Paired. Two-hinged doors are paired for various reasons. You might need a wider opening to move items too wide for a single door. Perhaps the doorway leads to an outside deck or patio that you want to use to open up the inside room in good weather. Or you may want a double door for a main entrance because it looks more important than a single door. One door of the pair is named the "fixed" door, normally held closed by flush bolts that lock into the head and sill. The edge of the fixed door is fitted with an astragal into which the "active" door latches. When you want to open both doors, you first have to release the flush bolts.

Bifold. Doors can be hinged from each other, as well as from a jamb, to create a pair of bifold doors. The outer door of a bifold pair contains a pin at the top that rides in a track, keeping the doors aligned as they move. An opposing pair can hinge off the opposite jamb, yielding a set of four door panels. Depending on the number of panels and width of each panel—which can range from 1 to 2 feet—the opening size can be 2 to 8 feet. Bifold doors suit locations where a single-hinged door would be cumbersome and, when grouped in sets, in places where you need a lot of access width, such as a shallow but wide closet.

Sliding. Some doors open and close without hinges by sliding back and forth within tracks at the head and sill. (Doors other than cabinet doors actually roll, rather than slide, on rollers mounted in the door head.) Sliding doors are mounted in pairs, with one or both doors sliding past the other, or in groups of three, with various opening combinations. Like bifold doors, sliders suit applications where space is short for a swing door in the open position or where a large opening is desired. Closets and patio/deck entries are common locations.

Pocket. Single doors can also slide, disappearing into a pocket in one jamb. The advantage is that the door is always out of the way when it's open. Pocket doors fit locations where the door is likely to remain open for most of the time, such as between a dining room and kitchen. Two things to consider: First, opening and closing a pocket door requires more effort than opening a single-hinged door; second, you must have a portion of wall on the pocket side at least as wide as the door. (The wall doesn't need to be wider than standard thickness, though.)

Door Styles

Doors vary in design and construction, as well as operation. The following is a rundown of some of the door styles you'll need to consider. Most styles can be obtained as doors to be installed in a separate frame or prehung in frames for easier installation.

Flush face. If your addition is contemporary in style, flush-face doors will maintain design consistency. The

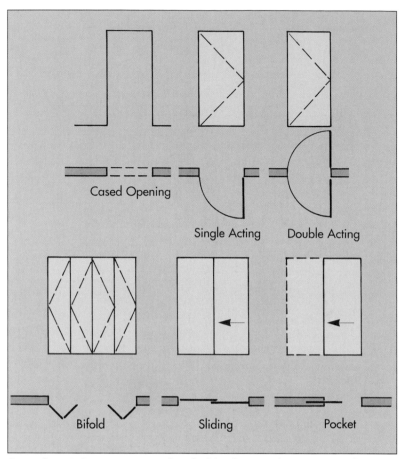

Drawing 6-26 *Doors are classified by the way they operate. The main types are shown here by their standard symbols in elevation and plan.*

most economical type consists of a honeycomb cardboard hollow core sandwiched between thin veneer facings and edged with solid wood. Hollow-core (HC) doors are okay for light-duty interior applications but won't withstand abuse and won't work for outside doors. The better grade (and heavier duty) solid-core (SC) flush-face door can be used for exterior or interior applications. This type contains a core of wood staves, particleboard, or other wood-composition material. Flush-face doors are available faced with hardboard for a paint finish and in a variety of wood veneers that can take a natural finish.

Panel. Panel doors are the style that most often comes to mind when people think of doors, and they are appropriate for a traditional-style addition, such as a Cape Cod, colonial, bungalow, or cottage. Also known as stile-and-rail doors, panel doors are made of raised panels inset between horizontal rails and vertical stiles—all neatly glued together with mortise-and-tenon joinery. Interior panel doors are typically 1⅜ inches thick; exterior doors are 1¾ inches. You can get them prehung or not.

Traditional panel doors are made entirely of solid wood in pine, fir, and various hardwoods. You can paint them or apply a natural finish. For exterior

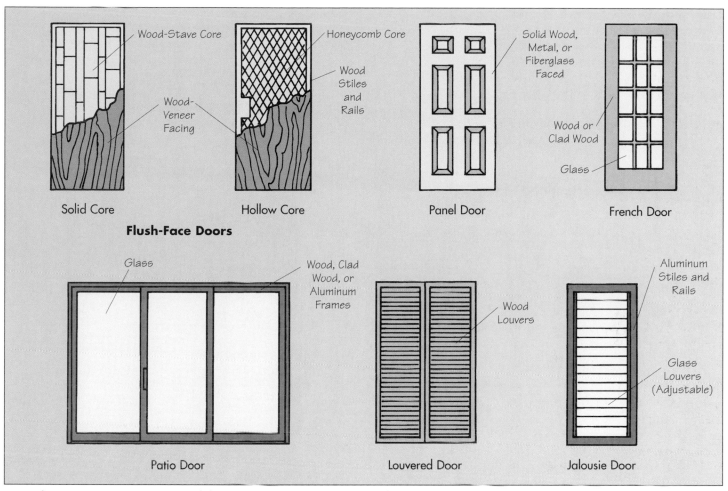

Drawing 6-27 *Here are some of the most common door styles used in homes today.*

applications, there are panel doors made of other materials that offer better resistance to heat loss, water, and sunlight. Another advantage is that unlike wood, these doors will not shrink and warp under exposure to heat and moisture. All of these supplant stile-and-rail construction with a core of some material faced with a skin formed to resemble a panel-door design. The skin of fiberglass-faced doors is embossed to look like wood grain. Painted, it succeeds. Finished naturally, the match is less convincing. Another type is faced with a stamped-steel sheet and comes primed for a paint finish. The core of nonwood panel doors is a solid material such as particleboard or foam plastic, which is a better insulator.

French. Panels in panel doors can be glass to permit light and view. But if you want glass over most of the door's face, consider a french door. The glazing can be an unbroken sheet of tempered (or insulated) glass or can be divided into small panes by muntins. Traditional muntins contain the panes, much as a traditional multi-pane window. A newer, more energy-efficient version contains the muntin grid inside an unbroken insulated glass panel with secondary grids married to the inside and outside faces. French doors are made of all wood or wood clad outside with aluminum or vinyl.

Patio. Patio doors offer maximum openness between the interior and a patio, deck, or garden area. Also known as sliding glass doors, they actually glide on rollers in the sill. Mostly glass, patio doors are available with frames of aluminum, wood, or wood clad with vinyl or aluminum. Heat loss and gain is always a concern with glazed windows and doors, and glazed doors offer a huge area of concern. That's why it's important to tailor the glazing to the requirements of your climate, as described in the next section on windows. Aluminum-frame doors also suffer because metals conduct heat well. If you are located in an area with a cold climate, choose the type that has a non-conductive thermal break sandwiched between the inside and outside portions of the frame.

You can get patio doors paired or in three-panel units. The width of a patio-door unit is the sum of the widths of the individual panels (plus the jambs). Standard leaf widths are 30, 36, and 48 inches, so the smallest single unit would be 60 inches wide (a pair of 30-inch leaves). The widest unit would be 12 feet (three 48-inch-wide leaves). Heights are 80 and 96 inches. Units can be ganged together to create a glazed opening of any width. When ordering, you have to designate which leaf of a unit is the active (movable) one.

Louvered and mirrored. Closet doors are often louvered to ventilate the interior or fronted with full-height mirrors. Mirrors can be mounted to the surface of any door, but the doors you buy already mirrored look as if they were designed that way because the mirrors are glazed into the door frame.

Jalousie. Natural ventilation is a time-honored (and cheap) way to cool a house. It works in every climate during some parts of the year. But to be effective, the openings have to be large enough. Jalousie doors and windows glazed with continuous glass strips 3 to 4 inches wide offer maximum ventilating area. Mounted in an aluminum frame, the strips are opened by a crank or rotor to tilt outward. They close like fish scales, each strip overlapping the one below. They are never very airtight, though, so don't use them if winter heat loss is a big concern.

Entrance Combinations

Main entrances need something more than a single door to signal their status as the principal place of arrival. Architectural features such as porches and canopies can go far to create importance, but a grand porch leading to a simple door falls short. The rest of the goal can be met by other design elements. The door itself can be embellished with a pattern or inset glazing. Flanking the door with sidelights and maybe a transom above makes it more of a focus. More ornate trimwork surrounding these items adds to the effect. You can get the main entrance you want by putting elements together, one by one, or by selecting complete entrance units from various suppliers—the best approach if you do your own construction. Many combinations in a variety of styles are available.

Combination entrances offer many possibilities, from single doors prehung in frames to one or more doors surrounded by sidelights and transom windows.

Planning Doors for Accessibility

Going through a doorway is the main obstacle for wheelchair-bound persons. Making doors accessible requires adequate width and space to maneuver while operating the door. The minimum required clear width of 32 inches grows to 36 inches when two ½-inch stops and the width of the open door are added in. An 18-inch-wide clear space next to the latch of an inward-opening door and 60 inches of space in front of the door are necessary for maneuvering. Another solution is to make the door double-acting by using spring hinges. A simpler solution, if privacy is not a problem, is to do away with the door completely.

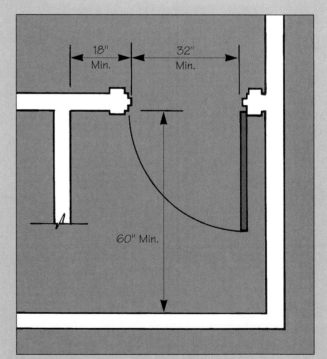

Drawing 6-28 Doors for wheelchairs require a clear space of 32 in. Achieving this while allowing for the width of the open door and the stops usually means using a 36-in.-wide door. A clear distance of 18 in. is necessary at the knob side of an inward-opening door to afford maneuvering space for the wheelchair. (The side space can be eliminated if the door is made double-acting.)

WINDOWS AND SKYLIGHTS

The windows of your addition are among the most important parts of the envelope. The window placement and style you choose are crucial to how the addition will look from the outside as well as the views, light, and ventilation you'll get on the inside.

First decide where you want light, views, and ventilation. It will help you if you know how the house sits with respect to the sun's seasonal path and the prevailing breezes (see Drawing 3-4). When you know where you want each opening and how big it is to be, you can decide what kind of window to put into the opening. The style of architecture can suggest whether one large window of a certain shape and style is better than, say, a group of several smaller units. You'll also need to choose among various types of sash and frame construction and the type of glazing. First pin down the window type.

Window Types

Windows are classified by the way they open and close. Windows that don't open at all are called "fixed." Because they are more economical than their operable counterparts, fixed windows make sense in a grouping containing other windows that open. You can get fixed units that match any type of operable unit.

Double and single hung. When people think of house windows, they usually imagine a vertical rectangle with an upper and lower sash that is sometimes divided into multiple smaller panes. Double-hung windows are fundamental to houses built in colonial, Cape Cod, and cottage styles. In traditional double-hungs, each sash is hung separately by ropes attached to counterweights unseen inside the jambs. The ropes ride on pulleys in the top of the jamb, allowing either the top or bottom sash to be raised and lowered. Single-hung windows are similar, except that only the bottom sash moves.

For all their popularity, traditional double-hung windows have some major flaws. First, the side pockets that contain the rope-and-pulley suspension systems are a nortorious source of heat leaks. Second, cleaning the outer panes from the inside requires the skill of a contortionist. Today's versions offer the same historical charm without the defects. Instead of ropes and pulleys, sashes glide up and down in weathertight channels with clock-spring counterbalance systems. For some models (called "tilt-turn"), the sashes can be released and tilted in so that the outside surface can be cleaned from inside the house.

Sliding. Turn double-hung windows on their sides, and you have sliding windows. The horizontal shape looks more at home with contemporary styles than with traditional ones. Sliders are often used where a horizontal strip suits the room inside, such as high above a tub or shower or above a kitchen sink.

Casement. If you seek a vertically shaped window but want a single rather than double sash, consider a casement window. Hinged at the side, the entire sash of a casement opens outward by a crank on the sill. The sash funnels passing breezes inside for ventilation. Casements offer twice as much ventilation opening as double-hung windows of the same size. The unbroken appearance of casements without muntins agrees well with modern-styled houses. However, casements can also suit traditional styles if the sash is subdivided into several smaller panes by muntins.

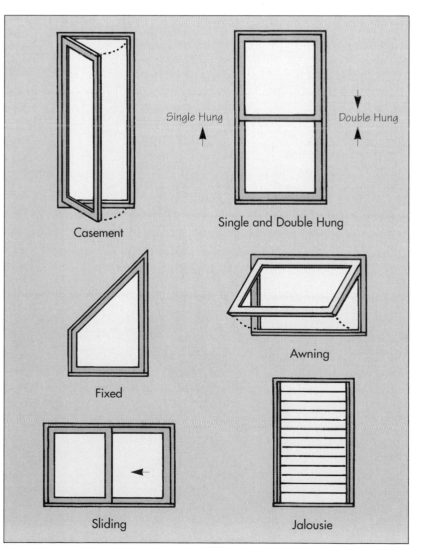

Drawing 6-29 *Here are the available window types as viewed from outside the building.*

Awning. Just as sliders are akin to double-hung windows turned sideways, awning windows are like casements on their sides. The shape varies from square to horizontal. Awning windows work well as the vented units of a group of windows. Another plus is that when open, awnings shed rain better than any other type except jalousie windows.

Jalousie. Like jalousie doors, jalousie windows are composed of many narrow glass strips set in an aluminum frame. Widths are limited to around 3 feet, but heights are unlimited.

Window Construction

Wood has reigned as the material of choice for windows for good reason. It has always been available, can be milled to make any shape down to the profile of the most intricate muntin, and can take a variety of natural and paint finishes. On the downside, wood needs periodic refinishing and swells when damp, causing moving parts to bind. You can get all-wood windows made of ponderosa pine, precisely joined and tightly weatherstripped. Mahogany windows are also available, with better weather resistance and at higher cost. If you want the appearance of wood but are just as happy to escape regular outside maintenance, choose wood windows with the wood exposed inside but protected outside by a plastic or aluminum cladding. Clad windows come in white, tan, or brown and

withstand the elements for many years. Aluminum-clad windows are the most durable and also the highest priced type of window.

Most residential windows are also available in materials other than wood, including aluminum and all-vinyl. If you don't like the silver color of mill-finished aluminum, you can get tan, bronze, or black applied by an anodized (electrostatic) or baked-enamel process. As with aluminum patio door frames, aluminum windows in cold climates need thermal breaks to stem heat loss. All-vinyl windows are made of extruded PVC plastic to look like their wood counterparts—but they don't. To achieve the required stiffness, the sashes and frames end up too fat to look natural. If you don't mind this, you'll get windows in a choice of white, tan, or brown that never need painting, inside or out.

Selecting Window Glazing

The window glass you choose will affect your comfort and fuel bills for many years to come. Less obviously, your glazing choice will affect how much outside noise will intrude and how quickly your furniture will fade.

The ability of the glazing to insulate against heat loss or gain is what affects your comfort and fuel bills most. A square foot of single-glazed window (R-1) wastes more than 19 times as much winter heat than an adjacent square foot of wall insulated to R-19.

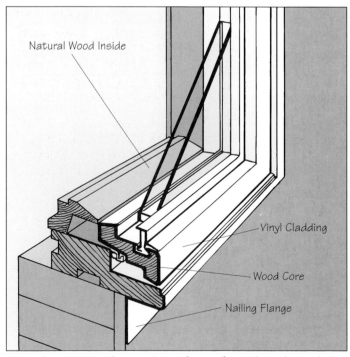

Drawing 6-30 *The exterior surfaces of wood windows clad on the outside with vinyl or aluminum never need painting. Inside, the wood core is left exposed for staining or painting.*

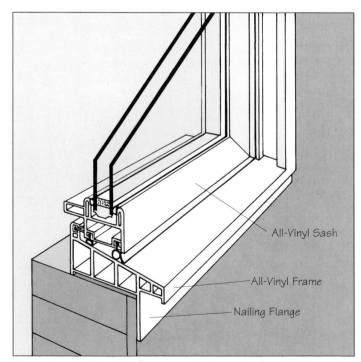

Drawing 6-31 *Windows extruded completely of PVC require no maintenance, inside or out. Standard colors are white, tan, and brown.*

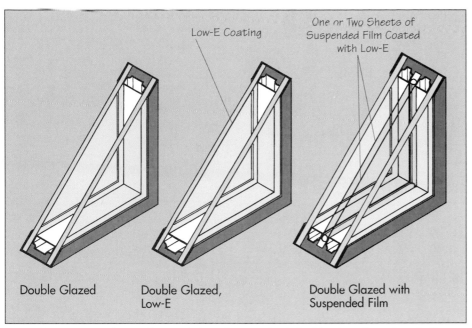

Drawing 6-32   *The insulating ability of a standard double-glazed window (R-2) is increased by half again when the outer surface of the inner pane is coated with low-E oxide. It increases even more when one or two low-E-coated polyester films are suspended in the air space and the air is replaced with a heavy gas, such as argon. The best-performing window currently available rates a total-window R-value of R-5.*

A double-glazed window comes in around R-2. Even cut in half, the window's heat loss is still more than 9 times the wall's.

The second pane of a double-glazed window doubles the window's R-value, due to the dead air space trapped between the two panes. Adding a third pane (triple glazing) increases the R-value to around R-3, and a fourth pane (quadruple glazing) reaches R-4. Each layer makes the window more resistant to noise penetration as well. But adding more panes makes the window bulkier and heavier—not to mention costlier—and each successive layer cuts the amount of useful solar heat that comes inside.

Three advances in recent years make it possible to get a window with an overall R-value as high as R-5 (as opposed to the center-of-glass reading, which is usually higher). The first is a microscopically thin metallic oxide coating called low E (for low emissivity), which makes the window act like an energy traffic cop, allowing the sunlight and heat in while preventing heat from escaping back out. The low-E coating also bars the ultraviolet rays that fade fabrics. Coating one surface of a double-glazed window with low E boosts its R-value from 2 to 3. The second advance is substituting thin polyester sheets for glass in the inner panes of triple- and quadruple-glazed windows, saving weight. Replacing the dead air space between panes with a heavier gas, such as argon, is the third advance.

Today's multiglazed windows offer various combinations of these advantages. The R-5 window, for example, is a quadruple-glazed unit with the two inner panes made of polyester (each coated with low E) and argon gas between. The added cost of this quality might pay off over time in fuel savings in Minnesota, but not in Alabama. Another type of low-E coating, suited to avoiding solar heat, is a better answer in hot climates. The advice of one or more window suppliers can help you choose the right glazing for your climate.

Roof Windows

Glazed openings overhead are a good way to bring sunlight into parts of rooms remote from a window or outside wall. Deploying them on a roof with a cathedral ceiling is as simple as providing an opening in the roof framing with doubled joists at the sides and headers at the top and bottom of the opening. The same framing is needed for a window in a sloped roof above an intervening attic, except that a shaft is necessary between the opening in the roof and flat ceiling below. The walls of the shaft can be vertical or splayed to get more light into the room.

Today's residential skylights have been pretty much taken over by window manufacturers, and the products look like real windows. They are even called roof windows. You can get them as fixed or operating with the sash tilted outward when open. Frames and sash are usually wood clad with aluminum or vinyl outside. Single or double glazing is available, along with low-E coatings. Codes require overhead glass to be laminated or tempered to prevent shards falling inside if the sash is broken.

Roof windows are often an alternative to dormers in an attic. Each has pros and cons. Here are a few things to consider when deciding which to choose.

Advantages of dormers:

▲ Dormers enhance the appearance of traditional-style homes more than roof windows do.

▲ The vertical face of a dormer offers more viewing area than does the sloped face of a roof window.

▲ Both roof windows and dormers of equal quality offer the same resistance to water penetration when closed. When open, dormer windows are less vulnerable to a sudden squall of wind-driven rain.

▲ Dormers let less unwanted heat inside during summer than roof windows.

Advantages of roof windows:

▲ Roof windows are far more economical than dormers for the same glazing area.

▲ Roof windows are easier to install in a cathedral ceiling than dormers, an important consideration if you are doing your own work.

▲ Roof windows spread their light more widely into the room than do dormers, but the light and glare are harder to control, usually requiring accessory blinds.

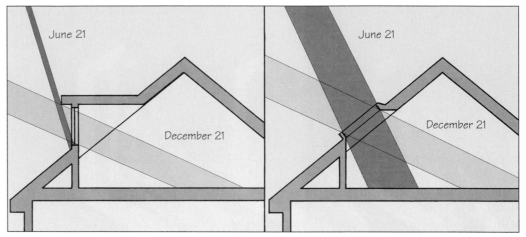

Drawing 6-33   *The sun's angles at the longest and shortest days at noon (at the latitude of Chicago and Boston) illustrate the difference between dormers and roof windows. Dormer windows allow less sunlight inside, but their geometry makes the sun's glare and heat easier to control than that of roof windows.*

Modern roof windows can turn an attic into an airy, elegant space. The fixed windows shown here are sized to fit between rafters, which greatly simplifies installation.

ROOFING

Because most houses have sloped roofs you can see from the ground, appearance matters. The steeper the slope, the more important it is either to match the main house convincingly or at least to blend well. Roof slope is described by how many inches the roof rises vertically for every 12 inches it travels horizontally. A roofer will talk about a "4 in 12" roof (often written 4/12 or 4:12) or perhaps he will simply describe it as "a 4." Whatever the slope, all roofs also have to stand up to water, wind, and strong sunlight. Resistance to fire may be important. And you would probably like a roofing material that you won't have to worry about for many years. A tall order.

Materials for Sloped Roofs

Sloped roofs shed water by virtue of their geometry, so they adapt well to many roofing materials, including shingles, slates, and panels. All of these have one thing in common. Each piece must overlap the piece below to shed water.

Asphalt and fiberglass shingles. The quantity of asphalt shingles installed each year in the United States would cover Lake Tahoe. Low cost, ease of installation, and a range of colors, patterns, and textures contribute to this popularity. Even repairing asphalt shingles is something home-owners can easily do with a few simple tools and a can of roofing cement. Traditional asphalt shingles are made of an organic fiber mat saturated with asphalt and topped with mineral granules. A more recent version substitutes fiberglass for the organic mat, saving weight and petroleum. Though stronger than their heavier antecedents, the first generation of fiberglass shingles didn't seal as well and tended to blow off in a heavy wind. Today's fiberglass shingles reportedly do not have this shortcoming and have eclipsed asphalt in popularity. Asphalt and fiberglass shingles offer styles ranging from flat to a highly profiled rustic appear-ance (sometimes called "architectural"), with surface granules in many colors, especially in tan, green, red, gray, and black.

Wood shingles and shakes. No question about it, wood shingles spell quality in a house roof. If the existing roof is shingled with wood and you want to use wood shingles on the addition, you should first evaluate the condition of the current shingles (with the aid of a roofer, if necessary). If the shingles are in poor shape, your best bet is to reroof, which will add to your costs but result in a homogeneous roof. Even if the shingles are in relatively sound shape, it will take a few years before the new wood of the addition grays enough to look like the old. If this bothers you, consider another roofing that will blend, such as asphalt shingles. (See "Shingles and Shakes," beginning on page 106, for species and grades of wood shingles.)

Metal roofing. Metal roofing, once associated only with commercial and industrial buildings, now graces many luxury homes. The priciest metal roofing is made of terne metal and copper, but more economical

Through texture and color, these fiberglass shingles echo the traditional look of slate.

choices in steel and aluminum are available in a range of baked-enamel colors. Metal roofing is available in shingle form, but using it can make your roof look like a fast-food restaurant. The predominant (and more attractive) form is panels (24 inches wide and up to 18 feet long) that are ribbed to prevent them from dimpling; their outer edges turn upward in some way to keep water out of the joint. Metal connectors, which are spaced along the sides, grab the upturned edges and secure them to the roof. Then the edge of the adjacent panel is crimped over the preceding one to make a weather seal. The ribs that run up and down metal roofing give it a highly distinctive appearance, which if used only on the addition may not blend with the existing house.

Standing-seam metal roofing, once seen only on commercial buildings, is now becoming popular on homes.

Roofing tiles made of fiber cement are less expensive than natural slate. Tiles from this manufacturer are predrilled for installation and come in muted shades of gray, green, and red.

Slate. If your home has a slate roof, slate on the addition will maintain the character. You will probably be able to make a credible match in color and pattern if your budget can stand it. If cost rules out slate, the next best bet might be asphalt shingles. If, on the other hand, the house roof is not slate, roofing the addition with slate might make the house look like a poor relative. As a roofing material, slate has kept water out of buildings for centuries, but it needs careful installation and regular maintenance. Slate is also fireproof. On the downside, it is brittle and not a good choice in a hurricane-prone areas or under a large tree.

Tile. Tile's distinctive appearance is associated with California Mission and Mediterranean architectural styles. If it doesn't already occur on the house roof, it will look out of place on the addition. If you want to roof the addition with tile, first make sure the structure can handle the heavy load, which can vary from 8 to 16 pounds per square foot. To find a close match for existing tile in terms of shape, size, and color, ask a roofer who specializes in this material for recommendations.

Topping a Flat Roof

Flat roofs (less than 1-in-12 slope) are rare on houses, except for urban row houses and International-style houses built in the 1930s. Even if your house has a sloped roof, the roof of the addition may be flat, such as a first-floor addition with a walk-out deck above. Overlapping roofing systems, such as shingles, that are designed to shed water on a sloped roof won't work on a flat roof. Instead, you need a roofing system that acts like an unbroken membrane.

COMPARING ROOFING FOR SLOPED ROOFS

Characteristic	Asphalt Shingles	Wood Shingles	Metal	Tile	Slate
Minimum roof slope[1] (inches of rise per horizontal foot)	2 to 3	4	¼ to 2½	2½ to 4½	5
Cost of materials (per square foot)	Low	Medium	Medium	High	High
Cost of installation (per square foot)	Low	Medium	Medium	Medium	High
Can be installed by homeowner	Yes	Yes	No	No	No
Life span (years)	15 to 20	10 to 40	15 to 40+	20+	30 to 100
Weight (pounds per square foot)	2.25 to 3.85	3 to 4	0.5 to 2.7	8 to 16	5 to 10
Fire rating[2]	A	B	A	A	A

[1] *A slope of 2 in 12 is possible with asphalt shingles if the guidelines for "low-slope" applications are followed. Clay tiles require a minimum slope of 4¼ in 12; concrete tiles can go down to 2½ in 12.*

[2] *An A rating is best. Wood shingles and shakes are treated with fire retardant and rated B. Combustible untreated wood shingles and shakes carry no fire rating.*

Asphalt roll. Asphalt roll roofing is made of the same material as asphalt shingles, except it comes in 3-foot-wide rolls. Cheaper both in cost and appearance, it can cover a lot of roof quickly and can be used for slopes down to around 1 in 12 if applied as directed for low-slope applications.

Built up. The traditional favorite for roofs with slopes of less than 1 in 12 is built-up roofing (BUR), which consists of several layers of asphalt-impregnated felts applied by mopping on melted asphalt. The top layer can be left exposed or covered by a layer of gravel to protect it against deterioration from ultraviolet rays. Applying a BUR roof requires the skills and equipment of a professional roofer.

Membrane. BUR roofing has been gradually replaced in recent years by single-membrane roofing made of elastomeric materials such as EPDM or neoprene. The membrane bonds to the roof by mechanical anchors or adhesive, or it is unattached and held in place by the weight of gravel. A membrane roof is a good way to cover a small addition that must have a flat roof. You may be able to obtain the materials from a supplier, but the material cost is the lion's share of the total cost, so you'll be better off having the supplier install the roofing rather than doing it yourself. And you'll get a guarantee besides.

Drawing 6-34 *If your addition abuts a house wall with second-story windows, you may be limited to a flat or nearly flat roof. Roll roofing can be applied to roofs with slopes as low as 1 in 12. Built-up roofing works on roofs with slopes of as little as ¼ in. per foot. Single-membrane roofing can be applied to dead-level roofs. All roofing should be installed according to the manufacturer's instructions. It may be necessary to have a licensed installer apply membrane roofing for the guarantee to be effective.*

Flashing

A good roof depends as much on what happens at the edges as on the surfaces. Every place where roofing meets a wall, valley, chimney, vent pipe, or fan is especially vulnerable to leakage and requires careful flashing. The flashing might be made by the roofing itself (as in asphalt shingles bent around to form a valley) but more often requires a material that can be formed into a special shape. Copper is the flashing of choice for quality roofing (wood shingles, slate, and tiles). Aluminum, galvanized steel, and PVC make good flashing for other roofing. Nails used for metal flashing must resist rust and not corrode the metal of the flashing. Copper nails are used with copper; aluminum nails are used with aluminum. Steel nails go with galvanized steel and vinyl flashing. Steel nails should be hot-dipped galvanized or, preferably, stainless steel.

The completion of roofing, siding, trim, and flashing on the outside marks a major milestone. With the envelope in place, interior work can proceed without threats from the weather. The next chapter will look at the choices of interior finish materials awaiting you.

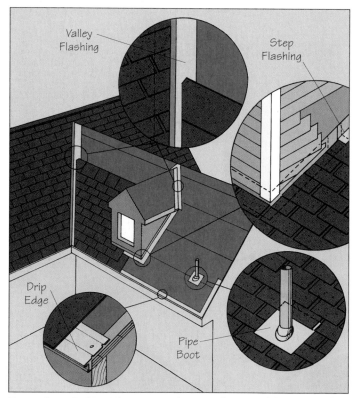

Drawing 6-35 *The watertightness of your addition's roof depends on how well the joints between abutting materials are flashed. Valleys at roof intersections can be flashed with organic sheet stock set in roof cement or with aluminum or copper sheet stock. Aluminum sheets (5 in. x 7 in.) are bent over each roof shingle and side wall. The wall stems are then capped by overlapping siding. A variety of boots (jacks) are available to flash pipes and flues to roofing. Metal or vinyl drip flashing makes roof edges watertight.*

Installing Roofing Yourself

Putting up your own roofing can be challenging, satisfying, and money-saving. The first challenge is height. A sloped roof two stories up is no place for an acrophobe, and even the fearless should be wary. There are old roofers and bold roofers, but few old, bold roofers. At the minimum, you should have a good, steady ladder and possibly a roof ladder. You'll need a steady work surface below the eaves—a scaffold or planks set on pole jacks—and another atop the roof. A plank stretching across the immediate work surface resting on movable brackets usually serves this purpose. How much extra protection you need depends on the height and slope of the roof and how much risk you can accept. Some professional roofers protect themselves against falling by wearing harnesses attached to ropes akin to mountain climbing gear. Whether or not you go this far, you won't lose anything by consulting an experienced pro before going it alone.

Cool, overcast, calm weather is best for roofing. Working in rainy or snowy conditions is begging for trouble. Strong sunlight soon makes dark-colored roofing materials too hot to handle. Wind that is scarcely noticeable on the ground can whip things around like confetti on the roof—and you with it. Then there's the weight of the material. Each bundle of asphalt shingles weighs more than 30 pounds, not too heavy to carry on the ground but tough to tote up a ladder and onto a sloped roof. Monotony is another challenge to people who are easily bored.

And the rewards? Well, because shingle roofing is labor intensive, it is an area where you stand to save on construction cost. Nailing down asphalt shingles is relatively easy and quick. Even wood shingles may be within your ability. And you won't get a better view from anywhere else on your project.

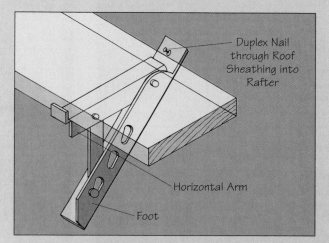

Drawing 6-36 *A plank supported by a roof bracket provides a horizontal work surface on a pitched roof. Brackets such as this one are nailed through the roof deck into rafters. The angle between the horizontal arm and foot can be adjusted to different roof slopes.*

Chapter 7

FINISHING THE INTERIOR

Everything up to this point was aimed to help you build a weatherproof box. Now it's time to turn the box into a living space. Planning the many interior finishes, trim details, cabinetry, and built-ins will require not only design skill but information and patience. If you rely on professional help, your designer will take the initiative and guide you through the decision process. If you are flying solo, first find out as much as you can about all the options, then be prepared to spend the time necessary to sort through a pile of product information, samples, pictures, and cost data. The challenge is to create an environment that reflects your design goals.

Wood flooring. The color and pattern of wood makes a floor look warm and homey. Its hard surface transmits more noise than carpet, but you can get around the noise by placing throw rugs in high traffic areas. Choices to make include unfinished or prefinished flooring, the species of wood you want, and the size and shape.

Unfinished wood flooring comes in random-length strips or planks with tongue-and-groove edges. Standard strip flooring is 2¼ inches wide and ²⁵⁄₃₂ inch thick. The widths of plank flooring vary from 4 to 10 inches, nominal size. You'll probably find maple and oak at your lumberyard, but you'll have to order walnut, fir, and cherry from a specialty supplier. Installing strip flooring is something you can probably do yourself if you don't mind the slow,

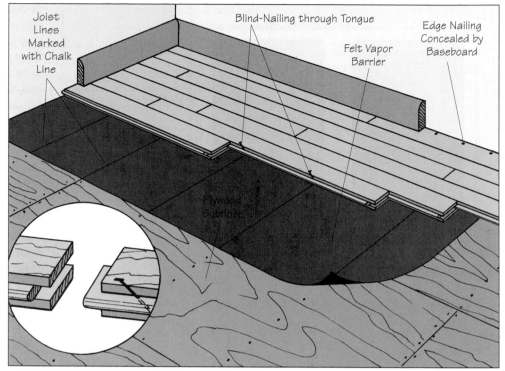

Drawing 7-11 *Wood-strip flooring comes in random lengths with tongue-and-groove edges. It is attached to the joists by blind-nailing through the tongue of each piece with a power nailer or hammer. A felt vapor barrier keeps moisture from migrating through the floor from below.*

Nothing warms a room like the natural color of wood flooring.

back-straining pace. After coaxing each strip into the grooved edge of the previous one, you drive a nail at an angle through its protruding tongue, which will be concealed by the groove of the next strip. Finishing a wood floor starts with filling cracks and sanding the surface smooth with a floor sander, which you can rent. You can then apply a penetrating oil to the wood for a deep matte finish or brush on two or three coats of clear nonpenetrating coating. Clear polyurethane is the easiest to apply and yields a very durable finish in satin or gloss sheen. Concerns over the hazards of volatile organic solvents have spurred the increasing use of water-based clear finishes, which are harder to apply than polyurethane and result in a different appearance.

Parquet flooring installs the easiest. It comes in 12-inch squares in a variety of shapes and species. Parquet tiles go down into troweled-on adhesive, similar to resilient floor tiles. You can buy parquet prefinished or as raw wood to be finished after installation.

If you want prefinished wood flooring, parquet tiles are only one of many options available. There are also prefinished laminated strips and planks (⅜ or ½ inch thick) and solid-wood strips and planks (¾ inch thick) available in widths of 3 to 7 inches in various light and dark hardwoods. The finish is a satin-sheen acrylic impregnated into the surface. Laminated products are installed in adhesive or "floated" over a foam pad. Solid strips and planks (¾ inch) must be blind-nailed through the tongue in the same way as unfinished flooring.

Tile. The choices and installation methods for floor tiles are the same as for wall tiles, with two

exceptions. First, glazed tiles should never be used on the floor. Their slick surface poses a hazard when wet. Second, tiled floors inside shower and drying areas should be set in mortar (mud set) rather than adhesive (thin set). Mud-set tiling is best left to professionals. A waterproof shower pan of copper or heavy vinyl must first be installed over the subfloor. Mortar is then built up over the pan to create a surface that slopes to the drain, and the tiles are set into the mortar.

Tile is a natural choice for greenhouse spaces. Thick tiles, such as these Saltillos set in a thick masonry base, have a lot of thermal mass that will absorb the sun's heat during the day and release it at night, moderating the temperature in the sun space.

COMPARING FLOOR FINISHES

Characteristic	Resilient floorcovering	Carpeting	Wood strip flooring	Parquet tile	Tile
Acceptable Substrates					
Plywood subfloor without improvement		✓	✓	✓	
Asphalt-saturated felt over subfloor material			✓		
Plywood subfloor with imperfections filled and sanded	✓				✓[1]
Particleboard underlayment		✓		✓	
¼-inch luan veneer underlayment	✓				
Cement board, gypsum backerboard					✓
Mortar bed over PVC or copper shower pan (mud set)					✓[2]
Suitable Locations					
Kitchen floors	✓		✓	✓	✓
Shower floors and drying areas					✓
Active areas above quiet areas		✓			
Ease of Installation by Homeowner					
Easy, even for beginners	✓[3]			✓	
Can probably do it without outside help	✓[3]	✓[4]	✓		✓[5]
Difficult, better done by a professional	✓[3]	✓[4]			✓[5]
Relative Cost[6]					
High				✓	
Medium		✓	✓		✓
Low	✓				

[1] *For floors in dry areas only.*
[2] *Shower and drying areas.*
[3] *Tiles are easy; sheet flooring is difficult.*
[4] *Difficulty depends on many factors; if in doubt, hire a pro.*
[5] *Thin-set tile can probably be done by a homeowner; for mud-set tile, hire a pro.*
[6] *Cost of the lowest-price option in each category.*

TRIMMING THE INTERIOR

Trimwork includes all the linear components that make the transition from one material to another. It also includes built-in finish carpentry, such as stairways and mantels. Modern-style homes use trimwork sparingly. A one-story contemporary addition might require only baseboards around the floors and casings around the doors and windows. More elaborate trimwork adorns the interiors of many older homes. A two-story Victorian, for example, might contain crown molding around the edges of the ceiling, a horizontal band (picture rail) a few feet down on the walls, and yet another band (chair rail) about 3 feet above the floor, which might separate the flat wall above from the wainscoting below. The stairway in a home such as this would be a real showplace of the carpenter's art. Hundreds of pieces, each shaped, cut, and fit with precision, went into the assembly of treads, side trim, balusters, and newel posts. An ornately carved wood mantel might frame a fireplace. The trimwork in the existing home should guide your decisions for the addition if you want a seamless transition. But matching the elaborate woodwork of a traditional home can be difficult and expensive. Compromise may be inevitable. An architect, interior designer, and fine carpenter might show you how you can blend with the existing trimwork without slavishly copying it.

Some trim is a special shape or color of the same material used on the surface, such as the base and cap pieces used to terminate ceramic tile or the vinyl base that might edge resilient floor coverings. You can install this type of trim yourself if you can apply the adjacent surface material of which it is a part. Most interior trim, however, is wood. And it's always exposed to view, unlike studs and joists. Where approximate cuts may pass muster for rough framing, trim pieces have to be cut and joined precisely, or you'll be reminded of the misfit every time you look at the joint. Good finish carpentry depends on quality materials put together to fit exactly. That doesn't mean you can't handle some trim work yourself. Trimming around windows, doors, and floors demands far less skill and fewer special tools than, say, building a staircase.

The cherry wood casework and trim in this room was certainly costly. The result can only be described as elegant.

Materials and Tools

Trim pieces can be custom cut and milled to the required profile or bought premilled to various standard profiles in lengths of up to 16 feet. Your lumberyard probably stocks a selection of the most common molding shapes in ponderosa pine. It may stock many of these shapes in oak as well. If they don't have a shape you need, they can probably order it for you.

When choosing a wood species, start at the surface. If the wood is to be painted, you want the most economical species that takes paint well. Paint-grade pine and poplar fit the bill, though poplar is not as readily available in premilled moldings.

Choosing a species for a natural finish is more complicated. Staining can tweak the wood's color darker or lighter, and the finish can be anywhere

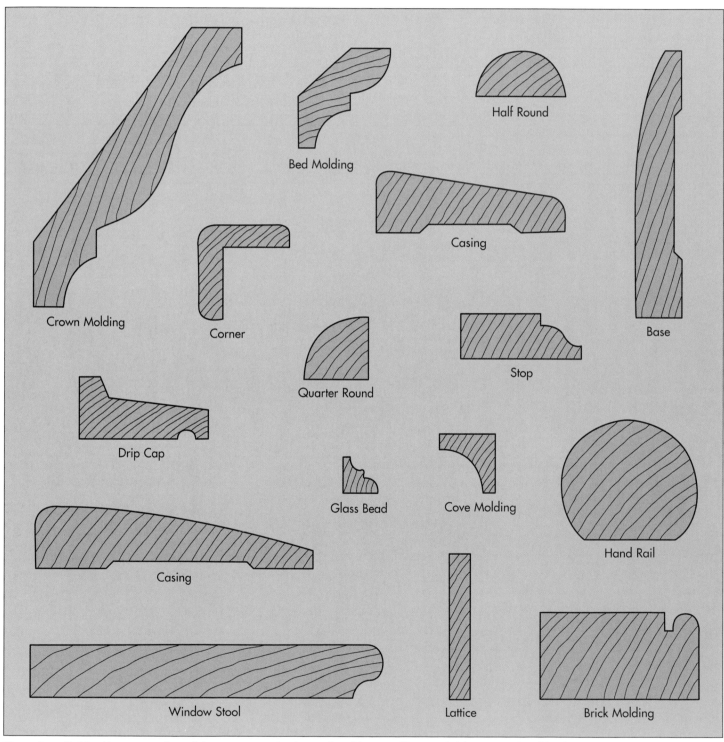

Drawing 7-12 *Here are a few of the many standard wood molding profiles available at your local lumberyard. Pine is usually stocked; other species may have to be special-ordered.*

from matte to shiny gloss. Woods with interesting grain patterns are often preferred for natural finishes. Oak, cherry, mahogany, and walnut are oft-chosen woods. Woods with subtler grains, such as maple and birch, aren't as popular for stand-alone applications but make good choices for natural edging around cabinets, doors, or floors of the same species.

Pine, fir, and spruce can also be naturally finished, but each has limitations. Premilled pine moldings are made by joining random lengths of rough stock with interlocking finger joints, which will be apparent through a natural finish. If you want to finish stock pine moldings naturally, specify "clear," which has no finger joints. (Poplar doesn't make a good candidate for natural finish.) If you mill your own trim pieces of pine lumber and want a knot-free material, you'll have to pay the premium for select-grade pine. On the other hand, tight knots will be acceptable (even desired) in the trimwork around knotty pine paneling. Fir and spruce also contain knots, so order a clear grade if desired.

Installing premilled moldings and trim requires basic carpentry tools—hammer, measuring tape, pencil, and try square—and a few special but economical tools. You'll need a miter box and backsaw to make angle cuts and a coping saw for curves. If your only hammer is a heavyweight framing hammer, you should get a lightweight claw hammer and one or more nail sets to countersink nails.

Types of Trimwork

Here are some of the most common trim options.

Base trim. Two pieces usually make up the trim between the floor and wall surfaces: a flat-profile baseboard and a smaller base shoe. Both pieces are nailed through the wall finish into the framing, never into the floor. Outside corners are mitered. Inside corners can also be mitered, but coping is the preferred method. If joints are required along the length of a wall, they must occur at a stud so that both trim pieces have something to attach to.

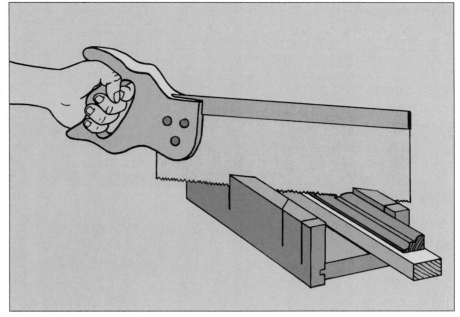

Drawing 7-13 A backsaw and miter box make accurate cuts on moldings for butt or mitered joints.

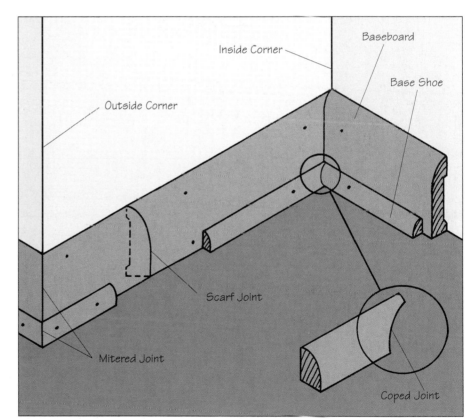

Drawing 7-14 Most wall bases consist of a wood baseboard nailed to the studs and a base shoe applied after the flooring is in place. Corners can be mitered, but mitering inside corners risks a gap when both pieces contract. Coping one piece to fit against another reduces the gap by half.

In quality work, the pieces are joined with an angled "scarf" rather than simply butted together. With a scarf joint, a gap won't open if the molding shrinks slightly in length.

Door and window trim. The pieces that trim a door or window at the wall go on after the unit has been secured into the rough opening and the wall substrate material has been installed. If other wall finishes such as tile or wallcovering are planned, they are typically applied later and abut the edge of the trim. The trimwork can be as simple as a single flat 1x4 or stock casing that runs around three sides of the window or door, or as complex as an assembly of fluted moldings and rosettes.

Plastic Moldings

It might be possible to match ornate wood or plaster trimwork by joining several stock wood moldings into composite assemblies, though this can get costly. Instead, you can get classical moldings made of polyurethane or fiberglass-reinforced polyester. Cornices, columns, friezes, niches, and medallions are some of the many shapes available. The plastic materials are preprimed, and they can be cut with the same saw as you'd use for wood molding. After installation, plastic molding can be painted with latex or oil paint. Unlike wood, plastic moldings won't expand and contract with humidity changes, so gaps won't develop after installation.

A wide, detailed crown molding, such as this one, would be very expensive to produce in wood. This plastic version is cheaper and you won't have to worry about gaps when the humidity changes.

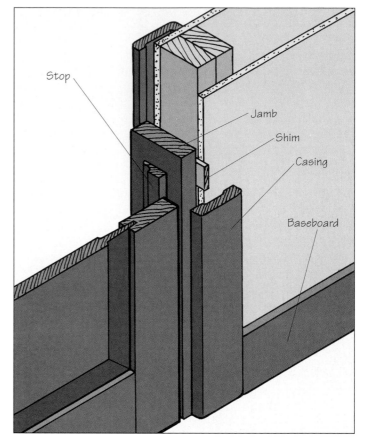

Drawing 7-15 *Here are the typical door trim elements.*

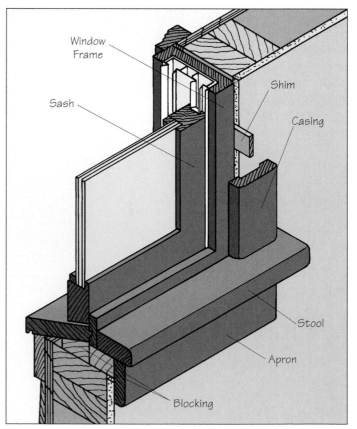

Drawing 7-16 *Here are the trim pieces used for a typical double-hung window.*

When the machine age made detailed molding affordable in the 1880s, clever carpenters realized that molded casings with decorative corner blocks at windows and doors would be handsome and easier to install than casings that met with miters. This type of molding is still widely available. A handy homeowner might want to tackle its installation.

Stairways. The simplest stairway is a straight run of stairs between two walls. After the supporting members (notched stringers) are in place, the risers and treads are installed. Trimming this type of staircase can be as simple as installing side pieces (skirting) and a molding between each riser and tread. A single handrail attached to the wall completes the installation. You don't have to be a skilled finish carpenter to put this type of stairway together. Stairways get more challenging when they turn corners or contain winders (angle-shaped treads), and open stairways flanked by balustrades test the mettle of even the savviest craftsmen.

Mantels. A fireplace is the focal point of a room. The design of the parts that frame the opening determine how well it fulfills this role. The frame, or mantel, should fit the overall architecture. Contemporary styles lean toward simplicity, maybe just a border of tile or other trim around three sides of the firebox with a simple wood shelf above. A hefty timber shelf, three or four courses of corbeled brick, or a stone ledge could create a more rustic mantel. But the image that usually comes to mind when we think

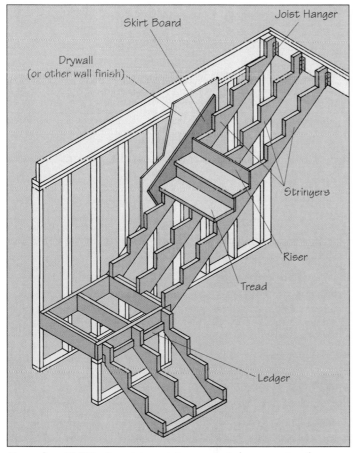

Drawing 7-17 *Framing a stairway starts by spanning three stringers between each run. Stringers usually consist of notched 2x12s. The wall finish and skirt board may be installed next, followed by stair risers and treads that butt into the skirt board. The skirt board can also be cut to fit around the risers and treads.*

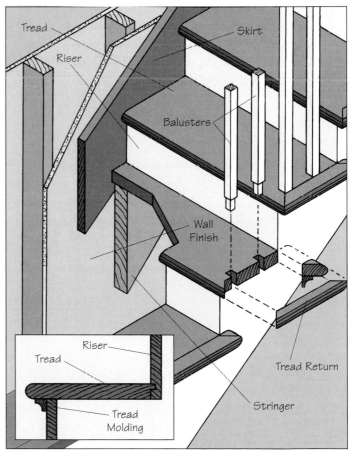

Drawing 7-18 *Stairs enclosed by a wall can abut a skirt board applied before the treads, as shown, or after. A handrail is mounted to the wall above the stairs. The open side of a stairway requires a handrail supported by balusters as well as a tread return to cover the exposed edges of the stairway.*

of a mantel is an assemblage of embellished wood panels and moldings capped by a shelf. The traditional wood mantel reached its height of popularity in Victorian homes. The highly skilled craftsmen who put these mantels together often built in columns and brackets and added mirrors above the shelf. You can obtain a traditional wood mantel the hard way by building it from scratch. An easier way, and one you can probably install yourself, is to use a mantel kit. If you are an antique buff, you might find a period piece that will suit your addition by scouting out antiques and architectural salvage stores or looking through a catalog of antique home accessories.

Cabinetry

Cabinets for your addition might be as simple as a shelf inside a bedroom closet or a vanity for a bathroom or as elaborate as a full set of kitchen cabinets. Whatever the scope, you'll need to decide the type, style, finish, and storage capacity of each item and how best to obtain it. Today cabinetry comes in a variety of styles and quality. Unless you have a space that won't work with standard cabinet sizes, or you have a very unusual design in mind, prefabricated cabinets will most likely be more cost-effective than custom-made cabinets. You can probably put up shelves yourself, but making complicated cabinetry requires advanced joinery skills and a well-equipped woodworking shop.

Shelving

The first design question for shelves is what is to be supported. The answer determines the depth, width, and thickness of the shelves and whether they should be fixed in place or be adjustable. Shelves that sag toward the middle point out a common mistake: underrating the load. The table "Shelf Loads" (below) can guide you in suiting the shelf thickness and width to the load.

Fixed shelves can be supported in various ways. The simplest is to cut the shelves to the exact width between the supports and insert screws through the supports into the ends of the shelves. Before installing the screws, glue the joint to help make it stronger.

A stronger way is to glue the shelves into dados in the supports. The grooves can be made with a power saw or router, or you can set the shelves on cleats attached

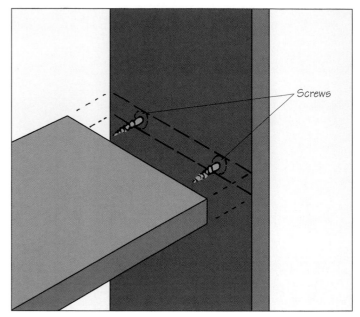

Drawing 7-19 *The easiest way to attach fixed shelves is with two or three screws. Glue the joint before installing the screws for a stronger joint.*

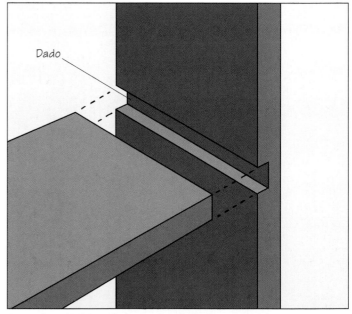

Drawing 7-20 *Shelves set into dados create the strongest, most stable units.*

Shelf Loads

Loading	Examples	Shelf Thickness (inches)	Shelf Width (inches)
Light	Books shorter than 10", knickknacks	¾	30
		1	36
Heavy	Record albums, books taller than 10"	¾	24
		1	20
		1½	36

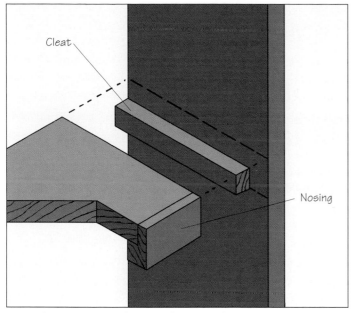

Drawing 7-21 *Shelves can bear on cleats attached to the sides of the unit. If appearance is important, conceal the cleat by attaching a nosing to the shelf.*

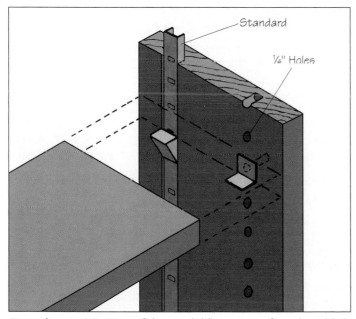

Drawing 7-22 *Two of the available supports for adjustable shelving. A metal standard fits into a groove in the support and clips can be placed into the slots at 1-in. intervals, or ¼-in.-diameter holes can be drilled into the support to receive another type of clip.*

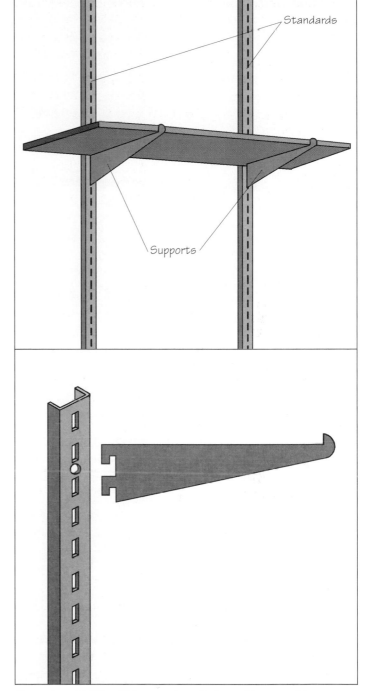

Drawing 7-23 *Sides can be eliminated by attaching metal standards directly to the wall and supporting the shelves with brackets. The standards require solid backing, such as a stud. Brackets come in lengths to support shelves from 6 to 12 in. wide.*

to the supports. But if you have ever lived with fixed bookshelves, you know how the spacing never quite seems to fit the books you have at any one time. Adjustable shelves are the way out of this problem. You can choose a system that uses slotted uprights (standards) to support metal clips or brackets, or you can drill holes in the supports and insert clips into the holes.

Shelves and supporting side pieces can be made out of any species of wood. But solid-stock hardwood is more expensive than hardwood veneer, so to get the wood appearance you want at the least cost, use veneer edged with a thin piece of solid wood of the same species. If the shelves are to be painted, you can save money by making them out of particleboard or plywood edged with solid wood.

Prefabricated Cabinets

Cabinets are the heart and soul of a kitchen. Their layout and interior amenities determine how well your kitchen will work, and because cabinets consume most of the wall space, they also create the mood of the kitchen. Prefabricated kitchen and bath cabinets come in numerous styles and finishes. Modular widths allow you to tailor the arrangement to suit your needs and style of cooking. Visit the showroom of a kitchen and bath store or home center early on to see what's available. Then decide on a cabinetry budget, and pass your findings on to your designer or use them as a starting point if you are designing your own project.

The variety of styles and finishes is one of the first things you'll notice in the showroom. Yet the many options spring out of two basic types of cabinet construction: face framed and frameless. Face-framed cabinets contain a narrow frame around all openings in the front to which doors and, sometimes, drawers are mounted. The frame creates a sense of depth and imparts a traditional look to the face pieces, which are available in a number of wood species and in panels or flush surfaces. If contemporary is your theme, look at frameless cabinets. They eliminate the face frame so that the doors or drawers cover the entire front surface. You can still get the same surface options and wood species, or choose the clean, unbroken, appearance of a flat laminated plastic front.

Kitchen cabinets fall into two basic categories: base and wall cabinets. Base cabinets are open at the top to receive a

This traditional-looking kitchen features cabinets with face frames. The drawers are fully inset flush to the outside of the frames. The doors overlap the face frames but don't fully cover them.

Frameless cabinets with full-overlay doors present a sleek modern look. Flat surfaces are, of course, easiest to clean.

countertop after the cabinets have been installed. The space just below the top edge is usually filled by a drawer, except where there is a sink or cooktop. The lower portions of the cabinet can contain more drawers, shelves, bins, or pull-out devices for waste-baskets, vegetable bins, and other items. Corner base cabinets often contain revolving shelves (lazy Susans). Bathroom vanity cabinets are similar to kitchen base cabinets and offer much the same interior options.

Wall cabinets typically contain shelving, left exposed or concealed behind doors. Spice racks, slots for plates, wineglass racks, and wine-bottle ports are some of the many specialty devices available. You can also get wall cabinets that extend all the way to the floor to house wall ovens, pantries, and brooms. And if the variety of wall cabinets is lacking, there are wall cabinets, such as appliance garages, that make use of the space at the back of the countertop.

Base cabinets are typically 24 inches deep and 35 inches high (without the countertop). Order 33-inch-high units if you are planning the kitchen for wheelchair access. Wall cabinets are 12 inches deep and 24, 27, 30, 36, or 42 inches high. Full-height wall cabinets are 24 inches deep and 84 inches high. Each separate base or wall cabinet is typically available in widths from 1 to 4 feet and in modular increments of 3 inches. If your room size doesn't match one of the increments, the supplier

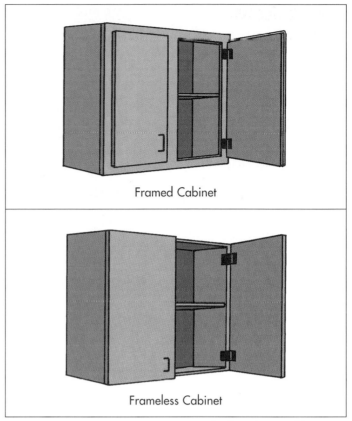

Framed Cabinet

Frameless Cabinet

Drawing 7-24 *The doors mount to the face frame of framed cabinets and to the case of frameless cabinets.*

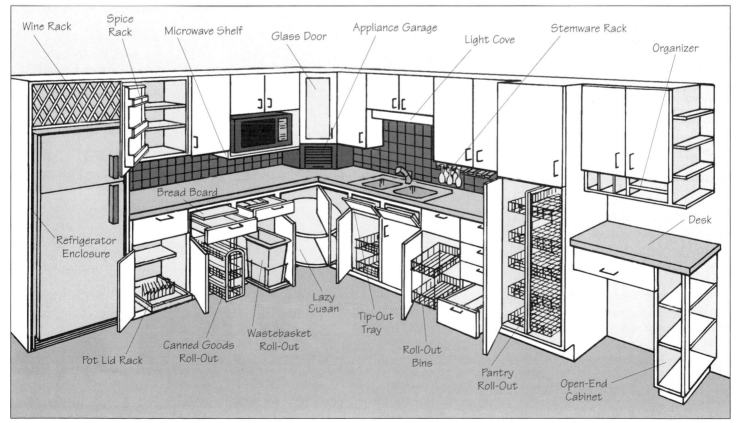

Drawing 7-25 *Even though prefabricated cabinets are made in standard modular sizes, you can create a design to fit the needs of your kitchen or bath by choosing from among the vast number of cabinet styles and storage options.*

will provide end panels to fill in the remaining gap. Or you can get a custom-size end cabinet to fit exactly but at additional cost.

Installing manufactured cabinets is not particularly difficult, but precision and know-how are necessary to make the units plumb and level. The cost of installing a full set of kitchen cabinets is small compared with the material costs, which can run into several thousand dollars, so you'll come out ahead by having the supplier install the units. You can probably install a single unit such as a bathroom vanity cabinet yourself, though, with a how-to book to guide you.

Getting the Most from Kitchen Cabinets

To make your kitchen addition hum with efficiency, start with a good layout. (Heed the planning advice in Chapter 4 under "Kitchen Additions," beginning on page 66.) Then select cabinets to serve the needs of their location. Here are some things to consider:

▲ Choose cabinets whose internal storage components are adjustable rather than fixed, to allow you to change the storage as your needs change.

▲ Lazy Susans make the best use of corner cabinets, even though the circular shelves don't use up the entire rectangular space.

▲ Select a sink base cabinet that uses the space at the top, in front of the sink, for storage. Even though it's shallow, this space is just right for dishwashing tools.

▲ Choose 24-inch-deep cabinets above refrigerators rather than keeping them at the 12-inch depth of the other wall cabinets. The extra foot doubles their storage capacity and makes the inside more accessible.

▲ Explore all the choices available for the insides of cabinets. Rather than limit yourself to shelves and drawers, consider pull-out shelves, bins, slots, and racks.

Another thing to consider is how best to use the foot or so of space just below the ceiling. Because most adults can't easily reach items higher than about 7 feet, this is the most common height of wall cabinets. One way to use this otherwise wasted space is to select wall cabinets that extend to the ceiling. Even if you have to stand on a stool to reach it, the highest shelf is a great place to store infrequently used items such as a punch bowl or picnic gear. Another possibility is to keep the cabinets at 7 feet but lower a portion of the ceiling to this height to house lighting fixtures.

Countertops

The field of countertop choices is wide, with abundant variation in cost, appearance, and performance. The right choice for you depends largely on how you rank each quality. Here's how some of the most likely choices stack up.

Plastic laminate. Low cost, durability, a seamless surface, and a variety of colors and patterns have ensured plastic laminate's popularity for countertops since the 1950s. The material you may know by the brand name Formica consists of several layers of kraft paper and a layer of decorative paper combined with a clear plastic, wedded under intense heat and pressure to create 1/16-inch-thick sheets that are up to 5 feet wide and 12 feet long. Plastic laminate comes in matte and gloss finishes. Matte shows fewer scratches. A pan of boiling water probably won't harm plastic laminate, but a hot frying pan will scorch the surface. Site-applied plastic laminate can be edged with a strip of the same material, but when the overhanging countertop piece is cut back and finished flush with the edging, a dark line (the thickness of the top piece) is inevitably revealed. Edging the countertop with hardwood, as shown in Drawing 7-26, still leaves the dark line but yields a nicer detail. One way to eliminate the line is to trim the top laminate flush to the edge of the substrate and apply a wooden edge that butts into the laminate. But this creates a top seam that can sometimes collect grime. You can avoid the dark line completely by ordering a prefabricated countertop faced with plastic laminate. This is called a "post-formed" countertop. The facing is continuous over a 4-inch-high backsplash, top surface, and front nose. You can order prefab stock in lengths up to 12 feet, with holes for sinks or cooktops cut out to your specifications.

Ceramic tile. Practical as it is, laminated plastic still evokes tabletops in fast-food restaurants. Tile is classier and homier but more expensive. It comes in

Plastic laminate is a practical, affordable countertop material that can be quite attractive. If you have a tight budget and a lot of surface to cover, it may be the only choice.

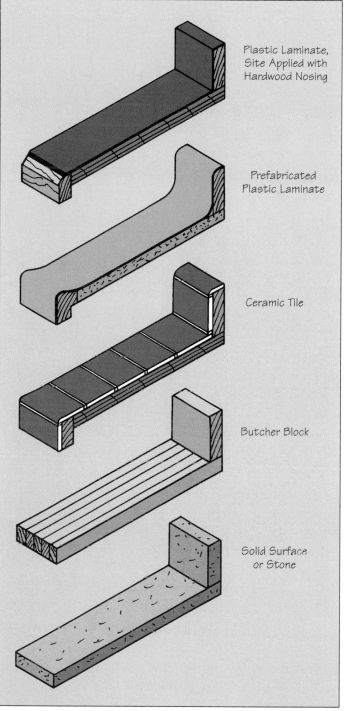

Plastic Laminate, Site Applied with Hardwood Nosing

Prefabricated Plastic Laminate

Ceramic Tile

Butcher Block

Solid Surface or Stone

Drawing 7-26 *You can obtain a plastic laminate countertop by applying the laminate to a wood base or ordering it prebonded in the length you want. Other options include tile, butcher block, solid surface, and stone.*

Using tile opens up a world of creative possibilities. The back counters are simple white tiles that draw attention to the island. The tiles on the island were custom designed as a set to create what amounts to an original artwork.

a range of colors and patterns and is generally easy to clean (except for the grout, which traps grease and grows mildew). Epoxy grout in the joints makes them easier to clean. Most homeowners can probably install a tile countertop by following the instructions supplied by the tile dealer or from a how-to book. Bullnose shapes can edge the countertop, or you can use another material such as hardwood.

Butcher block. If you really detest a kitchen that looks antiseptic, butcher block may be just the right choice. It comes in 1½-inch-thick slabs glued up from narrow strips of hard maple. Butcher block is the only countertop that you can cut against if you finish the top with a penetrating, nontoxic oil such as tung oil. Cutting against it will take a toll, though, making the surface look used. Burn and stain marks will also accumulate, and the rougher surface will trap odors and even salmonella bacteria. Preventing these problems requires regular sanding, bleaching, and reoiling, which can get tiresome. You can dodge these problems by finishing the wood with glossy urethane and using a separate cutting board.

Solid surface. One of the fruits of the plastics revolution is a countertop material that resembles but outperforms real stone. Sold under trade names such as Corian and Avonite, this solid-surface material gets its looks from the stone dust that forms its basis but gains its advantages from the acrylic or polyester matrix in which the dust is embedded. Solid surfacing can be cut, drilled, and shaped in much the same way as wood, and because it is manufactured, it can be cast to contain sinks. When cracks or blemishes occur, they can be filled in with a plastic repair material. Solid-surface stock comes in sheets of ⅛ to ¾ inch thick, widths of 30 or 36 inches, and lengths up to

12 feet. If joints are necessary, they can be chemically bonded, making them almost invisible. You might be able to install a surface countertop yourself, but some manufacturers will guarantee the product only if it's installed by a professional.

Stone. Marble and granite will impart real prestige to your kitchen if you are willing to pay the price. Heat and stains won't hurt stone, and it doesn't scratch or scar easily. If you bake, you won't find a better material on which to roll out dough than the cold, polished surface of marble. (You might consider a marble countertop only in the baking area.) It takes a substantial blow to crack the surface. Stone is thick enough to form its own front edge. Backsplashes can be a strip of stone or another material. Stone is heavy and difficult to install—a job for a professional.

Putting It All Together

When you have selected all your finishes and pinned down cabinet styles and countertops, you will need to select the colors and patterns for each material. Picking out a carpet is daunting enough. Coordinating it with the rest of the room is even more so. A sensitive architect or interior designer will help you make decisions that best suit your needs and tastes. If you are designing your own addition, here's a way to manage the task.

Because solid-surface material can be shaped easily, you can create any edge detail you like.

Stone is quite expensive, so you might not want to bust the budget by using it for all your counters. Here, the island is stone while the counters are plastic laminate edged with wood. Notice that the table was custom-made to match the counters.

COMPARING COUNTERTOP CHOICES

Characteristic	Plastic Laminate	Ceramic Tile	Butcher Block	Solid Surface	Stone
Installed cost[1]	X	1.5X	2X	3-5X	4-6X
Resistance to abrasion	G	M	G	M	M
Washability	G	M	P	G	G
Ease of repairing surface defects	P	M	G	G	P
Resistance to heat[2]	P	G	P	M	G
Cutting on the surface	P	G	P[3]	M	G
Need of a separate substrate	✓[4]	✓[5]			

G-good, M-medium, P-poor

[1] *Relative to the cost of plastic laminate, given as X dollars.*

[2] *Hot frying pan.*

[3] *Cut marks change the appearance of the surface and invite bacteria.*

[4] *Prefab countertops come with a particleboard substrate attached; site-applied plastic laminate requires particleboard (preferred) or plywood.*

[5] *Plywood preferred.*

As you deliberate on each item, collect samples. Begin with the materials that are least likely to change over time, such as carpeting, countertop materials, and wallcoverings. A carpet supplier should be willing to cut off a small swatch of any carpet you want to consider. (If not, take your business elsewhere.) You may not be able to get small samples of some materials, such as solid-surface countertops, so do the next best thing: Collect brochures. Sales brochures often show the colors and patterns in a series of chips that you can clip out. Then get sample swatches of wallcovering and color chips for paint.

The next task is to arrange the samples onto a sample board. Any white-colored 8½-by-11-inch (or larger) surface will work. Foam-core board, available at an art or hobby store, is best. Use rubber cement or other glue that isn't permanent. You'll need a separate sample board for each room or color scheme. Organize the samples on the board in the approximate arrangement in which you will see them in the room, with the floor material at the bottom and ceiling color at the top. Place each sample next to the samples of the materials that it abuts. For example, from bottom up you might see floorcovering, base, lower wall, chair rail, upper wall, and ceiling (see Drawing 7-27). Loosely position each sample on the board. Explore different combinations until you get a scheme you like, then glue everything down. The completed board will show you and your household what the rooms will look like. If and when you want to change the scheme, simply pluck out and replace samples until you are satisfied.

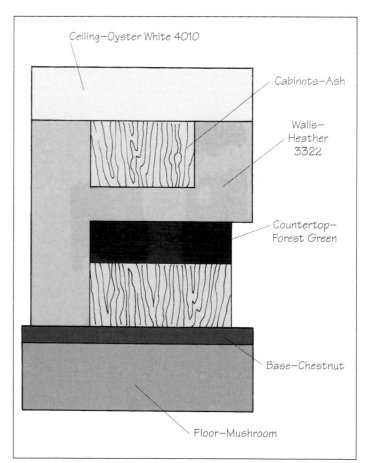

Ceiling—Oyster White 4010

Cabinets—Ash

Walls—Heather 3322

Countertop—Forest Green

Base—Chestnut

Floor—Mushroom

Drawing 7-27 *A sample board for each room shows how the colors go together. Mount color chips or material swatches on a neutral board in the arrangement in which they'll be used. A kitchen is shown here.*

Chapter 8

CREATING COMFORT IN YOUR ADDITION

Feeling comfortable indoors means more than just making sure it's not too hot or cold. It also means clean air and enough of the right kind of light in each area. If a kitchen or bath is part of your project, you'll expect the various networks of pipes, wires, and equipment to deliver comfort reliably and constantly. You probably know which systems in your home work well and which ones are troublesome. You can use this knowledge in planning the mechanical and electrical systems in your addition, perhaps improving shortcomings in your existing house while you are at it.

CONSERVATION FIRST

Comfort costs, like everything else. There are direct costs you bear and indirect costs to society that result from your decisions. Your costs begin when you shell out for equipment and distribution systems then continue indefinitely in the form of operating expenses. The societal costs are harder to control, even if you have the will to do so. For example, you may want to reduce your dependence on fossil fuels for heating. But selecting electric heat over, say, gas or oil isn't necessarily the most environmentally sound choice. Electricity generated from coal or nuclear energy is neither sustainable nor environmentally benign (not to mention the energy wasted over the transmission lines). Similar dilemmas beset almost every decision if you trace the consequences far enough. Still, some choices are more socially responsible than others. Some of them will cost you a bit more up front but save dollars in the long run—and benefit the environment.

Conservation is the key. Plan your addition to need less energy in the first place. This means taking full advantage of passive methods of making your home comfortable year round. When applied to heating and cooling your home, the word passive means without mechanical systems and the fuel it takes to run them. To create a structure that works passively, you must plan actively. Begin by orienting your addition to take the best advantage of the sun's path for heating and cooling (Chapter 3). Insulate walls and roof to meet the rigors of your climate (Chapter 6). Finally, select energy-efficient heating, cooling, and lighting systems.

The Passive Path to Comfort

Every climate has assets and liabilities. By designing and building your addition to take advantage of your climate's assets and defend against its liabilities, you can make your addition more comfortable year round, whether you live in Minneapolis or Miami. And if you do, you'll also continue to reap the gains in the form of greater comfort and fuel savings for as long as you live in the house. After locating your climate region in Drawing 8-1, heed the guidelines on pages 156–157.

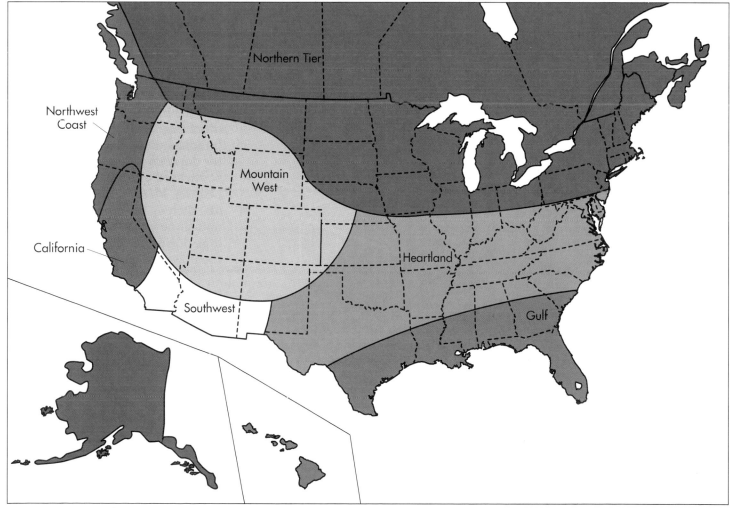

Drawing 8-1   *A house in North Dakota deals with a much different climate than one in Florida. Designing your addition to respond to its climate is the best way to ensure year-round comfort with the least dependence on mechanical systems.*

only the size of the stove but proper clearances. And don't neglect to check on firewood prices—they vary greatly from rural to urban areas.

Fireplaces have much in common with stoves, as far as operation and maintenance. But as heat sources, they suffer. Whereas stoves heat the room both by radiating and warming the air by convection, fireplaces heat mostly by radiation. Standard open-faced fireplaces usually suck out more warm air from the house than they return. If you do want useful heat from your fireplace, you can add features that make it work more like a stove. First, isolate the fire chamber from the room with glass doors. Provide outside combustion air to the chamber through a 4-inch-diameter duct. Vents fitted with blower fans at the sides of the chamber can draw room air from below and return warm air above. (Recirculating fireplace kits are available.) Or you can check out some of the Russian fireplace designs that draw hot exhaust gases through several channels in the masonry and radiates it to the room over several hours.

Room air conditioners and heat pumps.

The warmer your climate, the more you need cooling rather than heating. You can select separate equipment to heat and cool your addition or devices that package everything in one unit. Units that cool only are called air conditioners. They mount in an existing window opening, but if you plan one from the beginning, you'll get better performance by creating a special opening higher up on the wall. (Cold air drops naturally.) By installing the unit in its own opening, it will be easier to seal around the opening and won't consume part of a window. You can cool any size room you are likely to build with a single air conditioner as long as you match the size of the room to the capacity of the unit. Heating and cooling capacity is measured in British thermal units per hour (BtuH). The cooling capacity of room air conditioners ranges between 5,000 and 29,000 BtuH. If your room is well insulated, figure around 20 to 40 BtuH for each square foot of area to be cooled. Air conditioners use electricity for fuel—some more efficiently than others—so you should also check the energy-efficiency rating (EER) of any unit before buying. EER values vary from 7 to 11—the higher the EER number, the greater the efficiency.

Some air conditioners are equipped to reverse their cycle to provide heating. These heat pumps circulate heat into or out of a space. They heat efficiently when outside temperatures are above 45 degrees or so. Lower than this, efficiency drops off until a point at which the unit shifts to an electric resistance coil, which increases its operating costs, making this a poor choice in a region with a long winter. Another type of package heating/cooling unit uses gas rather than electricity during periods too cold for the heat

pump to work. Like the units you may have seen in motel rooms, these devices mount on an outside wall and must be connected to a natural gas or propane source.

Systems for Multiroom Additions

The same approaches to heating and cooling a new home apply to an addition with several rooms. You'll need a space for the equipment and provisions for running distribution pipes or ductwork. You'll also need to decide whether you want heating, cooling, or both. A good place to begin is to decide how you want the heat to be distributed.

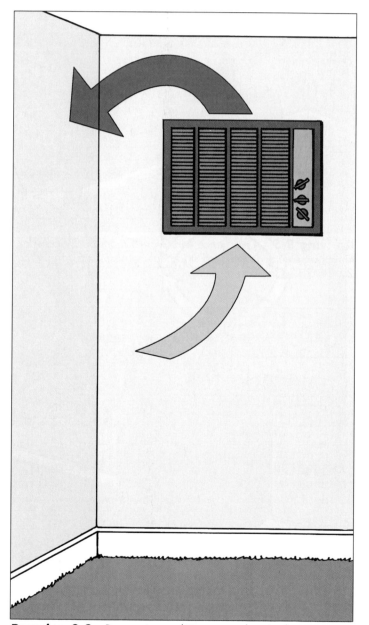

Drawing 8-8 Room air conditioners cool a single room. Heat-pump units also provide heat. In building an addition, you can plan an opening in the wall for the unit rather than sticking it through a window.

Hot air. Hot-air heating is so popular because of the other functions an air system can perform. Besides delivering heat, an air system can cool, humidify, dehumidify, filter, and ventilate. The heated and/or conditioned air reaches each room of the addition via a system of ductwork. Air is also returned to the furnace by ducts, usually connected to a centrally located grille. You may remember the octopus in the basement of the home you grew up in. This behemoth of a furnace sprouted huge tentacles in all directions, through which heated air rose by convection to get to the rooms above. Today, we use fans to force the air, thereby getting by with smaller ducts.

Hydronic. Just as the old vision of hot-air systems resembled an octopus in the basement, the old-style hydronic system conjures up clunky radiators that never seemed to keep the room at just the right temperature and pipework that made thumping noises. Today's hydronic heating systems offer improvements on all fronts. They use hot water rather than the steam that was used in some old systems. The water

is heated to around 180 degrees F by a central boiler. Small circulator pumps move the hot water through a loop of piping. Baseboard fin-tube or wall-mounted radiators (smaller and better looking than the old cast iron ones) tap heat off of the pipe loop and distribute it evenly in each room. If you are one of the many people who aren't comfortable with air blowing over their skin, consider a hydronic system. Hydronic systems don't stir up dust, as do forced-air systems, and generally run more quietly.

Central heating. Whether you choose a forced-air or hydronic heating system, the heat comes from a central source. Air systems use furnaces to heat air in a combustion chamber. Room air picks up heat by circulating through a heat exchanger. Hydronic heating systems depend on boilers, which heat the water by blowing a flame into the combustion chamber. Both air furnaces and boilers can use a variety of fuels. Gas and oil are the most preferred fuels, but wood-burning furnaces are also available. (Some draw on oil or gas for a backup fuel.) Furnaces and boilers

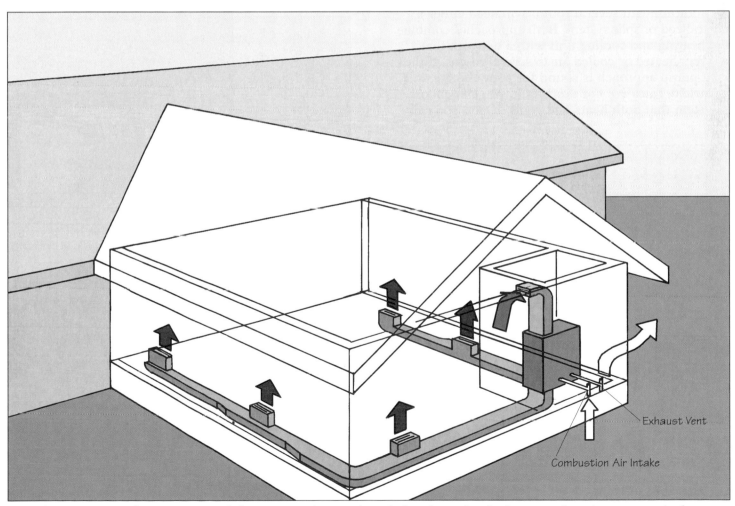

Exhaust Vent

Combustion Air Intake

Drawing 8-9 *Forced-air systems supply heat to several rooms through ducts located in the floor or ceiling. Air returns to the furnace through a centrally located vent. Standard gas and oil furnaces require flues through the roof to exhaust gases. High-efficiency gas condensing furnaces, as shown, need only two small-diameter PVC pipes through an outside wall to exhaust the low-temperature gases and bring in combustion air.*

with a separate circuit breaker. The panel, itself, has a maximum rating, usually 100 or 200 amps. Circuit breakers come in capacities of 15, 20, 30, 40, and 50 amps, according to the load connected to them.

There are three types of circuits in residences. Lighting circuits serve light fixtures hard-wired into them. Single-purpose circuits serve only one outlet for a specific appliance, such as a water heater, clothes dryer, or range. General-purpose circuits are connected to various outlets intended for portable lighting and small appliances. The continuous loading on a circuit should not exceed 80 percent of its rating. So a 15-amp

circuit can have a continuous load of 12 amps—enough for eight convenience outlets (assuming each outlet draws no more than 1.5 amps). For kitchens, code requires a minimum of two separate 20-amp, 120-volt circuits for small appliances such as toasters and blenders.

If the panel's total capacity is shy of the new added load, you'll have to replace it with one of larger capacity. If it is also outdated (containing fuses rather than circuit breakers), this is a good time to upgrade it anyway. On the other hand, your main panel may be up to date with ample capacity but still lack spare slots. One way to solve this problem is to replace single breakers with devices that contain two breakers that work independently but fit in a single slot. Another solution is to tap off of the main panel to feed a new subpanel (or branch panel)—a kind of little brother—that will contain the circuits in the addition. You'll need the help of an electrician to evaluate your panel and advise on how best to power the addition. If a replacement is in the works, by all means hire an electrician to do that, whether or not you do the branch wiring.

PLANNING THE LIGHTING

Good lighting goes beyond sufficient lighting for the occupants to see. It also creates a visual environment that suits the room. Bathroom lighting differs from lighting for a home office, and a good lighting scheme provides enough of the right kind to suit the function of the room. Lighting has two purposes and there are two types of lighting to serve those purposes. Ambient light is the general lighting in the room. Task lighting provides more illumination for tasks that will take place in the room, whether it be reading, cooking, or sewing. Most rooms need both types of lighting, although sometimes ambient and task lighting can be provided by a single source.

Ambient Lighting

Every area needs a general source of light for just getting around without bumping into walls. The best ambient lighting scheme also creates the mood you seek. Think about your favorite restaurant. How much of the special mood was created by effective lighting? The lighting probably had a lot to do with the mood, but because it was sensitively done, you didn't notice it. The sun can provide most of your ambient lighting during the day if you locate windows and skylights with that in mind. Backup and night lighting can come from direct, indirect, or combined sources. A ceiling fixture that throws its light downward is an

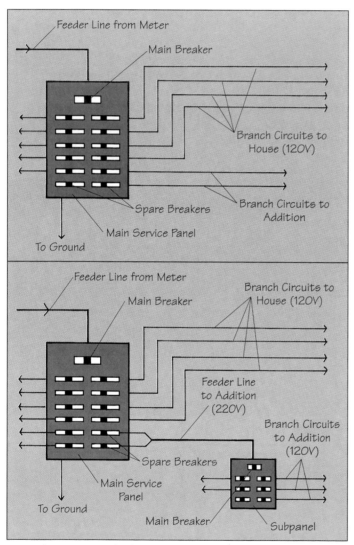

Drawing 8-18 *The house's main service panel may have enough spare circuits to power the addition. If so, each new 120-volt branch circuit will require a separate supply cable from a spare breaker at the panel (top). If the existing service panel doesn't have enough spare breakers or if the addition is too far from the main panel to make separate branch circuit runs practical, you can tap off two 120-volt breakers with a 220-volt supply that feeds a new subpanel located in the addition. The feeder cable contains two hot wires and neutral and ground wires. The subpanel should be sized to carry the quantity of branch circuits required for the addition. Some local codes require branch panels to have a main breaker switch, as shown here on the bottom.*

example of direct lighting. A lamp that illuminates the ceiling, which in turn diffuses the light to the room, exemplifies indirect lighting—a softer light that promotes relaxation. Some fixtures throw light both up and down, combining direct with indirect light. Often, they can be switched to select one or the other.

Task Lighting

Reading, writing, or any other focused work requires more light at the work area than you need for general vision. Task lighting can be fixed, such as below wall cabinets to illuminate a kitchen counter, or portable, such as a desk lamp. Another type of task lighting—accent lighting—is used to draw attention to specific objects such as a painting on a wall.

In this kitchen, fixtures built into the soffits over the cabinets provide ambient lighting by bouncing light off the ceiling. Task lighting for the counter is provided by fixtures under the cabinets while pendants provide task lighting for the island.

Light Sources

To get the lighting quality you want at each point of delivery, you need to select both a bulb (professionals call them lamps) and a fixture to hold and direct its light. Choosing a lamp in the past boiled down to matching the wattage of an incandescent bulb to a particular application. The warm, friendly color and universality of incandescent lamps still make this type the most preferred for applications in homes, but incandescent lamps use a lot of energy, much of it wasted as heat. Other recent types offer much better energy efficiency, but all do not equally suit every application.

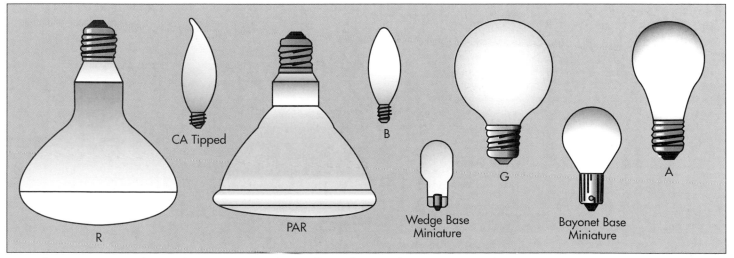

CA Tipped

B

R

PAR

Wedge Base Miniature

G

Bayonet Base Miniature

A

Drawing 8-19 *Incandescent lamps are somewhat inefficient but are also inexpensive. They come in many shapes and wattages. Bulbs that have a screw-in base include the standard A and G (globe) bulbs. R (reflector) and PAR (parabolic reflector) lamps are used in spot and floodlight fixtures. B and CA-tipped bulbs are used in decorative applications. Miniature bayonet- and wedge-base bulbs work off a transformer that steps the voltage down to 12 volts. Miniature lamps are used for accent locations.*

Fluorescent lamps provide up to five times as much light for the same power as incandescent, and they last longer, which is why they are ubiquitous in offices, stores, and factories. Until recently, though, fluorescent lamps threw a cold, bluish light that made skin look dead and turned red meat gray. That's why you didn't see them in homes and restaurants. Also, they were available only in long straight or circular tubes, neither of which fit well into residential lighting fixtures. But that's all changing. The newer compact fluorescents come close to the warm color of incandescents and are available in shapes that fit into many common household fixtures.

Halogen lamps, the newest type, use a tungsten-based filament surrounded by gas to achieve a bright, white light within a small bulb. Halogen lamps are available in reflectorized bulbs for focused lighting and in tiny tubes for accent lighting. The PAR types have screw-in bases for use in any 120-volt fixture. The bi-pin and MR halogen lamps must be wired to 12-volt transformers that, in turn, connect to the 120-volt house wiring.

Matching Fixtures to Applications

Visiting a well-supplied lighting showroom is like walking through a jungle. Fixtures of every conceivable shape and style hang from the ceiling or off the walls. To avoid being overwhelmed when choosing your lighting from this confusing array, set your lighting goals for each new room, then have in mind the general type of fixture you want. Here are some things to think about for different areas.

Family, living, and entertainment rooms. You don't want to look up into a bright light source while relaxed in a sitting position. Indirect lighting in the form of cove lights or spots that throw light onto a wall provide ambient lighting that is out of direct view. If the room is used for viewing TV or videos, consider putting the ambient lighting on a dimmer switch. Track lighting or fixed spots can add special interest at focal points along the walls. You can also use this type of lighting above activity areas, such as pool or table-tennis tables. Portable floor or table lamps provide flexible task lighting in these rooms.

Drawing 8-20 *Fluorescent lamps use as little as one-third the energy of incandescents. Today's fluorescents have excellent color rendition, and some can be screwed into standard screw-in fixture sockets. Fluorescents are best used where they will be left on for long periods.*

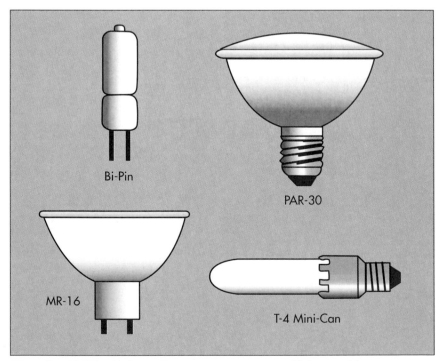

Drawing 8-21 *Halogen lamps are more energy efficient and have more precise beam control than incandescents. Low-voltage types like the bi-pin and MR-16 require a transformer to reduce the voltage to 12 volts. The MR-16 and PAR-30 have built-in reflectors for spotlight applications. Bi-pin and T-4 mini-can bulbs are used in multiples for accent lighting.*

Spot lighting provides illumination exactly where needed. Here, spots provide light for the entertainment center components, highlight a picture, and make it easy to read the titles on the bookshelf.

Dining rooms. If there will be a designated position for the dining table, a chandelier centered on the table can be a source of both task and ambient lighting. Recessed lamps around the edges can provide supplemental ambient light in a large dining room. If your dining room contains a hutch or china cabinet, you can feature it by mounting track or spots on the ceiling above. Accent the china inside with minihalogen lamps. Consider switching all dining-room lighting to a dimmer so that you can vary the mood.

Kitchens. First, what not to do. Don't mount a single ceiling fixture in the center of the room where it will guarantee a shadow on the countertop, no matter where you stand. Put the light where you need it. Recessed or surface-mounted cylinders around the edges of the ceiling can provide ambient lighting as well as task lighting for the countertop. You can add more task light in the form of strip fluorescent fixtures concealed under the wall cabinets above the countertop.

Baths. A single, ceiling-mounted fixture is inefficient for baths. Since bathrooms are usually small, you will probably get enough ambient light from the task lighting at each activity center. The goal at the vanity and sink area is to light your face, not the mirror. A variety of fixtures can be mounted at the sides of or above the

"Hollywood" lights surrounding bathroom mirrors are an ideal way to provide light for grooming.

The Color of Light

Cool lighting makes salad greens look fresh and inviting, but it makes red meat look gray. The lighting that makes meat look appealing browns a salad. Lighting color varies with the source and dramatically affects our response to our environment. We measure this quality in degrees Kelvin, even though this rating is not the actual heat temperature. Lamps with a color temperature above 3600K are too cool for most rooms in homes, except, maybe, the basement or garage. Warm-temperature lamps, below 3400K, create a friendly, intimate environment and enhance the color of skin. Even if they don't show off your salad to its best, it is the best all-round color light for the living areas in your addition. Incandescent lamps always emit warm light. Halogen light is slightly cooler. Fluorescent lamps are available in all color ranges. Usually, it's best not to mix lamp colors in the same room.

mirror to do the job. In the shower, consider using a recessed ceiling fixture rated for wet-area use or an exhaust fan that contains a lamp. If the toilet is enclosed, provide a ceiling lamp above the stall area.

Bedrooms. For bedrooms, softness should rule the ambient lighting, from recessed ceiling fixtures to cove lighting or wall sconces. Wire the ambient lighting to a

Ceiling cove fixtures provide soft yet dramatic lighting for this bedroom.

dimmer for greater control. For task lighting, you can mount fixed sources above the bed or use adjustable table lamps at the sides for more flexibility.

Home offices. Consider first the effect you want: how much formality you want and how much you want the space to feel like an office rather than a study. Ceiling-mounted fluorescent fixtures promote an office mood as well as provide all-round lighting for most tasks. But with more office work done on computers, the glare and reflections of overhead lighting can actually be a liability. Consider wall-mounted sconces instead—or, if wall space is scarce, a few recessed ceiling spots around the edges. For task lighting, it's hard to beat swivel desk lamps for portability and control.

Wiring Lighting Fixtures

Each lighting fixture on your plan requires a power source and a method of switching. The switch can be in line, between the power source and the fixture, or on a separate loop from the fixture. It can be a simple on-off switch or a two- or three-way switch that allows you to control a fixture at two or three different locations, such as you might want at the bottom and top of a stairway. You can even wire certain items together. In a household with small children, for example, it's fairly common to connect a bathroom exhaust fan to the light switch so that the fan automatically goes on with the light. The electrical plan shown in Drawing 8-17, for example, controls the lighting in the screened-in porch from both the bedroom and office by way of a three-way switch in each room.

Chapter 9

BUILDING THE ADDITION

Your home not only is where you live but is most likely your single largest investment. It's normal that any alteration to it may cause you some amount of worry. Your concern is justified. In the real world, things can and do go wrong. The construction work can upset your household's routine. Delays, glitches, and cost overruns can sour the experience and rob you of the satisfaction of seeing your dream take physical shape. But all these problems can be minimized or avoided if you know what to expect, maintain a positive attitude, and plan carefully. Knowing what to expect begins with

planning your family's routine for the anticipated disruptions. Remodeling an existing kitchen or bath might require major adjustments, while an addition that is separate from the house may be only a minor inconvenience. This chapter will help you plan for the turns in the road ahead by telling you what plans and specifications you'll need, the basics of construction contracts, and tips for finding and working with contractors.

CONTRACT DOCUMENTS

Your preliminary floor plan and exterior elevations show how the addition will look. They do not show or tell how it is to be built. That information is conveyed by working drawings—or plans—and specifications. A good set of these "contract documents" is necessary to secure accurate bids and a building permit and to serve as a road map for whoever constructs the project.

Working Drawings

Even minor additions need to be described sufficiently to build them. If you build the project yourself, you will naturally need far less information in the form of written plans and specifications than if you hire a contractor (assuming that you have worked out all of the kinks). Remember, though, you'll still need a set of drawings to apply for a building permit. If you want to prepare your own working drawings, you should start with a basic understanding of the techniques and conventions for architectural drafting. Look through books on drafting and borrow a good set of plans from a builder or architect. Or you can hire a drafting or plan service to produce a set based on your preliminary drawings or ideas. If an architect did the preliminary design, it

makes sense to have him or her make the working drawings. A basic set for an addition should include the drawings mentioned on the following pages. Check with your building department to make sure your set of working drawings will include everything required to obtain a building permit.

Site plan. The site plan shows how the addition joins the house and how it fits on the property. Basic information will show dimensions from the house and other structures to the property lines. Lines showing the required setbacks from property lines indicate that the project conforms to the zoning ordinance or that a variance is required. Your site plan should also show any power, water, sewer, gas, or telephone lines in the area near the

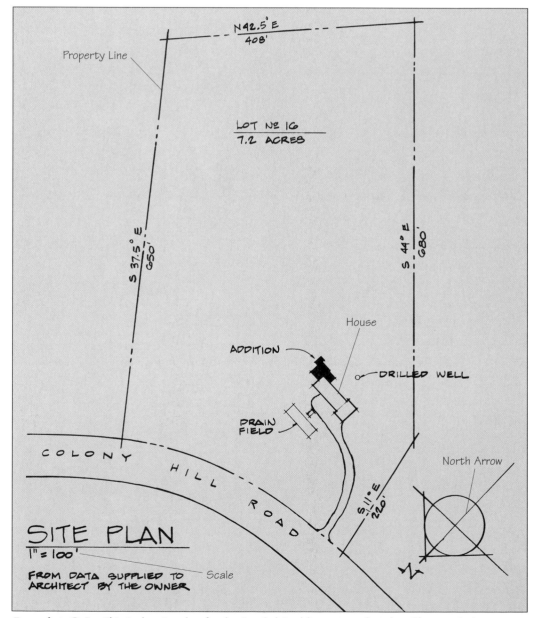

Drawing 9-1 *This is the site plan for the Frankels' addition, introduced in Chapter 4. A septic tank and a drain field dispose of sewage, and a drilled well is the source of water. On an urban lot, sewer and water pipes would be shown running out to connect with lines in the street.*

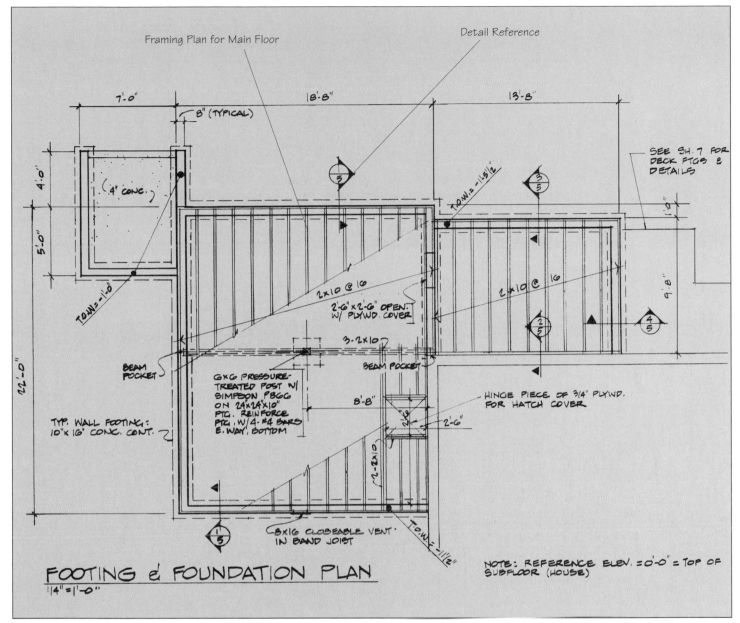

Framing Plan for Main Floor

Detail Reference

7'-0"   18'-8"   13'-8"

8" (TYPICAL)

SEE SH. 7 FOR
DECK FTGS &
DETAILS

4'-0"

(4" CONC.)

5'-0"

T.O.W.=-1'-0"

T.O.W.=-1'-5½"

2×10 @ 16

2×10 @ 16

2'-6"×2'-6" OPEN.
W/ PLYWD. COVER

BEAM
POCKET

3-2×10

BEAM POCKET

22'-0"

6×6 PRESSURE-
TREATED POST W/
SIMPSON PB66
ON 24×24×10"
FTG. REINFORCE
FTG. W/ 4-#4 BARS
E. WAY, BOTTOM

8'-8"

HINGE PIECE OF ¾" PLYWD.
FOR HATCH COVER

2'-6"

TYP. WALL FOOTING:
10"×16" CONC. CONT.

2-2×10

8×16 CLOSEABLE VENT
IN BAND JOIST

T.O.W.=-1'1½"

NOTE: REFERENCE ELEV. =0'-0" = TOP OF
SUBFLOOR (HOUSE)

FOOTING & FOUNDATION PLAN
¼"=1'-0"

Drawing 9-2 *The Frankels' addition sits above a crawl space, instead of a full basement. Floor framing for the main floor was shown on this drawing rather than a separate one.*

addition. Site plans are drawn at much smaller scales than building drawings, and the scales are based on tenths of an inch, rather than multiples of sixteenths of an inch. Common scales for site plans are: 1 inch = 10, 20, 30, 40, or 50 feet. An engineer's scale is the tool used for these ratios. The scale is similar to an architect's scale, except for one major difference. Because 1 foot is so small on an engineer's scale, a portion of it is not subdivided into inches at one end of the scale.

Basement, foundation, and footing plan. At the core of your set of drawings are several plans that represent horizontal slices through the addition at different levels. The lowest of these cuts through the foundation walls, which are shown as solid lines.

Dashed lines inside and outside the foundation lines represent the footings. If the footings have to drop up or down to accommodate a sloping site, the point of drop, or "step," is shown by a line crossing through the footing. The floor framing for the floor above the basement might be shown as dashed lines on this plan, unless it is complicated enough to require a separate drawing. Other items that can be shown on this drawing include the ductwork or piping layout for plumbing, heating, and electrical systems if these will not be shown in a separate drawing.

Floor plans. Subsequent horizontal slices through the addition cut through each floor level. All interior and exterior walls are first drawn in and dimensioned. Stairways come next, followed by windows and doors.

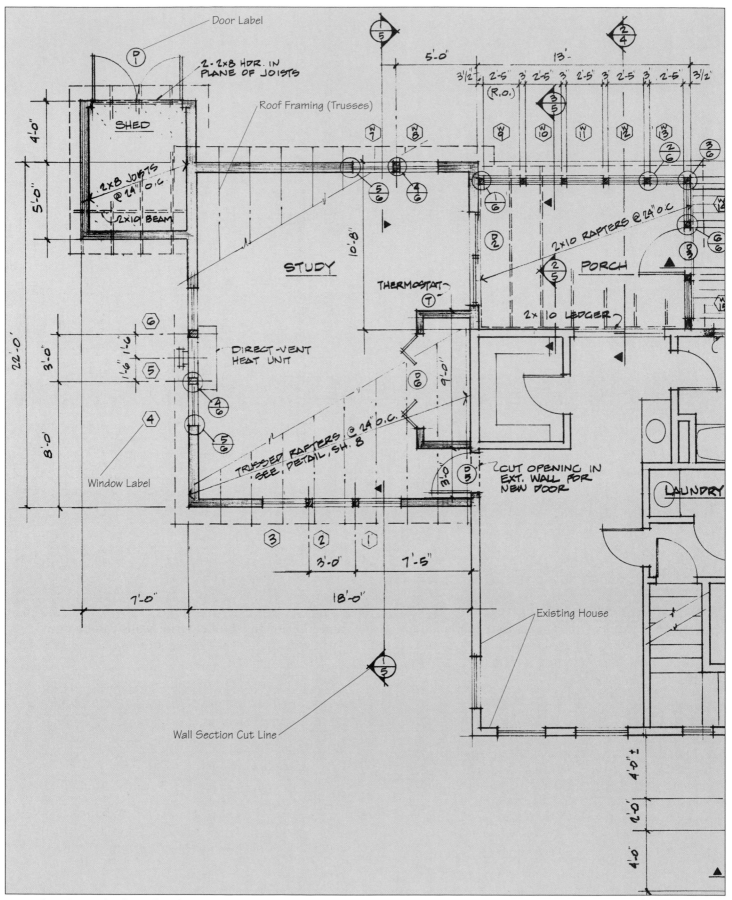

Drawing 9-3 *The floor plan shows the walls of the main level. Roof framing for this project was simple enough to be overlaid on the floor plan rather than on a separate drawing.*

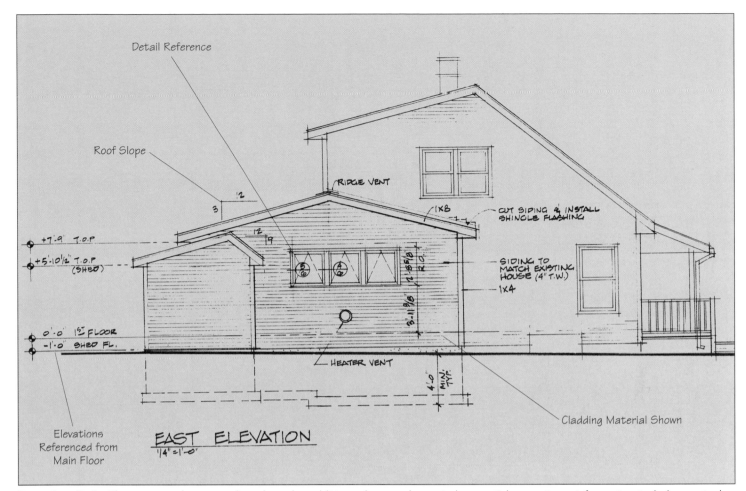

Labels on drawing:
Detail Reference
Roof Slope
RIDGE VENT
1x8
CUT SIDING & INSTALL SHINGLE FLASHING
SIDING TO MATCH EXISTING HOUSE (4" T.W.)
1x4
+7'-9" T.O.P
+5'-10½" T.O.P (SHED)
0'-0" 1ST FLOOR
-1'-0" SHED FL.
12 / 9
12 / 3
HEATER VENT
4'-0" MIN. TYP.
Elevations Referenced from Main Floor
Cladding Material Shown

EAST ELEVATION
¼"=1'-0"

Drawing 9-4 *The exterior elevations show how the addition relates to the main house. Other pertinent information includes vertical dimensions, roof slopes, and references to details.*

Each window and door can be identified by size and type right on the plan or tagged with a code that refers to a separate schedule. Other features, such as fireplaces and built-in cabinetry, round out the plan. Room finishes can be noted on the plan or listed in a separate schedule. Other items that can be added to the plan or shown separately include the structural framing for the next level up (such as a second floor or roof) and the location of electrical outlets and lighting fixtures.

Exterior elevations. The working drawing set should include one head-on view, or elevation, of each facade, showing all pertinent features—windows, doors, siding, and roof lines, with their vertical dimensions referenced off horizontal lines at each floor level and with notes to indicate finish materials. The slope of roofs should be shown on any elevation that pictures the slope, such as a gable-end view. It is also common to indicate the opening direction of windows and doors.

Cross sections. A good cross section through the entire addition shows more about how the parts of the project fit together than any other single drawing. Whereas the plans slice through the structure

horizontally, sections cut vertically to show how walls, floors, and roofs all fit together. Horizontal dimensions are rarely shown on cross sections, but vertical dimensions referenced off the floor lines are always necessary. The siding, structure, insulation, and interior finish of exterior walls can be noted here, or they can be left to another section or detail drawn at larger scale.

The more complicated the project, the more drawings are required to explain it adequately. The following are some of the drawings that might better stand alone rather than be overlaid onto another.

Floor- or roof-framing plans. The floor plans for even simple additions often get cluttered with other data, making a separate framing plan worthwhile. A floor- or roof-framing plan usually overlays the structural members of a particular level on the walls and support of the level just below. The second-floor framing plan, for example, would be drawn onto the first-floor plan.

Wall sections. If more detail is needed than your cross section provides, a series of wall sections drawn at larger scale can answer the call. The larger scale allows for more detail and better notation.

Details. Your addition may contain several items needing more clarification than plans or sections offer—particularly if the items go together in a unique manner. Windows, doors, porches, decks, cabinetry, mantels, fireplaces, and any special construction details are among the items that might need to be drawn separately at large scale. To get an idea of the proper scale, refer to the table "Common Scales for Working Drawings," on page 181.

Schedules. When windows and doors can't adequately be described on other drawings, they are coded and listed in a schedule, as shown in "Window Schedule (Partial)" and "Door Schedule (Partial)," on page 182. Sizes given for width and height are usually the dimensions of the rough opening.

Room finishes for a simple addition can be shown right on the floor plans. A separate finish schedule for a more extensive addition might look something like that shown in "Finish Schedule," on page 182.

Plumbing and heating plan. Any heating system more complicated than a single unit heater or wood stove probably needs to be shown somewhere to avoid conflicts with other elements, such as structural framing. Ducts or heating piping can be overlaid onto the floor plans, but this can get messy. You can avoid the confusion with a separate heating system plan. There is usually more latitude for running pipes for plumbing, so you may not need a plumbing plan. If you do your own plumbing, though, you should have a three-dimensional diagram, as discussed in Chapter 4, beginning on page 55.

Electrical layout. Your lighting and power systems constantly affect the interior environment. That's why Chapter 8 suggested that you be heavily involved in their planning. The working drawings needed to describe electrical systems depend on their complexity and who does the work. Lighting fixtures, electrical outlets, and switches drawn right on the floor plan might suffice for a simple, straightforward project. The electrician will have to figure out the circuiting, but that's not unusual. If the systems are more complicated—three- and four-way switching, for example—a separate power and lighting plan makes better sense. This plan should

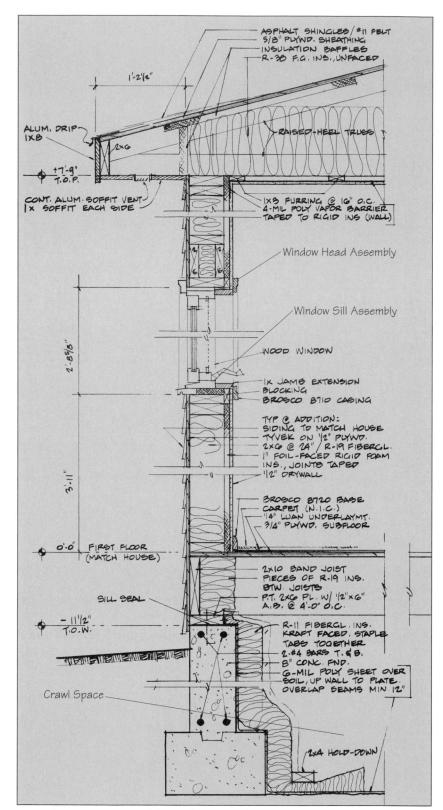

Drawing 9-5 *One of the wall sections for the Frankels' addition, this one was cut through a window of a typical exterior wall, showing the crawl space, main level, and roof.*

show every device, outlet, and type of switch, and how the devices are circuited for power. A lighting fixture schedule is often included, listing the type of each lighting fixture with the appropriate lamps.

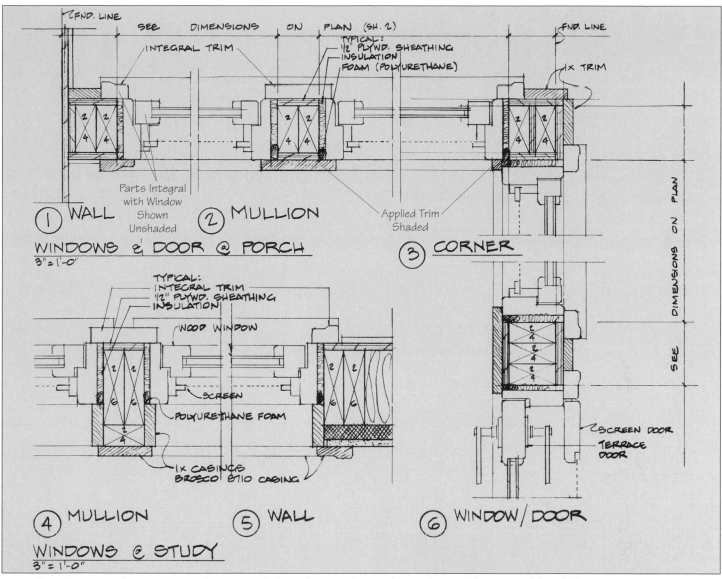

Drawing 9-6 *Detail drawings pin down exactly how the parts fit together so that as little as possible is left to chance.*

Specifications

Working drawings show graphically how the various parts of the addition go together. Specifications complete the picture, with specific information about the parts themselves and how they are to be installed. The shapes, sizes, and location of concrete work, for example, will show up on the drawings as footings, foundations, walks, and driveways. The specifications might spell out the type of concrete required for each use, type of reinforcement, strength, and finishes. Conformance to industry

COMMON SCALES FOR WORKING DRAWINGS

Drawing	Scales (in order of preference)
Site plan	1"=20', 1"=30',1"=40', 1"=50'
Floor plans	¼"=1'–0", ⅛"=1'–0"
Exterior elevations	¼"=1'–0"
Cross section	¼"=1'–0"
Framing plans	¼"=1'–0", ½"=1'–0"
Wall sections	¾"=1'–0", 1"=1'–0", 1½"=1'–0"
Details	3"=1'–0", 1½"=1'–0"
Window and door schedules	¼"=1'–0" (for depictions of each type of window or door)
Plumbing and heating plan	¼"=1'–0"
Electrical layout	¼"=1'–0"

WINDOW SCHEDULE (PARTIAL)

Mark	Type	Width	Height	Notes
W-1	A	2'-9"	2'-8⅝"	Flat trim on right side
W-2	A	2'-9"	2'-8⅝"	Flat trim both sides
W-3	B	2'-9"	2'-8⅝"	Flat trim on left side
W-4	B	2'-5"	4'-8⅝"	Flat trim on left side
W-5	C	2'-6⅜"	4'-1⅝"	Trim to match existing unit

DOOR SCHEDULE (PARTIAL)

Mark	Type	Width	Height	Thickness	Notes
D-1	AA	6'-2"	6'-10½"	1¾"	Pair hinged doors
D-2	BB	6'-2"	6'-10"	——	Sliding-glass door
D-3	CC	2'-11"	6'-8"	1¾"	Wood/glass terrace door
D-4	DD	2'-8"	6'-9"	1⅜"	Wood panel door
D-5	EE	6'-2"	6'-9"	1⅜"	Pair bifold doors

FINISH SCHEDULE

Room Name	Floor	Base	Walls	Ceiling	Notes
Basement	F1	B1	W1	C1	
Mud room	F2	B2	W2	C2	
Kitchen	F3	B2	W2	C2*	*Also in skylight shaft
Great room	F4	B3	W2	C2	
Bath 1	F5	B4	W3, W4*	C2	*See plan for walls to receive ceramic tile
Bath 2	F5	B4	W3, W4*	C2	*See plan for walls to receive ceramic tile
Bedroom	F6	B2	W2	C2	
Closets	F6	B2	W2	C2	
Garage	F1	B1	W2*	C1	*Insulate walls

KEY:
F1–Exposed concrete slab, no finish
F2–Quarry tile thinset on plywood subfloor
F3–Sheet vinyl over plywood subfloor
F4–¾" oak strip flooring
F5–Ceramic tile, thinset on plywood
F6–Carpet and pad over plywood

B1–No base
B2–4" pine, painted
B3–4" oak, natural finish
B4–Ceramic tile
W1–Unfinished concrete
W2–Drywall, ½", painted

W3–Ceramic tile over drywall
W4–Ceramic tile over backer board
C1–Exposed framing
C2–Drywall, ½", painted

standards, such as the American Concrete Institute, are often cited. Detailed specifications leave as little as possible to the person who orders and installs the items. Every material is described, either by an acceptable range of products or by a specific brand. Where the drawings call for "bevel siding," the specifications will describe the type, such as "number one grade select red cedar." Materials for which industry standards have been set can be referenced by the appropriate standard. Asphalt shingles, for example, can be described as "Class A, 235 pounds per square." If you have your sights set on a particular product, you can lock that one in by calling for "Acme, Homestead Series fiberglass shingles."

A complete set of specifications begins with a "boilerplate" section that spells out general requirements for the project.

Your responsibilities as owner of the project are spelled out, as well as those of the contractor and architect (if you have one). Insurance, payment provisions, and how changes are to be handled are also in this section. The following are detailed specifications for each category of work. The construction industry recognizes a standard format containing 16 divisions, as shown below in "Standard Architectural Specifications Format."

Do you need all this? Yes—at least the information. If you do everything yourself, you can call the shots as you see fit. If you have a general contractor bid the project, the more completely the project is spelled out, the more accurate the bid you'll get and the fewer surprises during construction. The specifications for a simple project can be brief, though. Specs can be typed up on standard paper or written on the last sheet of the set of drawings.

THE CONSTRUCTION PHASE

Maybe you can't wait to bang the first nail. Or you may be just as happy leaving town until the windows are cleaned. The extent of your involvement with the construction phase is up to you. Your time, interests, and abilities can help you decide how to get the project from lines on paper to reality. But building an addition requires more than putting pieces together. Whoever is in charge of the process must competently manage people as well as supplies, materials, and construction. He or she will have to

▲ Make a project schedule to plan the orderly progress of the work. This can be a bar chart that shows the time period of activity by each trade.

▲ Establish a budget for each category of work, such as foundation, framing, and finish carpentry.

STANDARD ARCHITECTURAL SPECIFICATIONS FORMAT

Division	Heading	Typical Content Topics
1	General requirements	Payments, coordination, warranties, bonds, insurance
2	Sitework	Demolition, excavation, paving, landscaping, utilities
3	Concrete	Formwork, foundations, footings, slabs
4	Masonry	Brick, stone, concrete block
5	Metals	Structural steel, steel joists, metal railings
6	Wood and plastics	Framing, engineered lumber, finish carpentry, paneling
7	Thermal and moisture protection	Waterproofing, moisture proofing, roofing, insulation, flashing, skylights, caulking
8	Doors and windows	All door and window types except skylights
9	Finishes	Drywall, plaster, floorcoverings, wallcoverings, painting
10	Specialties	Medicine cabinets, bathroom accessories
11	Equipment	Central vacuum systems, prefabricated cabinets, appliances
12	Furnishings	Fireplace accessories, window blinds and accessories
13	Special construction	Saunas
14	Conveying systems	Elevators, dumbwaiters, chutes, chair lifts
15	Mechanical	Heating, cooling, ventilation, plumbing
16	Electrical	Power, lighting, fire alarm systems

▲ Arrange for a source of construction financing.

▲ Get a building permit and post it conspicuously at the construction site.

▲ Line up a supply source and order materials.

▲ Find subcontractors and negotiate their contracts.

▲ Coordinate the work so that it progresses smoothly with the fewest conflicts.

▲ Notify inspectors at the appropriate milestones.

▲ Make payments to suppliers and subcontractors.

YOU AS GENERAL CONTRACTOR

You'll have to take care of every logistical detail yourself if you decide to act as your own general contractor. But along with the responsibilities of managing the project, you gain the flexibility to do as much of your own work as you want and subcontract out the rest. Before taking this path, however, be sure you have the time and capabilities. You probably already have a pretty good idea of your construction skills. Do you also have the time and ability to schedule the work, hire and coordinate subs, order materials, and keep ahead of the accounting required to manage the project successfully? If you do, you stand to save the amount that a general contractor would charge to take on these responsibilities, normally 15 to 30 percent of the construction cost. If you take this responsibility on but mismanage the project, the potential savings will erode and may even cost you more than if you had hired a general contractor in the first place. A subcontractor might charge extra for having to return to the site to complete work that was originally scheduled for a single time period. Or perhaps because you didn't order the windows at the beginning, you now have to pay for a recent cost increase. (If you hired a general contractor, he or she—not you—would have to absorb unexpected price increases.)

Managing even a small addition project may require coordinating up to six different subcontractors. Before taking on the responsibility, carefully evaluate your personal attributes. Make sure you will have the time, patience, and talent required. Involve other members of the household in the key decisions. Beyond their actual contribution to the work, bringing them in will make them a part of the process. The experience can be educational and satisfying to all. Take care, though, to create and maintain a single line of communication between you and your subcontractors. The potential for conflicts and confusion increases if more than one party deals with subcontractors.

When you act as your own general contractor, you first have to find subcontractors (subs), then negotiate and contract for their services. This process is similar to finding and hiring a general contractor (discussed below). But instead of turning the management of the project over to someone else, you'll have to schedule the work of each sub, coordinate it with other subs, and pay each one separately. The paperwork required to do all this efficiently can be daunting for even a small project, but it's still necessary. Get everything in writing, and create a system for filing data. A three-ring binder works well because the papers are all together, but you can add and subtract papers indefinitely.

Use the advice of your subs when creating your project schedule. Subs know what other work must be in place before they can begin and how their work affects that which follows. Subcontractors can also help you plan the construction sequence around the weather. In general, you should aim to get the exterior walls and roof up as quickly as possible. With the weatherskin intact, most other trades can proceed.

Your contract with each sub should spell out pertinent details of your arrangement. (See "Contract Content," beginning on page 185.) Make sure the scope of the sub's work is carefully spelled out as well as how payments are to be made. Also determine whether the sub has a worker's compensation policy to cover his or her employees. If not, you must secure coverage from your own insurer.

Pay subs only when you are satisfied with the work they have completed. Work that is completed all at one time, such as drywall, should be paid in full at completion (minus the 10 percent retainage, if any, as described under "Working with Your Contractor," page 186). Work that has to be phased should be paid for in installments. For example, a plumber should receive one payment after installing piping in the walls and floors (the "rough-in") and another after installing and hooking up the fixtures.

ENTRUSTING CONSTRUCTION TO A GENERAL CONTRACTOR

A general contractor will manage every aspect of the construction process. Your role after signing the construction contract will be to make regular progress payments and ensure that the work you are paying for has been completed. You will also consult with the contractor and agree to any changes that may have to be made along the way. If you retain an architect's services through the construction phase, the architect's services will normally include approving the contractor's payment requests and processing change orders.

Your architect may be able to help you find candidate contractors. Other leads might come from friends or neighbors who have had contractors build, remodel, or add to their homes. Real-estate agents and bankers may have some names handy but are more likely familiar with the contractor's ability to complete projects on time and budget than the quality of the work itself. The National Association of Remodeling Industry (NARI) can refer you to member contractors in your area. Call NARI headquarters at 800-440-6274 to get your local chapter's number.

The next step is to narrow your list of candidates to three or four who you think can do a quality job and work harmoniously with you. Phone each contractor to see whether he or she is interested in being considered for your project. If so, invite the contractor to an interview at your home. The meeting will serve two purposes. You'll be able to ask the candidate about his or her past work, and you'll be able to see whether your personalities are compatible. The contractor will have an opportunity to look over the contract documents and inspect the actual construction site as well as to feel you out about your expectations of time and costs—and how decisions will be made. Don't be afraid to ask "dumb" questions; that's how you learn. Ask how long the contractor has been in business and get names and phone numbers of a few prior clients. Ask the contractors how they handle complaints. Have they failed to complete any project? If so, why? Do they have any lawsuits or legal proceedings outstanding against them? After the meeting, call the referenced clients to ask about their experience working with the contractor. Would they do so again?

With a short list of capable contractors in hand, you will have to decide what type of construction contract best fits your project and financial needs. The two most-used types are lump-sum contracts and cost-plus-fee contracts.

Lump-Sum Contracts

A lump-sum, or fixed-fee, contract lets you know from the beginning just what the project will cost, barring any changes made because of your requests or unforeseen conditions. This form works well for projects that promise few surprises and are well defined from the outset by a complete set of contract documents. You can enter into a fixed-price contract by negotiating with a single contractor on your short list or by obtaining bids from three or four contractors. If you go the latter route, give each bidder a set of documents and allow at least two weeks for them to submit their bids. When you get the bids, decide who you want and call the others to thank them for their efforts. You don't have to accept the lowest bid, but it probably makes sense to since you have already

honed the list to contractors you trust. Inform this contractor of your intentions to finalize a contract.

Cost-Plus-Fee Contracts

Under a cost-plus-fee contract, you agree to pay the contractor for the costs of labor and materials, as verified by receipts, plus a fee that represents the contractor's overhead and profit. This arrangement is sometimes referred to as "time and materials." The fee can range between 15 and 30 percent of the incurred costs. Because you ultimately pick up the tab—whatever the costs—the contractor is never at risk, as he is with a lump-sum contract. You won't know the final total cost of a cost-plus-fee contract until the project is built and paid for. If you can live with that uncertainty, there are offsetting advantages. First, this form allows you to accommodate unknown conditions much more easily than does a lump-sum contract. And rather than being tied down by the project documents, you will be free to make changes at any point along the way. This can be a trap, though. Watching the project take shape will spark the desire to add something or do something differently. Each change costs, and the accumulation can easily exceed your budget. Because of the uncertainty of the final tab and the built-in advantage to the contractor, you should think twice before entering into this form of contract.

Contract Content

The conditions of your agreement should be spelled out thoroughly in writing and signed by both parties, whatever contractual arrangement you make with your contractor. Your contract should include provisions for the following:

▲ The names and addresses of the owner and contractor.

▲ A description of the work to be included ("As described in the plans and specifications dated . . .").

▲ The date the work will be completed if time is of the essence.

▲ The contract price for lump-sum contracts and the contractor's allowed profit and overhead costs for changes.

▲ The contractor's fee for cost-plus-fee contracts and the method of accounting and requesting payment.

▲ The criteria for progress payments (monthly, by project milestones) and the conditions of final payment.

- A list of each drawing and specification section that is to be included as part of the contract.

- Requirements for guarantees. (One year is the standard period for which contractors guarantee the entire project, but you may require specific guarantees on parts of the project, such as a 20-year guarantee on the roofing.)

- Provisions for insurance.

- A description of how changes in the work orders will be handled.

The contractor may have a standard contract you can tailor to the specifics of your project. Your architect, if you retain one, will probably suggest the Abbreviated Form of Agreement between Owner and Contractor, published by the American Institute of Architects. Version A107 is written for lump-sum contracts and version A117 for cost-plus-fee contracts. Both of these contain complete specific conditions with blanks you can fill in to fit your project and a set of "general conditions" that cover a host of issues from insurance to termination provisions. It's always a good idea to have an attorney review the draft of your completed contract before signing it.

Working with Your Contractor

The construction phase officially begins when you have a signed copy of the contract and copies of any insurance required from the contractor. Early on, the contractor should submit a schedule of values that breaks the construction cost down into subcategories by trade. When updated each month to show the percentage of completion for each category, the schedule of values serves as the basis of progress payments. It's not unheard of for a contractor to request an initial payment of 10 to 20 percent of the total cost to cover mobilization costs, those costs associated with obtaining permits and getting set up to begin the actual construction work. If you agree to this, keep a careful eye on the progress of the work to ensure that the total paid out at any one time doesn't get too far out of synch with the actual work completed. To protect yourself, you can include a clause in the contract to withhold 10 percent from each payment request until the end of the project (retainage). Monitoring the progress of the work with respect to the contractor's payments is the architect's responsibility if you retain one throughout the construction phase.

What about changes? From here on, it's up to you and your contractor to proceed in good faith and to keep the channels of communication open. Even so, changes of one sort or another beset every project, and they usually add to the cost of the project. In a cost-plus-fee contract, the cost is accounted for in the same way as any other item of work. In a lump-sum contract, you need to agree on a cost with the contractor then describe the change in a written change order, which also spells out the cost of the change and additional time, if any, to be allowed.

Light at the end of the tunnel. The contractor's request for a final inspection marks the end of the construction phase—almost. At the final inspection meeting, you, the contractor, and your architect (if you have one) will inspect the work, noting any defects or incomplete items on a "punch list." When the contractor tidies up the punch list items, you should reinspect to confirm or reject the corrections. Sometimes, contractors go on to another job and take forever to clean up the last few details, so only after all items on the list have been completed satisfactorily should you release the retainage.

SOME FINAL WORDS

This chapter began by suggesting that your attitude is as important as any external arrangements you make at the outset of the construction phase. A positive attitude can help you not only ride out the rigors of remodeling but get you the satisfaction you have worked so hard for.

Stay flexible. Expect problems because they certainly will occur. Weather can upset a schedule. An unexpected pipe may surprise you during excavation. The new construction might not align with the old where it was supposed to. Just as certain, every problem that comes along has a solution if you are open to it.

Be patient. The few extra days it may take to resolve a construction problem will be forgotten soon after the project is completed.

Express yourself. If what you see isn't exactly what you thought you were getting, don't be afraid to look into changing it. Or you may spot an unforeseen opportunity for an improvement. Changes usually cost, though, so don't make frivolous changes.

Finally, watching your addition go up is exciting, so stay upbeat. Get away from your project from time to time. Dine out. Take time to relax. A positive attitude will make for smoother relations with your contractor. An optimistic outlook will yield better-quality work if you are doing your own construction. And though the project might seem endless while it is under way, keep in mind that all the planning and construction will fade to a faint memory at some time in the future, and you will be getting a lifetime of pleasure from an addition that is just right for you.

Glossary

Construction terminology can be confusing. A "sill plate" in one area can be a "sole plate" in another. The following terms are defined according to the meanings commonly used, as the author understands them.

Astragal A vertical strip attached to the opening edge of one door in a pair, forming a jamb for the other door to close into.

Band Joist The joist that forms the outside perimeter of a floor framing system (also called rim joist).

Blueprint Any of the prints made by the Ozalid process (the image can be blue, black, or brown).

Bond The pattern in which bricks or other masonry units are laid up.

BtuH British thermal units per hour, a yardstick of heating and cooling capacity of equipment.

Cathedral Ceiling Any ceiling, flat or sloped, that attaches to the underside of the roof framing with no attic space above.

Collar Tie A cross member between two opposing rafters used to keep them from spreading apart.

Coping A method of joining two intersecting pieces in which the end of one piece is cut to fit the profile of the side of the other piece.

Cornice The trim where the exterior wall of a building meets the roof.

Dormer A structure that increases the useful height of a portion of an attic. Shed dormers have flat roofs that slope downward from the main roof but at a lesser pitch so that the bottom end is higher than the adjoining roof. A gable or doghouse dormer has a double-pitched roof that intersects the house roof at right angles.

Drywall A surface material consisting of a gypsum core sandwiched between paper.

Eaves The entire roof assembly that overhangs the sidewall.

Emissivity The ability of a material to emit heat. Black iron has high emissivity, while aluminum foil has a low emissivity.

Fascia The vertical trim piece (or face) of the eaves.

Flange The top or bottom of a joist or beam.

Footings Pads or strips of sufficient size and strength to transfer the load of the building safely to the ground.

Foundation The portion of the structure that extends into the ground and rests on footings.

Frame (structure) A structural system using multiple studs, joists, or rafters to carry the loads imposed (as opposed to post-and-beam or solid wall).

Frame, Door or Window The assembly attached to the structure that contains a door or window sash.

Furring Strips of wood or metal attached at a regular spacing to a wall or ceiling to provide an anchoring substrate for a new surface material, such as drywall. The space between the furring is often used to contain insulation, wiring, or piping.

Glazing Glass or plastic, translucent or transparent, used in walls to permit vision and/or the passage of solar light and heat.

Gusset Also called "gusset plate;" a flat piece of metal or wood used to connect the members of a truss to each other.

Jack Rafter One of a series of rafters used to frame the triangular portion of the intersection of two roofs or a hipped roof.

Jamb The top and two sides of a window or a door.

Joist A secondary structural member used repetitively to support floors or ceilings, usually spanning between beams or walls.

Joist Hanger A device made of galvanized sheet metal for attaching a wood joist to the face of a beam.

Kneewall A short wall often used in attics to block off the unusable angular space near the eaves. It may also help support the rafters.

Lally Column A trademark for a particular concrete-filled steel pipe used to support a beam.

Load The vertical weight imposed on a structural member by a floor or roof. Loads can be expressed in pounds per square foot (floor or roof surface), pounds per lineal foot (beams), or pounds (columns and posts).

Molding A thin strip, usually wood, that has been cut, shaped, and/or embossed in a decorative manner. Moldings are used as trim, and the two terms are often used interchangeably.

Mud Set A method of installing ceramic tile by first laying down a dry-mix mortar.

Mud Sill The horizontal member of an exterior wall frame that attaches to the foundation.

Muntin A small vertical or horizontal strip that divides window panes from each other.

Pier A short (less than 4 feet or so) support set on a square or round footing that is an alternative to continuous wall foundations.

Pitch The steepness of the roof, indicated by the ratio of rise (vertical distance) to span (horizontal distance), expressed in degrees. The "slope" is the more common way to express the steepness and is the rise in roof surface for each 12 inches of horizontal distance. For example a $5/12$ slope rises 5 inches for every 12.

Plate The horizontal pieces of lumber below and above the studs. The single piece below is called the sole plate. The two pieces above are called the top plate and the cap plate.

Post As used in this book, a post is a long, slender structural member used to support vertical loads. When used in place of foundations, posts are usually made of steel or wood set on concrete footings.

Rake The inclined edge of a pitched roof at the gable end.

Rebar A steel bar used to reinforce concrete, sized according to the nearest eighth of an inch of its diameter (a #4 bar is $4/8$ inch (or $1/2$ inch) in diameter).

Rise The vertical distance of a rise to run ratio, used to describe the slope of stairs or a roof.

Run The horizontal distance of a rise to run ratio, used to describe the slope of stairs or a roof.

Sash The part of a window unit that contains the glazing; the part that moves in operating windows.

Sidelight A window or panel mounted at the side of a door.

Sill Beam In a post-and-beam house, the horizontal member between the bottom of a wall and the foundation.

Sill The lowest horizontal member of a window or door.

Sleepers Wood framing usually laid in a gridwork over an existing sloping surface to level the surface for a new floor.

Sole Plate A horizontal member at the bottom of a wood frame wall is attached to the floor (also called sill plate).

Sone A unit that rates fan noise. The quietest exhaust fans are rated at about 1 sone; louder fans go up to 4 sones.

Stucco A mixture of cement, lime, and sand that is used to plaster exterior walls.

Stud A vertical framing member used repetitively and spaced 16 or 24 inches on center.

Subfloor The substrate material that supports the finish flooring.

Thin set A method of attaching tile to a substrate by means of a troweled-on adhesive.

Transom A window mounted above a door or another window. Transoms usually occur above head height.

Web The center portion of a beam between the top and the bottom of the flanges.

Index

A

Accessibility
in bathroom, 64, 65; planning doors for, 120
Accessory trim, 109
Additions
adding, 42–43; building, 175–86; conditioning single room, 158–60; downhill, 40; heating systems for multiroom, 160–62; piggybacking, 157; second story, 51–52; solar heat for, 158; supplying electric power to, 169–70; uphill, 39–40
Air, providing make-up, 164
Air conditioners
central, 162; room, 159–60
Ambient lighting, 170–71, 173, 174
Appealing case, 38
Architect-client relationship, 9
Architects, 30
bubble diagram used by, 41, 42; fees for, 30; landscape, 31; working with, 34
Architect's scale, 61, 177
Asphalt roofing, 127
Asphalt shingles, 125
Attic
ceilings, 51; expanding, 46–51; floor joists, 51; floors, 51; ventilation for, 113
Awning windows, 122

B

Backerboards, 132
Ballpark estimates, 26
Base cabinets, 148–50
Base drawings, making, 60–61
Basement, foundation, and footing plan, 177
Base trim, 143
Bath designers, 31, 64
Bathrooms
adding new, 24; exhaust fans for, 164; lighting for, 65, 173–74; planning layout for new, 64–65
Batt insulation, 110
Beams, 86–87
Bearing walls, 44
Bedrooms
lighting fixtures for, 174; planning layout for additional, 69
Bidding, role of architect in, 34
Bifold doors, 118
Blanket insulation, 110
Brick-and-mortar estimates, 26–27
Brick veneer, 90–91
British thermal units per hour (BtuH), 160
Bubble diagram, 41, 42
Building designers, 31
Built-up roofing, 127
Bumping out, 45–46, 53
Butcher block countertops, 151

C

Cabinets, 146
getting most from kitchen, 150; prefabricated, 148–50; shelving, 146–47
California climate, 157
Cape Cod transformation, 16–17
Carpeting, 137
Carports, enclosing, 53
Casement windows, 121
Cathedral ceiling, 51, 113, 123, 124
Ceilings, 130
attic, 51; backer boards, 132; cathedral, 51, 113, 123, 124; drywall, 130–31; finishes for, 132–35; insulation for, 113–14; plaster, 131
Central air conditioners, 162
Central exhaust system, 164
Central heating, 161–62
Ceramic tile countertops, 150–51
Civil engineers, 31
Climate control, 155–57
Closet doors, 120
Closets, walk-in, 69
Coal-burning stoves, 159
Cold basement, 114, 115
Columns, 86–87
Common wall, 93
Computer-aided-design (CAD) tools, 56
Concrete block, 91
Concrete-block foundation, 79
Concrete-block piers, 77–78
Concrete-filled steel columns, 87
Concrete floor slab, 83
Conditions, documenting existing, 58–60
Conservation, 155–57
Construction, entrusting, to general contractor, 184–86
Construction administration, role of architect in, 34
Construction documents, 34
Construction phase, 183–84
Consultants
finding right, 32–33; using outside, 30–34
Contract documents, 176
basement, foundation, and footing plan, 177; cross sections, 179; details, 180; electrical layouts, 180; exterior elevations, 179; floor- or roof-framing plans, 179; floor plans, 177–79; plumbing and heating plan, 180; schedules, 180; site plan, 176–77; specifications, 181–83; wall sections, 179–80; working drawings, 176–80
Contracts
content of, 185–86; cost-plus-fee, 185, 186; lump-sum, 185, 186; negotiating for design services, 34; with subcontractors, 184
Convection, 117

Cooling, ventilation for, 165
Cornices, 108
Cost analysis, 26
ballpark estimates in, 26; brick-and-mortar estimates in, 26–27; for second stories, 51
Cost-plus-fee contracts, 185, 186
Countertops, 150
butcher block, 151; ceramic tile, 150–51; comparing choices for, 153; plastic laminate, 150; solid-surface, 151–52; stone, 152
Crawl space, insulation for, 115
Crawl-space foundation, 76
Cross sections, 179

D

Damp proof, 80–81
Den, planning layout for, 70
Design, creating, 55–74
Design development, role of architect in, 34
Designer-builders, 31–32
Design programs, 56
Design services, negotiating contract for, 34
Details, 180
Dining rooms
lighting fixtures for, 173; remodeling, 16–17
Direct-vent heaters, 158–59
Doghouse dormers, 48, 49
Doors, 117
bifold, 118; double-acting, 117; flush-face, 118; french, 119; hollow-core, 118; jalousie, 120; louvered, 120; mirrored, 120; paired, 117–18; panel, 118–19; patio, 119; planning, for accessibility, 120; pocket, 118; purpose of, 117; single-acting, 117; sliding, 118; solid-core, 118; styles of, 118–20; trimming, 108–9; types of, 117–18
Door schedule, 182
Door trim, 144
Dormers, 97
advantages of, 123; doghouse, 48, 49; gable, 49, 97; shed, 48–49, 97
Double-acting doors, 117
Double-hung windows, 121
Downhill additions, 40
Drafting services, 31
Drain-waste-vent (DWV) system, laying out, 166–67
Drywall, 130–31
water-resistant, 134

E

Easements, 36
Electrical engineers, 31
Electrical layouts, 180
Electrical lines, 41
Electric strip heaters, 158

Electric systems, 168–70
mapping out power and lighting plan, 168–69; supplying power to addition, 169–70
Energy-efficiency rating (EER), 160
Engineers, 30
civil, 31; electrical, 31; mechanical, 31; structural, 30–31
Engineer's scale, 177
Entertainment center
lighting fixtures for, 172; planning layout for, 70
Entrance combinations, 120
Envelope decisions, 98–128
Estimates
ballpark, 26; brick-and-mortar, 26–27
Exterior elevations, 179
Exterior insulation and finish systems (EIFS), 100, 101
Exteriors
brick, 99; shaping, 73–74; shingles, 106; siding, 101–6; stone, 100; stucco, 100; synthetic stucco, 100; trimming, 107–9; wood shakes, 106

F
Family financial resources, 27
Family rooms
improving, 23; lighting fixtures for, 172; planning layout for, 70
Fans
fixed ceiling, 165; room exhaust, 164; whole-house, 165
Fiberglass insulation, 110
Fiberglass shingles, 125
Financing, 27
obtaining loans from lending institutions, 28; personal and family resources in, 27; using equity in, 27–28
Finish schedule, 182
Fireplaces, 159–60
Fixed ceiling fans, 165
Flashing, 128
Flat roof, topping, 126–27
Floor finishes, 136
floorcoverings, 136–39; subfloors and underlayments, 136
Floor framing plans, 179
Floor plans, 177–79
Floors, 83
attic, 51; beam, posts, and columns, 86–87; heavyweight, 83–84; insulation for, 114; tying new, to house, 86; wood-framed, 84–86
Fluorescent lamps, 172
Flush-face doors, 118
Footing drains, 80
Foundations and footings
attaching, to house, 82; building on existing, 76; grade-beam, 76; keeping dry, 80–82; materials for, 79–80; pier and post, 77–78; wall, 76–77
French doors, 119
Furring out, 91

G
Gable dormers, 49
Gables, 108
Garages, adding new, 23–24

Gas lines, 41
General contractors
entrusting construction to, 184–86; serving as own, 29–30, 181; working with, 186
Glazing, selecting window, 122–23
Grade-beam foundation, 76
Ground, adding over open, 46
Ground-fault interrupters (GFI), 169
Gulf climate, 157
Gypsum lath, 131

H
Halogen lamps, 172
Headroom problem, solving, 52
Heartland climate, 157
Heating
central, 161–62; direct-vent, 158–59; electric strip, 158; hot-air, 161; hydronic, 157, 161; mechanical, 157–62; solar, 158
Heating systems
for multiroom additions, 160–62; for single-room addition, 158–60
Heat pumps, 159–60, 162
split-system, 162
Heat-recovery ventilator (HRV), 164
Hollow-core doors, 118
Home designers, 31
Home-equity loans, 27
Home-improvement loans, comparing, 28
Home offices
adding, 26; lighting fixtures for, 26, 174; planning layout for, 62–63
Horizontal bracing, 89
Hot-air heating, 161
House, 41
adding over open ground, 46; adding space to, 42–43; adding story to, 51–52; attaching foundation to, 82; bumping out from, 45–46; converting roofed areas, 52–53; expanding attic of, 46–51; internal circulation in, 41–42; joining roof to, 96; tying new floor to, 86; and vertical access, 54
Housewrap, 117
HRVs, 164
Hydronic heating systems, 157, 161

I
Improvements
costs in making, 26–27; decision to move or make, 22; doing some of work on, 29–30; finding financing for, 27–28; payback potential of various, 22–26; using outside design help on, 30–34
Incandescent lamps, 171
Infiltration, blocking, 117
Insulation, 110
comparing types of, 112; materials for, 110–13; positioning of, 113–16; in stud walls, 89
Interior, trims for, 141–46
Interior designers, 31
Interior finishing, 129–53

J
Jalousie doors, 119
Jalousie windows, 122

Joists
attic floor, 51; manufactured, 86; steel floor, 89

K
Kitchen designers, 31, 64
Kitchens
getting most from cabinets in, 150; improving, 25–26; lighting fixtures for, 173; planning layout for, 66–68; remodeling, 20; work triangle concept in, 66
Kit house, expansion of, 11–14
Kneewalls, 94

L
Lally columns, 87
Laminated-veneer lumber (LVL), 85
Landscape architects, 31
Lateral bracing, 92
Latex paints, 132
Layout, planning, 61–74
Legal limitations, 36
Lending institutions, obtaining loans from, 28
Licensed design professionals, 30
Lighting, 170
ambient, 170–71, 173, 174; color of, 174; matching fixtures to applications, 172–74; sources for, 171–72; task, 171, 173, 174; wiring fixtures, 174
Lighting fixture schedule, 180
Light sources, 171–72
Living rooms
improving, 23; lighting fixtures for, 172
Loans
family, 27; home-equity, 27; home-improvement, 28
Loose fill and sprayed insulation, 113
Louvered doors, 120
Lumber, manufactured, 85
Lump-sum contracts, 185, 186

M
Mantels, 145–46
Manufactured joists, 86
Manufactured lumber, 85
Masonry walls, 90–91
Mechanical engineers, 31
Mechanical heating equipment, 157–62
Membrane roof, 127
Metal roofing, 125–26
Metal siding, 106
Mineral wood, 110
Mini-greenhouses, 45
Mirrored doors, 120
Moisture, controlling indoor, 116
Mountain west climate, 156
Mud-set tiling, 139

N
National Association of Remodeling Industry (NARI), 185
National Electrical Code, 169
National Forest Products Association (NFPA), 79
National Forest Products Laboratory, 80
Needs assessment, 6–20
Negotiation
of contract for design services, 34; role

of architect in, 34
Northern tier climate, 156
Northwest coast climate, 156–57

O

Oriented-strand-board (OSB), 85, 103–4

P

Paint, 132
Paired doors, 117–18
Panel doors, 118–19
Parquet flooring, 139
Patio doors, 119
Personal financial resources, 27
Piers and posts, 77–78
Plaster, 131
Plastic laminate countertops, 150
Plastic moldings, 144
Plumbing and heating plan, 180
Plumbing rough-in, 166–68
Plywood panel siding, 104–5
Pocket doors, 118
Porches
    converting, 52–53; enclosing, 53
Post-and-beam framing, 92
Post base, 87
Posts, 77–78, 86–87
Poured-concrete foundations, 79
Poured-concrete piers, 77–78
Power and lighting plan, mapping out,
    168–69
Predesign, role of architect in, 34
Prefabricated cabinets, 148–50
Prefabricated circular stairways, 54
Project, defining, 35–54

R

Radiant-barrier insulation, 113
Rafters, tying, 94
Recessed lighting, 173
Reconversion, as consideration in making
    home office, 26, 62
Refinancing, 27–28
Resilient flooring, 136
Ridge supports, 94
Rigid sheet insulation, 111
Rock wool, 110
Roofed areas, converting, 52–53
Roof framing plans, 179
Roofs
    asphalt roll, 127; built-up, 127; framing,
    93–97; insulation for, 113–14; joining, to
    house, 96; materials for sloped, 125–26;
    membrane, 127; metal, 125–26; self-
    installation, 128; site-framed rafter,
    93–94; slate, 126; tile, 126; topping flat,
    126–27; trussed, 95–96
Roof windows, 123–24
Room air conditioners, 159–60
Room exhaust fans, 164
R-value, 110, 113, 114, 123

S

Schedules, 180
Schematic design, role of architect in, 34
Scissors stairway, 54

Second mortgage, 27
Self-contracting, 29–30, 181
Septic systems, 41
Setbacks, 36
Sewer pipes, 41, 83
Shed dormers, 48–49
Shelving, 146–47
Shingles, 106; asphalt, 125; fiberglass, 125;
    wood, 125
Siding, 101–6
    metal, 106; plywood panel, 104–5; vinyl,
    105–6; wood board, 101–3; wood-com-
    position, 103–4
Single-acting doors, 117
Single-hung windows, 121
Single-membrane roof, 127
Single-room addition, heating systems for,
    158–60
Site features, existing, 40–41
Site-framed rafter roofs, 93–94
Site plan, 36–37, 176–77
Skylights, 64, 123–24
Slate roof, 126
Sleepers, 52
Sliding doors, 118
Sliding windows, 121
Sloped roofs, materials for, 125–26
Slope of land, 39–40
Soil testing, 41, 77
Solar heat, 158
Solid-core doors, 118
Solid-surface countertops, 151–52
Southwest climate, 157
Space utilization, 8–11
Specifications, 181–83
Stair rise and run dimensions, 54
Stairways, 54, 145
Standard architectural specifications
    format, 183
Steel floor joists, 89
Steel studs, 90
Stone countertops, 152
Story, adding second, 51–52
Stoves, 159–60
Structural engineers, 30–31
Structural walls, 89
    masonry walls, 90–91; post-and-beam
    framing, 92; stud walls, 89–90
Studs
    steel, 90; wood, 89–90
Stud walls, 89–90
Subcontractors, 184
Sun spaces, 53
    heavyweight floors for, 84; planning lay-
    out for, 71–72
Superstructure, defining, 75–97
Surface bonding, 79
Surface water, diverting, 82

T

Task lighting, 171, 173, 174
Telephone lines, 41
Tile
    as floor finish, 139; as roofing material,
    126; as wall finish, 134
Trims
    exterior, 107–9; interior, 141–46; types
    of, 143–46
Trussed roofs, 95–96

U

Uphill additions, 39–40

V

Vapor barrier, 110, 116
Variances, appealing for, 38–39
Ventilation, 163
    for attic, 113; for cooling, 165; exhaust-
    only, 163–64
Vertical access, 54
Vinyl siding, 105–6

W

Wainscoting, 133–34
Walk-in closets, 69
Wall cabinets, 149
Wallcoverings, 133
Wall foundation, 76–77
Walls, 130
    backer boards, 131; bearing, 44; com-
    mon, 93; drywall, 130–31; finishes for,
    132–35; insulation for, 114; masonry,
    90–91; plaster, 131; stud, 89–90
Wall sections, 179–80
Warm basement, 114, 115
Waste pipes, 64
Water pipes, 41
Waterproofing, 80–81
Water-resistant drywall, 134
Water-supply piping, 167–68
Water table, checking for, 41
Water vapor, 80
Well heads, 41
Whole-house fans, 165
Windows, 121
    awning, 122; in bathroom, 64; case-
    ment, 121; construction of, 122; double-
    hung, 121; jalousie, 122; roof, 123–24;
    selecting glazing for, 122–23; single-
    hung, 121; sliding, 121; trimming,
    108–9; types of, 121–22
Window schedule, 182
Window trim, 144
Wiring, for lighting fixtures, 174
Wood board siding, 101–3
Wood-composition siding, 103–4
Wood flooring, 138–39
Wood floor members, sizing, 84–86
Wood foundation, 79–80
Wood-framed floor, 84–86
Wood moldings, 108
Wood paneling, 133–34
Wood shakes, 106, 125
Wood shingles, 125
Wood stoves, 159–60
Wood studs, 89–90
Working drawings, 176–80
    common scales for, 181
Work triangle concept, 66
Wright, Frank Lloyd, 7

Z

Zoning ordinances, 36
    appealing for variance to, 38–39

Metric Conversion Charts

LUMBER

Sizes: Metric cross sections are so close to their nearest U.S. sizes, as noted at right, that for most purposes they may be considered equivalents.

Lengths: Metric lengths are based on a 300mm module, which is slightly shorter in length than an U.S. foot. It will, therefore, be important to check your requirements accurately to the nearest inch and consult the table below to find the metric length required.

Areas: The metric area is a square meter. Use the following conversion factor when converting from U.S. data: 100 sq. feet = 9.29 sq. meters.

METRIC LENGTHS

Lengths Meters	Equivalent Feet and Inches
1.8m	5' 10⅞"
2.1m	6' 10⅝"
2.4m	7' 10½"
2.7m	8' 10¼"
3.0m	9' 10⅛"
3.3m	10' 9⅞"
3.6m	11' 9¾"
3.9m	12' 9½"
4.2m	13' 9⅜"
4.5m	14' 9⅓"
4.8m	15' 9"
5.1m	16' 8¾"
5.4m	17' 8⅝"
5.7m	18' 8⅜"
6.0m	19' 8¼"
6.3m	20' 8"
6.6m	21' 7⅞"
6.9m	22' 7⅝"
7.2m	23' 7½"
7.5m	24' 7¼"
7.8m	25' 7⅛"

METRIC SIZES (Shown Before Nearest U.S. Equivalent)

Millimeters	Inches	Millimeters	Inches
16 x 75	⅝ x 3	44 x 150	1¾ x 6
16 x 100	⅝ x 4	44 x 175	1¾ x 7
16 x 125	⅝ x 5	44 x 200	1¾ x 8
16 x 150	⅝ x 6	44 x 225	1¾ x 9
19 x 75	¾ x 3	44 x 250	1¾ x 10
19 x 100	¾ x 4	44 x 300	1¾ x 12
19 x 125	¾ x 5	50 x 75	2 x 3
19 x 150	¾ x 6	50 x 100	2 x 4
22 x 75	⅞ x 3	50 x 125	2 x 5
22 x 100	⅞ x 4	50 x 150	2 x 6
22 x 125	⅞ x 5	50 x 175	2 x 7
22 x 150	⅞ x 6	50 x 200	2 x 8
25 x 75	1 x 3	50 x 225	2 x 9
25 x 100	1 x 4	50 x 250	2 x 10
25 x 125	1 x 5	50 x 300	2 x 12
25 x 150	1 x 6	63 x 100	2½ x 4
25 x 175	1 x 7	63 x 125	2½ x 5
25 x 200	1 x 8	63 x 150	2½ x 6
25 x 225	1 x 9	63 x 175	2½ x 7
25 x 250	1 x 10	63 x 200	2½ x 8
25 x 300	1 x 12	63 x 225	2½ x 9
32 x 75	1¼ x 3	75 x 100	3 x 4
32 x 100	1¼ x 4	75 x 125	3 x 5
32 x 125	1¼ x 5	75 x 150	3 x 6
32 x 150	1¼ x 6	75 x 175	3 x 7
32 x 175	1¼ x 7	75 x 200	3 x 8
32 x 200	1¼ x 8	75 x 225	3 x 9
32 x 225	1¼ x 9	75 x 250	3 x 10
32 x 250	1¼ x 10	75 x 300	3 x 12
32 x 300	1¼ x 12	100 x 100	4 x 4
38 x 75	1½ x 3	100 x 150	4 x 6
38 x 100	1½ x 4	100 x 200	4 x 8
38 x 125	1½ x 5	100 x 250	4 x 10
38 x 150	1½ x 6	100 x 300	4 x 12
38 x 175	1½ x 7	150 x 150	6 x 6
38 x 200	1½ x 8	150 x 200	6 x 8
38 x 225	1½ x 9	150 x 300	6 x 12
44 x 75	1¾ x 3	200 x 200	8 x 8
44 x 100	1¾ x 4	250 x 250	10 x 10
44 x 125	1¾ x 5	300 x 300	12 x 12

Dimensions are based on 1m = 3.28 feet, or 1 foot = 0.3048m

Dimensions are based on 1 inch = 25mm

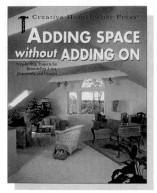

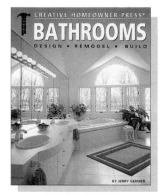

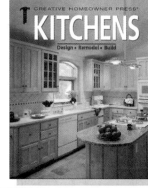

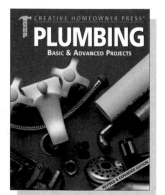
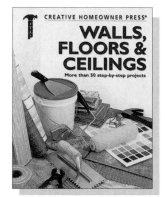